Six Capsules

TRUE CRIME HISTORY

SIX CAPSULES

The Gilded Age Murder of Helen Potts

George R. Dekle Sr.

The Kent State University Press

KENT, OHIO

Library of Congress Catalog Number 2018052217

ISBN 978-1-60635-370-7

Manufactured in the United States of America

Library of Congress Cataloging-in-Publication Data

Names: Dekle, George R., 1948- author.

Title: Six capsules : the gilded age murder of Helen Potts / George R. Dekle Sr.

Description: Kent, Ohio : The Kent State University Press, 2019. | Includes bibliographical references and index.

Identifiers: LCCN 2018052217 | ISBN 9781606353707 (pbk.)

Subjects: LCSH: Harris, Carlyle W., 1869-1893--Trials, litigation, etc. | Potts, Helen, 1871-1891--Death and burial | Trials (Murder)--New York (State)--New York--History--19th century.

Classification: LCC KF223.H3764 D45 2019 | DDC 345.747/02523--dc23

LC record available at https://lccn.loc.gov/2018052217

23 22 21 20 19   5 4 3 2 1

Contents

Dramatis Personae

ABBE, DR. ROBERT: Harris's preceptor in medical school

BANER, DR. WILLIAM: Physician called to assist Dr. Fowler

BAYHA, IDA: Defense witness before the Raines Commission

BELL, DR. EDGAR C.: Phrenologist who proclaimed Harris not a murderer

BELL, MASON (JOSEPH): Twelfth juror

BENSON, TILLIE: Serving girl seduced, impregnated, and abandoned by Harris

BERGSTON, MATILDA: Serving girl sexually assaulted and impregnated by Harris

BIGGS, DR. HERMAN M.: Defense pathologist

BROWN, HARVEY J.: Fourth juror

BROWN, WARDEN: Warden of Sing Sing at time of escapes

BRUN, CARRIE: Pseudonym that Carrie Bruning used to visit Harris in the Tombs

BRUNING, CARRIE: Frequent visitor of Harris in the Tombs

BYRNES, THOMAS: Chief of detectives, NYPD

CARMAN, ANNA B.: Defense witness before the Raines Commission

CARMAN, GRACE: Defense witness before the Raines Commission

CARSON, FRANCES: Helen Potts's roommate at the Comstock School

CHOATE, DILWORTH: *World* reporter who allied himself with the prosecution

COCHRAN, DR. JOHN ELWYN: Classmate of Harris

COGGESHALL, HENRY J.: Senator who introduced legislation favoring new trial for Harris

CONNAUGHTON, PRINCIPLE KEEPER: Supervisor of Death House

COOK, MR.: Prosecution witness before the Raines Commission

COOKSON, RACHEL: Helen Potts's roommate at the Comstock School

CRANE, JOHN D.: Sixth juror

CROKER, RICHARD: "Boss" of Tammany Hall

D., LILLIE: Purportedly wrote a letter saying she supplied Helen with morphine

DANIELS, DR. C. M.: Pronounced Harris dead

DAVIS, ELECTRICIAN: Pseudonym used by executioner at Sing Sing

DAVIS, VERNON M.: Assistant district attorney originally assigned to the case

DAVISON, CHARLES E.: Friend and lawyer of Carlyle Harris

DAY, LYDIA: Principal of the Comstock School

DIXON JR., REV. THOMAS: Pastor who criticized Harris's conviction

DREW, QUEEN: Harris's romantic interest in Canandaigua, NY

DURSTON, WARDEN: Replaced Warden Brown at Sing Sing

FALLON, WARDEN: Warden of the Tombs during Harris's incarceration

FIELD, ALBERT: Third juror

FITZGERALD, JUDGE JAMES: Issued warrant for Harris's arrest

FITZSIMMONS, FRANK: Lawyer who purportedly investigated Harris's conviction

FLOWER, ROSWELL P.: Governor of New York

FOWLER, DR. EDWARD: Physician who attended Helen Potts in her last illness

FRENETTE, MARY M.: Affiant who supported new trial for Harris

GARDNER, CHARLES: Investigator for Rev. Charles Parkhurst

GRAHAM, CARL: Alias used by Harris in Canandaigua, NY

GRAY, JUDGE JOHN CLINTON: Wrote the appellate opinion affirming Harris's conviction

HAAMAN, CARL: Friend of Harris who claimed Helen used morphine

HAMILTON, DR. ALLAN MCLANE: Performed autopsy on Helen

HAND, DR. DAVID: Physician who assisted in the delivery of Helen's stillborn child

HARKNESS, CHARLES W.: Alias under which Harris ran the Neptune Club

HARRIS, ALLEN: Youngest brother of Carlyle Harris

HARRIS, CARLYLE: Accused murderer of Helen Potts

HARRIS, CHARLES: Alias that Harris used to marry Helen

HARRIS, CHARLES L.: Father of Carlyle Harris

HARRIS, ETHEL: Defense witness before the Raines Commission

HARRIS, FRANCES MCCREADY: Mother of Carlyle Harris

HARRIS, ROBERT MCCREADY: Brother of Carlyle Harris

HAYDEN, DR. JAMES R.: Harris's personal physician

HILBERG, DAVID H.: Ninth juror

HINES, CHARLES H.: Fifth juror

HOWE, WILLIAM F.: Harris's lawyer in postconviction proceedings

HULSE, KEEPER: Guard at Death House during escape

HUMMEL, ABRAHAM: Law partner of William F. Howe

INMANN, ANNE E.: Claimed Helen's ghost exonerated Harris during a séance

IRVING, DR.: Doctor at Sing Sing

JACKSON, FRANCIS D.: Seventh juror

JACKSON, SUSAN F. R.: Defense witness before the Raines Commission

JEROME, WILLIAM TRAVERS: Assistant defense counsel for Carlyle Harris

JONES, CARRIE: Pseudonym under which Carrie Bruning attended Harris's funeral

KERR, DR. GEORGE: Physician called to assist Dr. Fowler

KINMOUTH, DR. HUGH: Defense witness before the Raines Commission

KROM, DR. CHARLES: Classmate of Harris

KUNN, ANNA: Claimed knowledge of Helen's use of morphine

LANGE, FRANCIS: Druggist, defense witness before the Raines Commission

LATHAM, JOHN F.: Friend of Harris from Canandaigua, NY

LATHAM, LIZZIE: Friend of Queen Drew from Canandaigua, NY

LeBRUN, ALEXANDRINE: Defense witness before the Raines Commission

LEDYARD, HOPE: Nom de plume of Frances McCready Harris

LEFFERTS, JOSEPH H.: Defense witness before the Raines Commission

LEWIS, MARY: Affiant who supported new trial for Harris

MacMULLEN, JOHN: Former teacher of Harris

MANSON, GEORGE: Clerk who double-checked compounding of Harris's prescription

MAPES, DR. JAMES J.: Classmate of Harris

MAPES, SAMUEL P.: Eighth juror

MASON, CRAWFORD: Eleventh juror

McCREADY, BENJAMIN W.: Grandfather of Carlyle Harris

McCREADY, MARY L.: Aunt of Carlyle Harris

McINTYRE JR., EWEN: Coowner of pharmacy that filled prescription for Harris

McINTYRE SR., EWEN: Owner of pharmacy that filled prescription for Harris

McKEE, S. B. W.: Jury foreman

MEEKER, MOLLY: Friend of both Helen and Carl Haaman

MELLVAINE, MURDERER: Previous occupant of Harris's Death House cell

MITCHELL, DR. DAVID: Pastor who criticized Harris's conviction

MOODY, REV. DWIGHT L.: Evangelist who petitioned for pardon of Harris

MORPHEUS: Claimed knowledge of Helen's drug use

MURPHY, KEEPER: Guard at Death House during escape

NICOLL, DE LANCY: Elected district attorney

NIELSON, HELEN: Alias that Helen used to marry Harris

OLIVER, CHARLES: Heard Harris's boasts about sexual conquests

OSMOND, J. L.: Contradicted Harris's account of Roehle and Pallister's escape

PALLISTER, THOMAS: Escaped from Death House at Sing Sing

PARKHURST, CHARLES H.: Pastor who led crusade against police corruption

PEABODY, DR. GEORGE L.: Professor of materia medica at the College of Physicians and Surgeons

PETERSON, CARL: Alias of Carl Haaman

PFINGSTEN, GUSTAVE: Chemist who analyzed Harris's capsule

POTTS, CYNTHIA: Mother of Helen Potts

POTTS, GEORGE H.: Father of Helen Potts

POTTS, HELEN: Secret wife of Carlyle Harris

POWER, HEARN: Clerk who compounded prescription for Harris

PRATT, JOHN J.: Affiant who supported new trial for Harris

PRESCOTT, FRANK: Alias given by Carl Haaman when arrested for gambling

REED, MISS: Assistant principal of the Comstock School

REILLY, DETECTIVE: Arrested Carlyle Harris

REYNOULS, DR. GEORGE B.: Affiant who supported new trial for Harris

RINCKHOFF, M. P.: Alderman who secretly married Harris and Helen

ROCKWELL, BERTHA: Helen Potts's roommate at the Comstock School

ROEHL, FRANK W.: Escaped from Death House at Sing Sing

ROGERS, DR. JOHN: Classmate of Harris

RUDOLPH, HENRY: Tenth juror

SCHEELE, DR. WALTER: Claimed it was impossible to tell if Helen had morphine in her body

SCHOFIELD, MAE: Friend of Helen to whom Harris confessed the secret marriage

SCHULTZE, LOUIS: Elected coroner

SCUDDER, REV. JOHN L.: Pastor who criticized Harris's conviction

SEXTON, JAMES H.: Undertaker who buried and later exhumed Helen

SIMMS JR., CHARLES E.: Assistant prosecutor of Carlyle Harris

SMITH, DR. GEORGE D.: Assisted with autopsy of Helen

SMYTH, RECORDER FREDERICK: Judge who presided over Harris's trial

STANGLAND, BENJAMIN F.: Second juror

TAYLOR, GEORGE B.: *New York Times* reporter

TAYLOR, JOHN A.: Lead trial counsel for Harris

THOMPSON, DR. ALLAN MCLANE: Performed autopsy on Helen

THOMSON, DR. WILLIAM H.: Professor of materia medica at New York University

TOMPKINS, DR. BYRON P.: Helen's personal physician

TRAINER, DETECTIVE: Arrested McCready Harris, thinking him to be Carlyle Harris

TREVERTON, DR. CHARLES: Helen's uncle who delivered her stillborn child

TSCHEPPE, ADOLPH: Toxicologist who assisted Dr. Pfingston in analysis of capsule

TUERKE, CHARLES: Clerk at McIntyre & Son's pharmacy

UNGER, HENRY W.: Assistant district attorney who first met with Harris

VAN BRUNT, JUSTICE CHARLES H.: Judge who transferred case to Court of General Sessions

VAN BUREN, A. H.: Lawyer who lobbied for a new trial for Harris

VAN MATER, MR.: Druggist who testified for prosecution before Raines Commission

VAN ZANDT, LULU (1): Daughter of Egbert Van Zandt; purported secret wife of Carlyle Harris

VAN ZANDT, LULU (2): Daughter of Thaddeus Van Zandt; cousin of Lulu Van Zandt (1)

VANNETT, WILLIAM: Undertaker who embalmed Helen Potts

VON GERICHTEN, DETECTIVE: Arrested McCready Harris, thinking him to be Carlyle Harris

WADDELL, ANNA: Affiant who supported new trial for Harris

WALLACE, FRANKIE: Affiant who supported new trial for Harris

WATSON, JAMES: Prosecution witness before the Raines Commission

WEILLS, REV. JOHN C. S.: Chaplain of Sing Sing

WELLMAN, FRANCIS L.: Lead prosecutor of Carlyle Harris

WESTON, ALBERT: Deputy coroner who investigated Helen's death

WHITE, DR. GEORGE: Classmate of Harris

WITTHAUS, DR. RUDOLPH: Toxicologist
WOOLMAN, HENRY M.: Defense witness before the Raines Commission
WORMLEY, DR. THEODORE: Defense toxicologist
WORRELL, REVEREND: Father of a fiancé of Harris

The Sleep of Morpheus

Lydia Day expected to spend the evening of January 31, 1890, in quiet comfort at her home, which also served as a boarding school. The Comstock School, located at 32 West Fortieth Street in New York City, a prestigious finishing school for young ladies, was usually filled with the sounds of energetic young girls, but on this evening the girls were at a concert by the New York Symphony[1] and wouldn't be back until late. Miss Day began her evening in the third-floor sitting room with a good book. One student, Helen Potts, skipped the concert due to a bad headache. Helen was a beautiful, talented young lady, the daughter of wealth and privilege, who had led a sheltered life in the seaside town of Ocean Grove, New Jersey. A recent enrollee in the school, she was a demure young lady who seemed to be well liked by her fellow students despite the fact that she was somewhat older than they. Helen was very cheerful that evening as the two women alternately talked and read.[2] Miss Day retired a little before 10:00 P.M., leaving Helen in the sitting room. Helen soon decided to go to bed herself.

As she made her way to the communal bedroom on the fourth floor, Helen saw Miss Reed, the associate principal. Helen stopped Miss Reed and said, "My young doctor friend has given me a prescription to cure my malaria. He says that I must take it just before going to bed and that I must not be awakened. If I wake up, he says, the medicine won't do any good. I wish you would warn my roommates not to wake me tonight when they come home from the concert."[3]

At 10:30 P.M. Helen's roommates, Frances Carson, Rachel Cookson, and Bertha Rockwell, arrived back at the school from the concert and went upstairs to go to bed. Miss Reed neglected to give them Helen's message.

When they entered the bedroom they found Helen asleep with the gaslight turned down. The girls turned the light up and began bustling around the room preparing for bed.[4] The noise woke Helen. "Girls," she said, "I have had such beautiful dreams, I could dream on forever. I have been dreaming about Carl." The girls laughed as they continued to get ready for bed.[5] Miss Reed came in and turned the gaslight off at 11:00 P.M.,[6] and about five minutes later Helen began to moan.[7] Frances Carson got out of bed and went to Helen.

Helen complained of numbness, and Frances began to rub her head to comfort her.[8] Helen began to have difficulty breathing and complained of a choking sensation.[9] She said she felt as if she were going to die. The girls tried to reassure her that she was all right, but she repeatedly said she thought she was going to die. "If you go to sleep," they told her, "you would be better." Helen replied, "If I go to sleep, it will be a death sleep."[10] She urged them, should she go to sleep, to periodically check to see if she were still breathing. "Carl said I could take one of these pills every night for twelve nights in succession and he had taken them himself. Carl would not give me anything that would hurt me—would he?"[11] The girls comforted Helen for approximately three-quarters of an hour. When it became apparent that Helen was worsening, they sent for Miss Day. When she arrived, Helen was unconscious.[12] Rachel Cookson later testified that when the gaslight was turned back on, "She looked like death. She was very pale and the veins all stuck out on her forehead and were blue, and even her hands were blue."[13] Miss Day wasted no time trying to revive Helen but immediately sent for Dr. Edward Fowler, who lived three doors down from the school on Sixth Avenue. No ordinary general practitioner, Dr. Fowler was an eminent physician, the author and editor of several medical books, and a founder of New York's Homeopathic Medical College.[14]

When Dr. Fowler arrived, he found Helen "in a state of profound coma," with cold, pale-blue skin and labored breathing. Her pupils were "both contracted to a point almost beyond being perceptible."[15] Fowler recognized the symptoms, which were all too common in Gilded Age New York City—opiate poisoning, probably from an overdose of the opium derivative morphine. During the Civil War, Union medical officers had liberally used morphine as a painkiller in the treatment of the horrific wounds inflicted by the 50-caliber Minié balls fired in the rifled muskets of the era. Because the addictive qualities of morphine were not fully understood, thousands of Union soldiers returned home hopelessly addicted to the drug.[16] From this core of addicts, the abuse of the drug spread, until by the 1890s, morphine abuse was rampant. Sale of the drug was for the most part unrestricted, and it could be bought in many drugstores without a prescription. Over-the-counter painkillers often contained morphine, and the well-to-do morphine addict could easily obtain the drug from multiple sources. The less well-off could make do with less expensive products containing opium such as paregoric and laudanum.[17] By the early 1900s morphine addiction had been proclaimed "one of the most serious menaces accompanying twentieth century civilization."[18]

Fowler almost immediately summoned Dr. William Baner to assist him.[19] Fowler called for black coffee[20] and gave Helen a coffee enema.[21] He also sent Miss Day looking for any kind of medicine container in the bedroom, and she immediately found an empty pillbox on Helen's washstand.[22] Dr. Fowler began administering artificial respiration as he waited for the arrival of Dr. Baner. Because mouth-to-mouth resuscitation wasn't invented until 1956,[23] Dr. Fowler used the old, inefficient method of pulling Helen's arms up over her head to extend her chest and pull in air and then pulling them back down to expel air.[24]

Miss Day brought the pillbox to Dr. Fowler and he examined it. The box came from a nearby pharmacy, McIntyre & Son's pharmacy on Sixth Avenue. The label on the box tended to confirm Fowler's diagnosis. It read:

1–20–91
Quin. Sulph. Gr. xxv
Morph. Sulph. Gr. i
Sig: One before retiring
(Signed) C. W. H., Student[25]

Fowler asked Miss Day if she had any idea who this "C. W. H., Student" might be, and she did. He was Carlyle W. Harris, a handsome, brilliant medical student at the College of Physicians and Surgeons who had visited with Helen the very afternoon before she fell ill. He was the grandson of Benjamin W. McCready, one of New York's most respected physicians, and the son of Frances McCready Harris, a temperance crusader who also wrote inspirational books under the pen name Hope Ledyard. Dr. Fowler wanted very much to meet Harris and find out what exactly was in the capsules from the empty box. Dr. Fowler sent for the young man, but it would be hours before he arrived.

When Dr. Baner arrived at the Comstock School at 1:00 A.M., he took one look at Helen and thought she was dead. Upon closer examination he determined that despite her cold, blue skin, she was breathing very slowly.[26] Her minutely contracted eyes led him to the same diagnosis made by Dr. Fowler—poisoning from some form of opium. During the night Dr. Fowler and Dr. Baner used every antidote to opium poisoning that they could: in addition to the coffee enemas and artificial respiration, they periodically gave her atropine, whiskey, and digitalis; they shocked her with a battery; and they gave her oxygen through a mask.[27] There was one other thing they could have done—they could have pumped Helen's stomach. Dr. Fowler later said that he decided against the stomach pump because "We discussed the matter of using it and concluded that the use of the stomach pump would kill the girl. [This was] because her respirations very soon came only one in two minutes, and any attempt of that kind would have to necessarily in part suspend the artificial respiration on which the girl's life depended."[28]

By 3:00 A.M. Helen began to show some improvement, breathing more rapidly, and Dr. Fowler took the opportunity to go home for a few minutes. The rally lasted only half an hour, and Dr. Fowler soon had to return.[29] Around 6:00 A.M., approximately an hour before sunrise,[30] Harris arrived at the Comstock School, and not long after that Dr. Fowler sent for Dr. George Kerr to come and assist with Helen. Dr. Kerr arrived at 7:30 A.M.[31] Dr. Fowler said to Harris, "We have a frightful case here, and there must have been some very great mistake. What was in these capsules?"

"I gave them for malaria, for headache and insomnia and the like," replied Harris. "I thought it to be the best thing for that. I ordered twenty-five grains of quinine and one grain of morphine to be equally mixed and to be divided into six capsules, with the direction that one capsule should be taken at night."

"A sixth of a grain of morphine or even one grain of morphine could not have produced the condition that we have here," Dr. Fowler said. "This is one of the most profound cases of opium poisoning that I have ever witnessed. Go at once to the druggist and ascertain what they put in the capsules. It appears that they have reversed the proportions of the drug and instead of four grains and a little over of quinine, she has taken four grains and a little over of morphine." Harris immediately left on the errand Dr. Fowler gave him, and Dr. Fowler returned to the task of trying to save Helen's life.

Harris soon returned and reported that the druggist had prepared the capsules exactly according to the prescription he wrote. "Are you a medical doctor?" asked Fowler. "No," replied Harris. "I wrote and signed the prescription as a medical student." At this point the conversation ended and Fowler returned to working on the stricken girl as Harris stood by with his hands in his pockets and watched.[32] Then Harris asked, "Do you think I could be held responsible for this accident?" Dr. Fowler told him, "I don't know who is responsible. I'm not occupied in that question. I am trying to save this girl's life. I only know that a frightful mistake has been made somewhere." During the course of the morning Harris asked the question another eight or nine times.[33] As the doctors worked over Helen, Harris did make some remarks other than to ask whether he might be held responsible. He told them he was somewhat interested in Helen. He said that if she survived, it was possible that he might become engaged to her after he concluded his medical studies.[34]

On one occasion Harris helped the doctors by holding one of the poles of the battery when they administered a shock to Helen. The only other assistance he offered was to suggest that the doctors perform a tracheotomy. Fowler declined to follow Harris's suggestion; he thought that a tracheotomy would kill the girl.[35] Under the ministrations of the three doctors, Helen began to rally. Her breathing became more rapid until around 10:00 A.M., when they reached eight or nine breaths per minute,[36] then she began to fade. At approximately 10:45 A.M. on the morning of February 1, 1890, Dr. Fowler stopped working, stepped back, and said, "Well, it's no use. She's gone." Harris asked, "Is she dead, Doctor?" Fowler replied, "Yes." Then Harris exclaimed, "My God! What will become of me?"[37]

Because Harris had shared his plans for the future with the doctors, they stepped back to allow him some time alone with the body of the girl he planned to marry. He hardly paid any attention to the body at all. The only emotion he showed was when Miss Day entered the room. "Oh, Miss Day," he said, "I am so sorry for you." Since it was obvious that Harris had no interest in Helen's body, Dr. Fowler stepped back to her bed and closed her eyes and arranged her hair.[38]

The battle for Helen's life being over, the doctors took their leave of the Comstock School, and Harris accompanied them. When they reached the sidewalk at the bottom of the stairs, Harris again asked Dr. Fowler, "Do you think I could be held in blame for this terrible catastrophe?" Fowler said to him, "I don't know who is at fault. I only know the young girl has taken a frightful dose of morphine, and that she is dead. I don't know where the fault lies at all. I presume the druggist must have made an error—that the druggist must have reversed the drugs in their proportions." Harris replied, "Yes, evidently it was a very profound case of morphine poisoning."[39]

Dr. Kerr told Harris to go to the pharmacy and get the original prescription, then go to his office and wait for him. Kerr said he was going to go to the coroner's office to report the death, and there was certain to be a coroner's inquiry into the circumstances. They would both need to go back to the Comstock School later in the day for the coroner's investigation, and the coroner would need the prescription. Harris agreed to go to the pharmacy and get the prescription. The group then split up and went their separate ways, with Kerr going to the coroner's office and Harris going to McIntyre & Son's pharmacy. When Kerr returned to his office, Harris was not there. He asked the receptionist if Harris had come by and was told that Harris had indeed come to the office and waited for him briefly before leaving.

Charles Tuerke started his shift at McIntyre & Son's pharmacy promptly on the morning of February 1. Tuerke was never late for work; he slept in the building. The morning passed uneventfully and unremarkably until 11:00 A.M., when a handsome young medical student sauntered into the building and up to Tuerke's counter. Tuerke had never waited on the man before but knew him by sight—he was Carlyle Harris, and he was making his first visit of the day to McIntyre & Son's pharmacy. "Sir, could you look up a prescription for me? The date is January 20th, signed 'C. W. H.,' student,' and it calls for six capsules of morphine and quinine." Tuerke went to the records and found the prescription. "Do you want it compounded?" he asked. "No," replied Harris, "I just want to know the contents." Tuerke read off the contents of the prescription as Harris jotted them down in his memorandum book. When he finished reading the prescription to Harris, Tuerke again asked if Harris wanted the prescription compounded. "No, thank you," said Harris, and then he left the store. Harris said nothing to Tuerke about why he wanted the information and nothing about the death of Helen Potts at the Comstock School earlier that morning.[40]

The coroner's office was one of three government agencies charged with the investigation of suspicious deaths; the other two were the police and the district attorney's office. Usually the police were the first on the scene at an unattended death, and it was their duty to notify the district attorney and the coroner. The coroner was an officer who performed an investigation into the death and presented the results of that investigation to a coroner's jury, which would render a verdict describing how the deceased came to die. Although the coroner was frequently a medical doctor, sometimes men became coroners solely on the strength of their ability to get votes. One infamous recent occupant of the coroner's office was an ex-prizefighter by the name of Richard Croker,[41] a Tammany Hall worker whom we shall encounter later in this narrative.

The police usually notified the district attorney before they notified the coroner because both agencies had small regard for a coroner's competence to investigate homicide cases. One assistant district attorney described his feelings about coroners in the following words: "The Coroner is at best no more than an appendix to the legal anatomy, and frequently he is a disease. The spectacle of a medical man of small learning and less English trying to preside over a court of first instance[42] is enough to make the accused himself chuckle."[43] Such attitudes led to rivalry, and there would sometimes be races to see who could get to the death scene first, the coroner or the district attorney. On one occasion a deputy coroner, racing to a death scene, galloped his horse down Madison Avenue so furiously that he collided with a trolley car and broke his leg.[44] There would be no race to the scene of Helen's death; the doctors attending her, being more comfortable with other doctors than with the police, notified only the coroner; and the coroner notified neither the police nor the district attorney. The ensuing coroner's investigation tended to validate the lack of trust that the police and the district attorney placed in the coroner's office.

Deputy Coroner Albert Weston arrived at the Comstock School at 2:00 P.M. to examine Helen's body and question the witnesses. He had already gone to Dr. Fowler's office and taken Fowler's statement there. At the scene Weston, who was a medical doctor, spoke with Lydia Day and then with Dr. Baner and Dr. Kerr. Harris was also present for the interview with Baner and Kerr. The first order of business was to establish cause of death. Weston asked Baner and Kerr their opinions as to cause of death, and they were unanimous—morphine poisoning. Since Harris was a medical student, his opinion might be of some value, so Weston turned to Harris. "Do you think it was morphine poisoning?" Harris answered, "Yes."[45] Having settled the cause of death to his satisfaction, Weston now turned to the manner of death. The key piece of evidence as to the manner of death was the empty pillbox. How could a capsule from a seemingly innocent pillbox poison a young, healthy girl? If it were the druggist's mistake, the case could be closed and the parties could settle their differences in a civil lawsuit. Given the facts as known to Weston at the time, accident seemed to be the most probable manner of death. Suicide would be the least likely manner. It was essential, however, to rule out homicide.

Weston asked Harris to tell him about the capsules. Harris said that Helen complained to him about headaches, and he prescribed twenty-five grains of quinine to be combined with one grain of morphine and divided into six capsules. He removed two capsules from the pillbox and gave her the other four on January 21, with instructions to take one each night before going to bed. The next morning, he left for a trip to Old Point Comfort and was gone for a week. While he was in Old Point Comfort, Helen had written him and told him the capsules seemed to be making her headaches worse. He wrote back advising her to continue taking the medicine. He visited with her when he returned to New York and had been with her the afternoon before she died.

Weston asked Harris why he wrote the prescription rather than having a licensed medical doctor write it. Harris replied that his preceptor at the medical school said he could write prescriptions, and he had been told that quinine and morphine were very good for headaches caused by malaria. Weston wanted to know the exact nature of Harris's relationship with Helen, and Harris said he was just a friend of the family. Weston asked about Helen's family. Harris said that Helen's mother lived in Ocean Grove, New Jersey, that she had been notified of Helen's death, and that she would be coming into New York that afternoon or evening.[46]

Weston wanted to know why Harris held back two of the capsules. Harris said he didn't want a full grain of morphine to be in a girls' school.[47] Did Harris still have the two capsules? He did. Weston said that he was coming back to the Comstock School that evening and that Harris should bring him the capsules he held back.[48] The two separated, and Weston ran into Harris about half an hour later at the bar in the Hotel Royal on the corner of Fortieth Street and Sixth Avenue. Weston spoke to Harris, and Harris told him that Mrs. Potts would be arriving in New York about seven thirty or eight o'clock that evening.[49]

New York Times reporter George Taylor was refreshing himself at the bar when he saw Carlyle Harris talking with Deputy Coroner Albert Weston and a reporter from a rival newspaper. He approached the group and joined the conversation. They were talking about the death of a pretty young girl at a nearby boarding school. Harris was telling this other reporter basically the same story he told Weston. Taylor asked a question. Was Harris courting the young lady? Harris ridiculed the idea. "I'm struggling for life, struggling for a profession. I haven't thought of doing anything of the sort." Harris said he was merely a friend of the family, and he occasionally visited the girl at the school with her mother's consent.[50]

That evening Weston was back at the Comstock School, where he met with Mrs. Cynthia Potts and Carlyle Harris. Helen's body was still at the school, and Mrs. Potts was anxious to have an undertaker remove it to prepare it for burial.[51] Weston said that he needed to ask her a few questions, and she agreed to be interviewed. They retired to a small room on the upper floor of the school and sat down. "Mrs. Potts," he began, "will you tell me if your daughter has ever been ill, and if so, what was the nature of her illness?" Harris began, "She had been suffering for a number of years from heart disease." Weston stopped him. "I wish Mrs. Potts to tell the story, and give me the history herself."

Although Harris's claim that Helen suffered from heart disease was untrue, Mrs. Potts backed him up on the story in order to avoid an autopsy, which she feared would reveal that Helen had undergone an abortion.[52] Mrs. Potts said that Helen caught scarlet fever at age five, and her heart had been weak ever since. Helen had been treated by a physician two years before her death, and the physician told her that she had heart disease and must avoid violent exercise. Helen studied very hard the previous school year, and Mrs. Potts thought she had been severely overworked. The interview took on something of the nature of a muted debate with Weston suggesting that Helen was poisoned and Mrs. Potts insisting that she died of heart disease. Weston then questioned Mrs. Potts about her confidence in Harris's ability to safely prescribe for her daughter, pointing out that the young man was a medical student and not licensed to practice medicine. Mrs. Potts assured Weston that she had perfect confidence in Harris's abilities.[53]

As Weston questioned Mrs. Potts about her confidence in Harris, the young man thrust his hand into his pocket and offered a capsule to Weston.

"Here is one of the capsules. You may take it and have it analyzed, and you will find that the capsule is alright." Weston wanted to know where the second capsule was, but Harris said that he could find only one of them when he went home to look for them. Weston took the capsule. Harris reminded Weston that the pillbox was marked as a student's prescription and that made everything all right. Weston decided to be blunt. "Mrs. Potts, I don't believe you understand what I am telling you, that she died of morphine poisoning." When Weston spoke those words, Harris sprang to his feet. Mrs. Potts would later testify that it was "as if he had been moved by electricity." Try as he might, Weston could not get Mrs. Potts to agree to an autopsy.[54]

Being unwilling to authorize an autopsy against the wishes of such a socially prominent lady as Mrs. Potts, Weston gathered up the capsule and the pillbox and released the body to undertaker William Vannett. He reported his findings to Coroner Louis Schultze, who arrived at the school around 9:00 P.M. Weston also turned all the evidence he collected over to Schultze.[55] Having taken the ball from Weston, Schultze then began to fumble it. One of the first things Schultze did was to lose the pillbox Weston gave him.[56] On February 2, Schultze called District Attorney De Lancey Nicoll and explained the situation to him. Could Nicoll get a court order to have the capsule taken by Weston examined? Nicoll would try. He assigned Assistant District Attorney Vernon M. Davis to the case,[57] and Davis filed an application for authorization to incur the expense of the test. The judge ruled that the evidence was insufficient to warrant wasting the county's money on an analysis.[58] Schultze persisted, and he was finally able to get the capsule analyzed.[59] It was made up exactly according to the specifications of Harris's prescription. Having failed to autopsy Helen, having lost the pillbox, and having fumbled the analysis of the capsule, Schultze plowed ahead and held an inquest before a coroner's jury composed of six pharmacists and six physicians, whom Schultze believed to be "some of the best in New York."[60] One of those physicians was Dr. George L. Peabody, professor of materia medica (clinical pharmacology) at the College of Physicians and Surgeons, who had recently given a series of lectures at the college on the subject of morphine poisoning. Carlyle Harris was one of the students attending those lectures. The coroner's jury returned a verdict stating, "We, the jury, find that Helen Potts met her death from opium poisoning. We also find that the amount of morphine in her possession was not sufficient to cause her death."[61] Harris testified before the coroner's jury, and it would be interesting to know what he had to say, but Coroner Schultze misplaced the transcript of Harris's testimony. He did deliver a copy of the transcript to Harris's attorney, but District Attorney Nicoll never got one.[62] Helen Potts had been buried without an autopsy; a major piece of evidence, the pillbox, had been lost; a judge had refused to allow the capsule to be analyzed; and the transcript of Harris's testimony had been lost. The press characterized the coroner's handling of the case as "farcical"[63] and "little less than criminal dereliction."[64] The case was so thoroughly botched that Assistant District Attorney Davis closed it without filing charges.

The authorities may have given up on the death of Helen Potts, but the newspapers of New York could not let it go. It was just the kind of a Gilded Age scandal that could keep them churning out copy for the next few weeks—a beautiful young girl, a handsome young medical student, both from prominent families, an upscale boarding school, a suspicious death, and a whiff of possible romance. As the reporters sank their teeth into the story, new allegations continued to be made, which merely added fuel to the fire—a secret wedding, unlawful abortions, adulterous affairs, bigamy, the seduction and ruin of innocent young girls. The media storm formed part of an odd chain of events that resulted in the reopening of the case, the indictment of Harris, and the trial of the first murder-by-poisoning case in New York City in twenty-two years.[65] The lurid trial that resulted garnered nationwide headlines and launched the careers of two of New York's most famous prosecutors, Francis L. Wellman and William Travers Jerome.

The *Irish American Weekly* called it "One of the most remarkable criminal trials that ever took place in this city."[66] The *New York Tribune* said of the case, "Rarely, if ever, . . . have so many elements of romance been united in one proceeding as in the trial of Carlyle W. Harris."[67] The *Harrisburg Patriot* said it was "probably one of the most sensational trials in all of modern jurisprudence,"[68] and the aftermath of the trial was as bizarre as the trial was sensational. The case spurred vigorous debate about Harris's guilt or innocence, the value of circumstantial evidence, the worth of expert testimony, press coverage of sensational trials, and the advisability of the death penalty. What was completely overlooked in the hue and cry was the decisive role that the second-class status of women in Gilded Age culture played in the death of Helen Potts and the downfall of numerous other women Harris seduced.

The Carlyle Harris case was a significant milestone in American courtroom history that has been all but forgotten. It deserves to be remembered, and this book seeks to ensure that it is. It will describe the sequence of events from the time Harris met Helen Potts at the Coleman House in Asbury Park, New Jersey,[69] and trace the case's passage through New York's labyrinthine court system. It will describe Gilded Age morals, journalism, religion, and politics, and show how these various aspects of nineteenth-century culture influenced the course of a high-profile murder prosecution; and it will describe the larger-than-life characters of the lawyers involved in the trial and appeal, chronicling and evaluating the stratagems they employed litigating the case.

CHAPTER ONE

The Secret Marriage

Dr. Benjamin William McCready, a lifelong resident of New York City, graduated from New York's College of Physicians and Surgeons in 1836 and went on to a long and distinguished career as a medical man. He was one of the founders of the Bellevue Hospital Medical College[1] and served on the faculty of the college as professor of materia medica.[2] His business interests extended far beyond medicine and medical education,[3] and by the time of his death on August 9, 1892,[4] he owned a sizable estate, none of which was left to his grandson Carlyle W. Harris.[5]

Dr. McCready had an intelligent, articulate, strong-willed daughter by the name of Frances. Frances did not marry well. Her husband proved incapable of supporting her, but she stayed with him through many years and several childbirths. Because she and her children received little or no support from her husband, she was forced to find a way to take care of her family, and it had to be a way that would be in keeping with the highest standards of Gilded Age propriety. Using the pen name Hope Ledyard, she eked out an existence as the author of inspirational books[6] and articles,[7] and as an itinerant speaker on such subjects as church work,[8] temperance,[9] social purity,[10] and the rearing of children.[11] She eventually parted company with her husband, but Frances McCready Harris did not divorce him—such a thing was out of the question for a lady who prided herself on being the model of Christian temperance, virtue, and deportment. There is no direct evidence as to why they separated, but Mrs. Harris may have left clues in her writings as to the issues that drove a wedge between them.

Writing as Hope Ledyard, Mrs. Harris penned a number of short stories about a virtuous housewife named Nellie Ryder. The stories dealt with such uplifting subjects as patriotism and temperance. One story written a few years before she separated from her husband, "Nellie Ryder's Tea Triumph," tells how Nellie's husband Ned, a two-fisted drinker, wants to serve wine at an upcoming party. Nellie gallantly talks him into serving tea instead, and it turns out to be a great hit with all of her husband's business associates. The story ends with one of Ned's friends telling him what a treasure he has in Nellie.[12] One is led to suspect that Nellie is Mrs. Harris's fictional alter ego and that the resolution of the story is one Mrs. Harris wished for in her own life.

An essay she wrote shortly before her separation from her husband renders up another clue. In "False Pride as to Work," Hope Ledyard fiercely criticizes the unemployed man who will turn down a job because he thinks that he deserves a larger salary than what is being offered. She describes Herculean efforts finding the man a job and intense disappointment when he turns down the job because the pay is beneath his dignity. Then she heaps praise on the woman who steps into the breach and does whatever it takes to support her family.[13]

From these two articles it is easy to infer the following scenario: Frances McCready Harris grew up in the lap of luxury and respectability as the daughter of a wealthy physician, but she married a man who couldn't keep a job worthy of his talents because he liked his liquor too much. False pride prevented him from taking a job beneath his perceived station in life, and the family saw hard times. Mrs. Harris swallowed her Victorian pride of station, rolled up her sleeves, and went to work to support the family. When she became self-sufficient, she realized that her husband was nothing more than an anchor around her neck and got rid of him. Separation from her husband, however, did not separate her from familial heartache.

Charles L. Harris and Frances McCready Harris had seven children, four of whom survived to adulthood.[14] Carlyle W. Harris, their oldest child, was born in Glenn Falls, New York, purportedly on September 23, 1869,[15] and to say he didn't turn out well would be an understatement. Before Helen Potts's death, in an unguarded moment Mrs. Harris confided to Helen's mother that Harris was "a constant source of trouble to me all my life," and his brother McCready Harris warned Helen's mother that his brother was a "polished villain" who could not be trusted.[16] Harris's two most apparent faults seem to have been an utter disregard for the truth and an insatiable appetite for sex. Harris left school at age thirteen and went through a string of jobs—as a jeweler's clerk, at a sugar refinery, and

Carlyle W. Harris
at the time of his
trial (Wellman and
Simms, *The Trial of
Carlyle W. Harris*)

as a sales representative for a sugar importer. Then, much to his mother's chagrin,[17] he became an actor and toured with a theatrical company putting on the play *Paul Kauvar,* a story of the French Revolution.[18]

Despite his proclivity for the Bohemian lifestyle, Harris had some good qualities. He was handsome, intelligent, charismatic, and industrious— capable of doing much good if his abilities were channeled in the right direction. It seemed that Harris was about to turn a corner in his career path when he left the *Paul Kauvar* company. He entered medical school at the College of Physicians and Surgeons, his grandfather's alma mater, and took a part-time job as a clerk at the Old Dominion Steamship Company to defray the costs of his tuition.[19] He did not need to work as a clerk for long because his grandfather was so delighted that he not only agreed to pay Harris's tuition, he allowed the young man to live with him while attending college.[20] Harris excelled in his studies at the College of Physicians and

Surgeons and became popular with both faculty and students. The only thing they disliked about him was his tendency to boast about his purported sexual conquests.[21]

In the summer of 1889, Frances McCready Harris rented a cottage in Ocean Grove, New Jersey,[22] where she was joined by her sons Carlyle and McCready. The municipality of Ocean Grove, New Jersey, began with the formation in 1869 of the Ocean Grove Camp Meeting Association of the Methodist Episcopal Church. They began holding tent revivals on six acres of land, then started selling lots, and by 1889 Ocean Grove had developed into a thriving religious retreat.[23] Such a location was a perfect fit for Mrs. Harris's work. While in Ocean Grove she gave a series of lectures on temperance, and the lectures were attended by George H. Potts, a wealthy railroad contractor and mine owner, and his wife Cynthia.[24] It was only natural that Mrs. Potts and Mrs. Harris befriend each other, as they had many mutual friends residing in the vicinity of Ocean Grove.[25] In this situation Mrs. Potts's beautiful daughter, Helen, could not possibly escape Harris's notice.

For those who wished to escape the summer heat of New York but did not care for the intensely spiritual atmosphere of Ocean Grove, there was the more secular neighboring community of Asbury Park. Harris met Helen when she was escorted to a dance held at the Coleman House in Asbury Park. Helen's escort, a friend of Harris, made the formal introduction.[26] Harris later described his first impression of her: "She was the most beautiful girl I had ever seen. She was tall, with remarkably large, dark eyes, an olive complexion, and possessed that crowning glory of all, a mass of chestnut hair."[27] He immediately began to court her. Harris began to attend the Young People's Temple in Ocean Grove, where Helen sang in the choir.[28] He took her boating, they went swimming in the ocean, they played tennis, and enjoyed all the "usual sea-shore pleasures," but always in the company of others.[29]

When winter came, George Potts moved his family to New York so his children could attend schools in the city, and Harris returned to medical school. Helen went to the College of Music and her younger brother went to the Columbia Institute, a military academy.[30] Because Mr. Potts was away from home for long periods on business, they took a small apartment not far from the College of Physicians and Surgeons.[31] Both Harris and his brother McCready visited the Potts family regularly, but Harris visited too

The Coleman House in Asbury Park, where Harris and Potts met (Courtesy of the Library of Congress)

regularly to please Mrs. Potts. She cautioned him about his frequent visits, and he promised to visit less often. He asked Mrs. Potts if he could become engaged to Helen, and she flatly refused to allow it. Harris wanted to know why she objected. "You're too young to speak of an engagement. You're only twenty years old, and it is nonsense to talk about an engagement. My husband won't consent to an engagement until Helen is older, and it would be better for both of you not to think of such a thing." She went on to say that she did not object to him; she thought he was a bright young man, but she knew his family would object just as strenuously to an engagement at that time. She said he was a handsome young man and well liked in society, and if he would wait, he could marry in a much better way.[32]

Harris told Charles E. Davison, a friend of his, that he wanted to become engaged to Helen but her mother wouldn't consent. Because Davison was a lawyer, Harris asked him about the advisability of secretly marrying Helen. Davison told Harris that it was a bad idea, that he shouldn't do it. "Wait," Davison said, "until you can get the consent of the girl's parents." By the time Davison finished counseling Harris, he was convinced that Harris was going to take his advice.[33]

It seems that McCready Harris was courting Helen also, and it may have been at this time that he warned Mrs. Potts about his brother being a "polished villain" who couldn't be trusted. Things came to a head on the evening of February 7, 1890, during a visit by the two brothers. McCready invited Helen to go to the stock exchange on the following day, where he worked, and Helen gladly accepted. Harris lingered at the Potts residence after his brother left and asked permission to escort Helen to the stock exchange the next morning to meet his brother. Mrs. Harris agreed. Bright and early the next morning, Harris called for Helen, and the two had not been long gone when McCready arrived to pick up Helen for the excursion. What Mrs. Potts and McCready Harris said about his brother's duplicity is lost to history because she wasn't allowed to testify about it at the trial.[34]

Harris didn't take Helen to the stock exchange. He took her downtown and, under the assumed names of Charles Harris and Helen Neilson, the two were married before Alderman M. P. Rinckhoff. Helen gave Harris the marriage certificate for safekeeping. When they returned to the Potts residence at 3:00 P.M., Harris told Mrs. Potts they had gone to the *Tribune* building and afterwards ate lunch together. Harris asked permission to sit with Helen for the afternoon and Mrs. Potts consented.[35]

Harris did a number of things after they were secretly married. He burned the marriage certificate.[36] He went to his lawyer friend and confessed that he had married Helen. Davison urged him to go to Helen's parents and tell them about the marriage. Harris promised he would do so, but he never quite got around to breaking the news to Mrs. Potts until circumstances forced his hand.[37] Most important, he impregnated Helen twice and twice convinced her to have an abortion. Over time his visits to the Potts residence steadily declined. Helen was no less interested in him, but his interest in her seemed to be waning.[38]

When summer came, Harris's life began to spin out of control. He was free from studies that summer, so he borrowed $600 from his grandfather and opened a business in Asbury Park.[39] He rented a three-story building near the Coleman House. On the ground floor he opened the Bijou Café, an innocent restaurant and candy store. He ran this store in his own name. Over the stairwell leading to the upper two floors he put a sign that said "Neptune Club—for members only." On the upper two floors, club members could gamble at the poker tables and refresh themselves with alcoholic beverages.[40] Harris tried to shield himself by running the Neptune Club under the alias of Charles W. Harkness, but his foray into the vice industry had set him on the pathway to a collision with the criminal justice system. But before he hit the landmine of an arrest for keeping a disorderly house, he hit another; Helen told him she was pregnant again, and she wasn't going submit to another abortion. Harris was desperate to keep his marriage a secret—possibly because of his recent engagement to the daughter of a Reverend Worrell, a Presbyterian minister[41]—and the impending birth of his child was going to make that impossible. Harris began a campaign to persuade Helen to have another abortion. She finally agreed, but it was a conditional agreement. She was not going to submit to the disgrace of another possibly fatal abortion until Harris acknowledged her as his wife to an impartial witness. He had no choice but to comply.

Helen invited her good friend Mae Schofield down to Ocean Grove for a visit, and after she had been there a few days, Helen asked Mae to take a walk on the beach. Just before they left for their walk, Harris came to call and Helen invited him to join them. Schofield started down the steps toward the beach, but she noticed that Helen and Harris were hanging back, having a whispered conversation. It is reasonable to infer that Helen was urging Harris that "Now is the time. You must tell Mae now." Schofield

Helen Potts,
the only known
picture (Wellman
and Simms, *The
Trial of Carlyle W.
Harris*)

stopped to wait for the two, and Helen called to her to walk on with Harris, that she needed to go back and finish writing a letter. Schofield said she would wait. "No," replied Helen. "Go on, I will join you in a moment." Harris and Schofield walked down Lake Avenue toward the beach.

"Can you keep a secret?" asked Harris.

"Not if it is a very big one," she answered. "Don't tell it to me, please."

Harris said, "I wouldn't could I help it, but Helen insists."

"Then let me tell you the secret," said Schofield, "You and Helen are engaged. I guessed that ages ago."

Harris said, "Perhaps you didn't guess that we were married last February."

"You can't mean that you were secretly married and have told no one!" she said.

"I do mean just that," he replied. "Do you suppose I would have anyone know of the marriage?"

Schofield answered, "If Miss Potts hasn't already told her mother, I shall beg her to do so!"

Harris became angry. "You will do no such thing! I put you on your honor not to tell. My prospects will be utterly ruined if this marriage is known! I would rather kill her and kill myself than have the marriage public! I wish that she were dead and I were out of it!"

"Carl Harris, even in anger you shall not say such things to me in my presence!" Miss Schofield turned to walk back to the Potts house and Harris followed. They walked in silence. When they got back to the house, they found Helen at the top of the steps.

"I have told her, Helen," said Harris.

"What do you think of it, Mae?" asked Helen.

Schofield said, "I'll tell you later." Harris began to walk off.

"Can't you come in, Carl?" asked Helen.

"Not now. I have an engagement. Remember your promise. Mae will urge you to tell your mother, but remember your promise; for we can't have the marriage known now, can we, Helen?"[42] Satisfied that she had an independent witness to the marriage, Helen did not tell her mother she was married and later that day allowed Harris to attempt the abortion.

When Harris came back later that afternoon, he and Helen took a solitary walk on the beach. They were gone for three hours, and during that time Harris performed what he thought was a successful abortion by inducing a bloody discharge, which he thought contained the fetus. Helen bled so profusely he thought she was going to die, but eventually he stopped the bleeding.

When Harris brought her home, Helen looked pale and ill and complained of a headache. Mrs. Potts told her she ought not to have taken so long a walk and asked her why she did so. Helen gave her no answer but went upstairs to bed and did not reappear until the next morning.[43] Harris went back to the Neptune Club, thinking his problems were solved, but instead of getting better, things got worse. Despite the fact that Helen was slowly sickening, or possibly because of it, Mrs. Potts sent Helen to her brother-in-law, Dr. Charles Treverton, who lived in Scranton, Pennsylvania.

When Helen arrived in Scranton, Dr. Treverton saw that she was in poor health. She had a pale complexion, no appetite, and seemed to be nauseated in the mornings. Dr. Treverton questioned her and learned that she was very weak and had a vaginal discharge. He said he needed to make a physical examination of her, but she refused. He continued to insist that he needed to examine her, and she continued to refuse. This went on for approximately one week before Helen finally relented and allowed him to touch her. Dr. Treverton put his hand on her stomach and began to palpate it. He soon discovered that his niece Helen, whom he believed to be a model of purity and deportment, was carrying a child.[44]

Treverton was surprised and disappointed. To these emotions he added disbelief when Helen confessed her secret marriage and told him that Harris had induced her to have three abortions, two performed by him and one by a doctor whom she didn't know. Treverton could not believe that any man would stoop so low as to perform an abortion on his own wife. Helen sat down and wrote a statement outlining all the particulars of her marriage to Harris and signed it with her full signature. She handed the statement to Treverton. "There, will that satisfy you?" she asked. It did.[45]

On July 29, almost immediately after confessing her marriage to Dr. Treverton, Helen went into labor. Because Treverton had only six years of experience as a medical doctor, he felt less than equal to the task of attending Helen without advice. He consulted with his mentor, Dr. David Hand, who recommended that Treverton ease Helen's pain by giving her deodorized tincture of opium.[46] Treverton began administering opium to Helen, but the opium didn't do much for the pain. He consulted with Hand again, and they decided to give Helen quarter-grain doses of morphine every three hours. This eased her pain. Treverton continued to administer quarter-grain doses of morphine to Helen for the next three days.

Sometime during the confusion of Helen's first day of labor, Treverton sent a letter to Harris, which was less than diplomatic. It betrayed three concerns: concern for Helen's health, concern for any possible scandal that might result from the pregnancy, and concern for the expense involved in treating Helen.

Scranton, Pa., July 29, 1890

Mr. C. W. Harris:

Dear Sir—As you are aware, Miss Potts is in a critical condition and you are all to blame. Things must be attended to at once, or you must know the result—disgrace for us all, and, above all, I shall need medical aid and money. Will you stand the bill? If you will, things can be made all right again, and no one be any wiser. If not, we will take other steps. I shall be pleased to see you in Scranton at once to see to this matter. If you come, dispatch when you will be here and stop at the Wyoming House and I will meet you there. If you can't come, dispatch and say whether you will bear expenses. If you [will], say yes; if not, say no; and may God help you to be quick about it and save any more trouble. Remember, I shall handle this thing to your sorrow if you fail to appear. Write to me, and don't fail to direct me what to do at once.

Yours truly,

Dr Treverton.

I mean business—[47]

It is open to question as to whether Harris would have responded to this letter if Helen herself had not sent him a telegram urging him to come and see her.[48]

On Saturday, August 2, 1890, matters came to a head. Treverton decided he needed more than Dr. Hand's advice, he needed Hand's active assistance. When Hand arrived at Treverton's home, he examined Helen and decided that they should change their strategy. Up to this point they were simply seeking to ease her pain as the natural contractions expelled the baby, but Hand decided that the intensity of Helen's contractions needed to be increased, not lessened. They began administering quinine and giving her rectal injections of hot water. Even with the stimulus, it was another twenty-four hours before the stillborn child was delivered.[49]

Harris was scheduled to arrive that Sunday, and Treverton had no time for him. He made arrangements for his nephew Charles Oliver to meet Harris. Oliver met Harris at the train station and took him to the Lackawanna Valley House, where Harris checked in, freshened up, and changed clothes. Oliver then took Harris to his uncle's home, where Harris and Treverton spoke briefly.[50] Upon being informed of the situation, Harris said that he was a student at the College of Physicians and Surgeons, that he had brought a valise of instruments with him to handle the situation, and that Dr. Treverton could use them if he wished. Did Dr. Treverton need his assistance? Dr. Treverton didn't need the instruments or Harris's assistance. They agreed to discuss the matter of Helen's predicament more fully the following day, and the two parted company.[51] Harris went sightseeing with Oliver, who knew nothing of Helen's predicament, and Treverton went back to Helen's sickbed.

The two young men toured the Bellevue Coal Mines that Sunday evening as Helen finally delivered Harris's stillborn child; and they toured the steel mills on the following day, staying at the mills until almost midnight. On the walk back from the mills Oliver asked Harris how he liked the study of medicine. Harris said that he liked it very well and that he had learned a great many interesting facts. Harris said he had made a special study of women, and there were a great many women who were willing to pay high fees for professional services. With this segue, Harris began to expound on his favorite topic. He told Oliver that he had a great deal of experience with women and that he had debauched more than a few. Harris explained how easy it was to mix alcohol into ginger ale, and when the alcohol took effect, he would roll them over on the floor and "screw" them.

Harris said that only two women were able to resist him, and he conquered both of them by talking them into secret marriage ceremonies. Oliver was shocked, but Harris assured him that he was ready to stand by them if he was compelled to do so. Oliver wanted to know how he could stand by two marriages at the same time. Harris said that wouldn't be a problem; the first "wife" was glad to be rid of him. And why was that? She got pregnant, and he forged a letter from his mother inviting her for a visit. He showed the letter to her family and took her away, but they didn't go to his mother's. They went to some sort of hospital in New York, where he had an abortion performed on her. When she was released from the hospital, he asked her if she wanted him to acknowledge her as his wife. She told him no, she was disgusted and wanted to have nothing more to do with him.[52]

Harris shoehorned an interview with Dr. Treverton between his visits to coal mines and steel mills. They met that Monday morning, and Dr. Treverton described how Helen finally delivered a stillborn child who had evidence of trauma to its head. It looked as though it might have been dead for two to four weeks, maybe even longer.[53] In his reply to Treverton, Harris sought to rehabilitate himself as a competent medical man in Treverton's eyes and to burnish his self-image as a Casanova. He told Treverton he was somewhat surprised by the nature of Helen's illness because he thought at the time he performed the operation, he removed it all himself. He said this was the second abortion he had performed on her. He did admit that this last abortion resulted in a lot of hemorrhaging and he was a little frightened, but he got it under control and everything seemed to turn out all right.[54] Treverton was appalled. Didn't Harris have any sense of delicacy about performing such an operation on someone whom he knew so intimately? Harris said he had no qualms at all. Harris said he had connection with five different young ladies and that one of them delivered as fine a little boy as he ever looked upon. He said he always got through things rather slick and he figured he'd get through this thing slick too.[55] When Treverton protested at the way he was treating Helen, Harris said he did not intend to drop her altogether. Whenever he got a girl pregnant, he never left her unprotected. He always looked after them until they were over it. Harris emphasized that he never deserted them until they recovered. To show Treverton what an honorable man he was, Harris told of his two secret marriages and how he stood by his first secret wife in her pregnancy. He told Treverton basically the same story he told Oliver with two exceptions. In the version he told Treverton his first secret wife delivered a child rather than having an abortion, and he said nothing about her leaving him in disgust.[56] To reassure Treverton that his intentions toward Helen were honorable, Harris said he liked Helen more than all the others and was sorry she was in that condition. Harris said they have even gone through a ceremony and were "virtually" married.[57] When the district attorney's office learned of Harris's statements to Oliver and Treverton concerning his secret marriages, they did their best to verify them, but given Harris's penchant for stretching the truth, they were unable to determine the exact number of times Harris had been secretly married.

After having reassured Treverton of his skill as a surgeon, his prowess as a Casanova, and his honorable intentions toward Helen, Harris departed for a tour of the steel mills with Charles Oliver. He spent Monday night at the Lackawanna Valley House, and on Tuesday morning he was back on the train headed for Asbury Park and the Neptune Club. When he got back to Asbury Park, he called on Mrs. Potts and told her that Helen was sick and wanted to see her. He said nothing about the abortion or the secret marriage. As Helen recuperated in Scranton, Harris settled back into running his twin businesses—but not for long. On August 20, 1890, police raided the Neptune Club and arrested Harris for keeping a disorderly house. When he was booked into jail, he gave the name Charles W. Harkness.[58]

CHAPTER TWO

The Sacred Marriage

When Mrs. Potts learned of Helen's illness, she rushed to her daughter's side. Mrs. Potts felt it was fortunate that Mr. Potts's job as a railroad contractor, which took him all over the country,[1] had taken him away from home during this trying time. There is no direct evidence of the discussions among Mrs. Potts and Dr. Treverton and her daughter. Our only evidence for the circumstances of her visit comes from the trial testimony, and the rules of evidence (especially the hearsay rule) sharply restrict what witnesses can say about conversations outside the presence of the defendant. Sometimes attorneys are lax in enforcing the rule, thinking they can gain a tactical advantage by letting the hearsay in. Harris's attorneys did not seem to have this attitude, and they were vigilant in objecting to any testimony that even remotely resembled hearsay.[2] This often gives testimony a fractured and disjointed texture, with much essential context omitted, and that is the case with many of the incidents relevant to our inquiry. It is often possible, however, to infer the conversation from the course of events. For example:

> Q: Officer Friendly, did you speak to Valerie Victim about her gunshot wound at the scene of the crime?
> A: Yes.
> Q: After speaking with her, what action did you take?
> A: I arrested Dan Defendant.

It doesn't take a rocket scientist to infer from this line of questioning that Officer Friendly asked Valerie, "Who shot you?" and she said, "Dan

Defendant." From a careful reading of the testimony of Dr. Treverton and Mrs. Potts, we can reconstruct a highly likely course of events for her visit to Scranton.

Now that Helen's health was on the mend, Treverton's objectives changed somewhat. He wanted to protect Helen from scandal, to recoup his financial losses, and to punish Harris in some way. The only feasible way to punish him without exposing Helen to scandal was to corkscrew money out of him under threat of reporting his misdeeds to the College of Physicians and Surgeons and to the Ocean Grove authorities. Mrs. Potts did not care about any of Treverton's objectives other than protecting Helen from scandal. She knew Harris to be dependent upon the generosity of his grandfather, and she knew that his grandfather's generosity would not extend to defraying the cost of one of Harris's amorous escapades. Mrs. Potts had a second objective, and getting Harris expelled from medical school and prosecuted for performing a criminal abortion would render both her objectives impossible. Hiding the scandal would protect Helen's reputation, but it would do nothing to erase the stain on her character. The only way to repair that blot was to have Harris marry her in a public, church-sanctioned wedding, and have them marry when they both had pristine reputations for social purity. Mrs. Potts persuaded Dr. Treverton to withhold any action until she went back to Ocean Grove and sorted things out with Harris. Although Mrs. Potts stayed in Scranton with her daughter as Helen recuperated from her sickness, she was not idle in pressing her agenda.

Helen wrote Harris and told him that the cat was irretrievably out of the bag. This prompted Harris to write Mrs. Potts in Scranton:

Dear Mrs. Potts: I have just learned from Helen that you have made a discovery that I did not intend that you should make for months. I can only crave your indulgent pardon for myself and Helen in having deceived you for so long under any circumstances. I must beg you for all our sakes to keep our secret, and that things can go on in the ordinary way, first the engagement and then the public ceremony. The proof of the first (the marriage) one may be had in the Bureau of Vital Statistics in New York. I wish I could see you and talk with you and I trust I may before long. In the meanwhile I can only hope for your forgiveness and try to win your respect, and I shall always be yours, affectionately, Carl.[3]

In a second letter Harris urged Mrs. Potts to tell her husband about the secret marriage. He was afraid that Dr. Treverton would write him, and he felt it would be much better if Mr. Potts heard the story from her. She was in the process of writing the painful letter to her husband when news came of Harris's arrest. Just when it looked as though things were at their worst, she learned that they could get much worse. Despondent, she abandoned the letter and resolved not to tell her husband anything.[4] She also resolved that her daughter would have a proper ministerial marriage. From that day forward until the day of Helen's death, Mrs. Potts was a woman on a mission, and that mission was to compel Harris to marry her daughter in a proper ceremony.

It was September 1, 1891, and the College of Physicians and Surgeons was about to reopen for the fall semester. Harris, who was busily avoiding court dates on his disorderly house charge, was back in New York to prepare for his final year of school. He asked Mrs. Potts to come to New York to settle the matter of the secret marriage. He was going to have enough trouble answering the school on the Neptune Club issue, and he could not afford to have Dr. Treverton writing the college about the abortion.[5] Mrs. Potts took her daughter, by this time fully recovered from her illness, to New York to discuss the matter with Harris. They took the train to the New Jersey ferry terminal and rode the ferry over to the city with the morning commuters. They met Harris at Altman's store on Sixth Avenue and then went to Clark's Restaurant on Twenty-Third Street where, just five years before, a group of descendants of the Dutch settlers of New Netherlands had formed the Holland Society of New York.[6] The society is still in existence today and has its headquarters at 708 Third Avenue in the city.[7]

At Clark's they ate a rather uncomfortable meal and then began to talk. Harris wanted to explain about his arrest for keeping a disorderly house. He swore that he had no idea what was going on upstairs over his innocent café and candy store. His first inkling that there was anything wrong came when a gentleman marched downstairs and accosted him with a complaint that he was cheated out of eight dollars at the gaming tables. Harris said that he was so shocked he didn't know what to do, so he reached his hand in his pocket and pulled out eight dollars and gave it to the man. Harris said he would take an oath to the truth of what he said. When Mrs. Potts broached the subject of Harris and Helen getting married properly, Harris assured her that the marriage was perfectly legal. He spoke so emphatically that he

Morning ferry docks in New York with commuters from New Jersey, 1904 (Courtesy of the Library of Congress)

attracted the attention of other diners. Mrs. Potts suggested that they go somewhere a little more private to discuss such delicate subjects. Harris agreed and suggested that they go to the office of a friend of his, and the friend could explain everything to her. Mrs. Potts said Helen had to go and make some visits, and she would go alone with him to the friend's office. First, she said, they needed to go to City Hall and see the official records of the marriage. Harris objected. He said it was very important that his friend

explain some things to Mrs. Potts before she saw the record of the marriage.[8] Mrs. Potts finally agreed, and they went to 170 Broadway to the office
of Charles E. Davison, attorney at law.

When they were seated in Davison's office, the lawyer began to explain to Mrs. Potts that the Neptune Club was incorporated in Harris's
name and was perfectly legal under New Jersey state law, but they overlooked the local borough ordinances. Mrs. Potts was not interested. She
wanted to talk to Harris about the marriage. Davison droned on about
the Neptune Club. In conclusion, he said, it would be far better for Harris
to forfeit his bail than to go to trial.[9] Davison then turned his attention
to Dr. Treverton. He told Mrs. Potts that Treverton had placed himself
completely within Davison's power, and if Treverton made any trouble
for Harris at the College, Davison would use that power against him. This
threat was completely wasted on Mrs. Potts. She had no idea what Davison was talking about.[10]

At this point Davison was called out of the room, and Mrs. Potts could
speak privately with Harris. He asked her if she had told her husband of
the secret marriage. She replied that it was not the right time to tell her
husband. She asked Harris if he had told his mother.

"No," said Harris, "I would not have the family know it for half a million
dollars."

Mrs. Potts said it would have been well if he had thought of that sooner.

Harris said, "If you're so unhappy about the marriage, it could very
easily be broken. If you had not found out and it became a bore, we could
have easily broken it and nobody would have been the wiser. We can break
it now if you wish."

Mrs. Potts replied, "I would call that legalized prostitution. I want it
made a ministerial marriage."

Harris replied, "I'm perfectly willing to make it a ministerial marriage at
any other time than the present time. Helen's name might get connected
with the Neptune Club scandals."

Mr. Davison returned and said that he had sent a clerk over to City Hall
to retrieve a copy of the marriage certificate and that the clerk had returned
with it. "Where is the original certificate, and why have we been waiting for
this?" Mrs. Potts wanted to know.

"I burned the original certificate." Mrs. Potts sat in a stunned silence,
which was broken by Mr. Davison saying he would put it in an affidavit if

Mrs. Potts would let the marriage stand as it was for the time being. Davison prepared an affidavit for Harris's signature and attached it to the marriage certificate. He then showed it to Mrs. Potts. She was horrified. Neither Harris's nor Helen's name appeared anywhere on the certificate. Attached to the certificate was an affidavit that read

> Carlyle W. Harris, being duly sworn, says that he resides at No. 28 East Seventeenth Street, in the City of New York; that on the 8th day of February 1890, deponent, under the name of Charles Harris, married Helen N. Potts under and by the name of Helen Neilson before W. P. Rinckhoff, the Alderman of the Seventeenth District in the City of New York, as appears by the annexed transcript from the records of the marriages reported to the Health Department of the City of New York, which is numbered 2062.

Mrs. Potts turned to Harris. "There is nothing sacred to me in such a marriage as this."

Harris said, "Well, I should say not. I looked the old fellow up, and he keeps a lager beer saloon."[11] Harris again promised definitely that he would have a ministerial marriage with Helen at any time after the Neptune Club scandal had blown over. Harris said that although the scandal had not hurt his standing in society, if word of the ministerial marriage leaked out while the Neptune Club case was pending, it might sully Helen's reputation.[12] Mrs. Potts grudgingly approved of Harris's plan with one proviso: as long as the marriage was secret they would live as friends—no sexual intercourse. Harris agreed to the stipulation.[13]

They left Davison's office together, and as they were going down in the elevator, Harris thanked Mrs. Potts for not pushing the ministerial marriage any further at that time. "If it had been pushed further," he said, "I would have been obliged to leave everything and go west."[14]

In an earlier letter to Mrs. Potts, Harris had urged her to enroll Helen in the Comstock School. Helen was impulsive, he wrote, and so natural that she revealed her emotions too readily. He wrote that the Comstock School would train her and fit her for the society he expected she would live in after he became a successful doctor. While they were in the elevator Harris returned to the subject, and Mrs. Potts agreed. She thought he was a brilliant young man with the potential to go far and Helen would profit from a first-rate finishing school.

Harris then turned to the subject of Dr. Treverton. Could Mrs. Potts write him and tell him she was completely satisfied with the marriage? If Dr. Treverton were to write the college, it would make him a great deal of trouble there. He was going to have his hands full dealing with the Neptune Club scandal, and answering Dr. Treverton's charges would be too much of a challenge. Mrs. Potts assured Harris she would make things right with Treverton. She would write Treverton a letter requesting that he not make trouble for Harris and send him a promissory note for his medical fees.[15] When Mrs. Potts later made good on her promise, Dr. Treverton immediately destroyed the promissory note and wrote a letter telling her he did not require such a thing from her.

Their business concluded, Harris escorted Mrs. Potts to the ferry that would take her back to New Jersey. When they got to the ferry, Helen was waiting for them. Seeing that they appeared to be friendly to one another, she broke into a smile. "Mother, are you satisfied with the marriage?" she asked. "For the time being," Mrs. Potts replied. Helen was happy. Mrs. Potts would later recall, "I never have seen her look so happy as she did that day."[16] When they boarded the ferry, Mrs. Potts gave them plenty of room to talk privately. They parted company when the ferry docked, and Harris went back to New York while they traveled on to Ocean Grove. Harris wrote both Helen and Mrs. Potts constantly from that time forward until Helen entered the Comstock School in December.[17]

Then Mrs. Potts, Helen, and Harris had a series of communications that is difficult to make sense of. Mrs. Potts destroyed all the letters she received, believing that they may someday be used as evidence that Helen had engaged in an unholy marriage. Harris retained his copies of the letters from Mrs. Potts. None of the letters survive, and we have only the portions of the letters read into evidence at the trial to sort out what was said. It seems that Mrs. Potts had been pressing Harris to at least tell his family that he and Helen were engaged to be married, and he complained in a letter to Helen about her mother's insistence. Helen made the complaint known to her mother, and Mrs. Potts responded with a letter to Harris:

Dear Carl: I learn, I see by the contents of your letter that you would prefer not telling your family of an engagement before the holidays, as I had expected you would do; I see no necessity for doing so, as your marriage is

New York–New Jersey ferry against the New York skyline, early 1900s (Courtesy of the Library of Congress)

already an assured fact; you owe your family gratitude and an expression of it rather than disappointment and disobedience; I am quite willing that there should be no engagement at this time.[18]

As Mrs. Potts had destroyed Harris's letters, his reply could not be read into evidence, but she could paraphrase it:

He said that he had enjoyed reading my letter, that he would now like to suggest that there be no further question of either marriage or engagement for two years. Let Helen remain at the Comstock School through the summer and be fitted for Wellesley and take a collegiate course and let everything just remain as it was for two years longer.[19]

Mrs. Potts did not reply to this letter. A couple of weeks passed, and Harris wrote another letter. Of that letter Mrs. Potts recalled:

He wrote me that he had seen Helen and found that his lawyer had worried me; he regretted this; he placed himself entirely in my hands to have any ceremony, religious ceremony that he had already promised at any time I might ask for it, even if it hindered his professional advancement.[20]

It was January 18 or 19, 1891, that Mrs. Potts replied to the second let-ter.[21] She would later recall that letter in the following words:

> I said to him that his letter to me made me very nervous, that he had
> asked me to allow my daughter to remain in the hardest position a woman
> could ever occupy, to remain three years an unacknowledged wife, and
> for no reason but a whim, it seemed to me; there seemed no reasonable
> reason that the marriage should be kept secret three years; I told him that
> her illness in Scranton had been commented upon and it was necessary
> that for such reasons it be not kept a secret so long; I told him what keep-
> ing it so long must mean to her; I told him how hard it was and what po-
> sition it placed her in to ask her to remain three years a secret wife—that
> there were too many questions involved in that time for me to be willing
> to allow it to remain a secret marriage. . . .
>
> I said that he might die, and I could not publish the marriage in the
> form of an affidavit, and the copy was so humiliating to me, the form of
> the marriage was so humiliating that I could not show the certificate to
> my husband; I could not ever let him know I doubted the legality of the
> marriage, at that time; he might meet Dr. Treverton of Scranton and be
> told of the illness and of the doctor's doubts that there was any marriage;
> I tried to show him in every way what it represented to her to be or to
> remain a secret wife for two years longer, making three years, and I asked
> him then to keep his word; he had always promised me on paper that he
> would do just as I said and placed himself entirely in my hands; I said,
> "Now I will ask you on the anniversary of the first marriage to go to a min-
> ister of the gospel and to be married in a Christian manner, and give me
> the certificate to hold, and I will choose my own time in making it public,"
> but I intended to keep it until he was graduated.[22] . . .
>
> I ask you to do as you often asked, take your wife and go, that he go
> and explain to a minister that they were already married [and have him
> perform a sacred marriage]. And then I said I would cheerfully wait for
> five years; I said "Take your wife and be remarried, and let me hold this
> certificate, and I will withhold it until my own time to publish it." I said
> then in the spring if he graduated and failed to get a hospital appointment
> he could have a run to Germany. . . . And I felt there could be no pleasanter
> way than to go with her husband; he answered back that he would do just
> as I said, and I suggested the eighth of February as the day because it was
> the anniversary of the marriage.[23]

There was one ominous proviso in Harris's agreement to a sacred marriage with Helen. Mrs. Potts recalled the proviso in the following language: "[H]e said he would do all I had asked of him, if no other means of satisfying my scruples could be found."[24]

Harris wrote something else about the same time that he wrote Mrs. Potts agreeing to marry Helen on February 8—it was a prescription. On January 20, between 10:00 A.M. and noon, Harris entered McIntyre & Son's pharmacy and asked Hearn Power, the prescription clerk, to prepare twenty-four capsules of oil of sandalwood. Power said it would take some time to prepare that many capsules. Harris asked him to prepare six immediately, and he would pick up the remaining eighteen capsules the following day. Harris also gave Power a prescription for morphine and quinine capsules. He then took a seat and waited for Power to make up the capsules.[25] Power called George Manson, another clerk who was on duty, to come and observe him as he mixed up the morphine and quinine. Manson stood by and observed as Power carefully weighed out the one grain of morphine, placed it in a mortar, and stirred it with a pestle; weighed out twenty-five grains of quinine and placed it in the mortar with the morphine; stirred the two powders together until they were thoroughly mixed; and filled six capsules with equal quantities of the mixture, carefully checking the weight of each capsule.[26] Power then placed the capsules into labeled containers and gave them to Harris. Harris took the six capsules of sandalwood and the six of quinine and morphine and left the pharmacy. He never came back for the other eighteen capsules of sandalwood.[27]

The next day Harris gave Helen four of the six capsules of quinine and morphine, telling her to take them before retiring for the night. Harris then took a break from his studies and departed for Old Point Comfort on the Hampton Roads Harbor in Virginia, the scene of the historic Civil War sea-battle between the *Monitor* and the *Merrimac*. Helen was not a compliant patient. She took the first two capsules in the morning, and the quinine nauseated her.[28] She wrote Harris at Old Point Comfort complaining about the ill effects of the capsules. Harris wrote her back, telling her to persist with the capsules and take them as directed. Harris was back in New York on January 31, and he saw both Helen and Mrs. Potts that day. Mrs. Potts had come to New York to visit with Helen.[29]

Mrs. Potts went up to Helen's room at the Comstock School to meet her roommates, but they were not there when mother and daughter first arrived. As they sat in the room waiting for the roommates to come back,

Helen told her mother about the medicine Harris had given her. As Helen reached into a drawer looking for something, she saw the pillbox and said, "That's the box there." She took it out and shook it. From the sound, Mrs. Potts concluded that there was a single capsule in the pillbox. Helen said she didn't like to take the capsules—that they made her sick. "I'm tempted to toss it out the window rather than take it."[30]

"Quinine is very apt to make one feel wretched," said Mrs. Potts, "your father always feels the effects of quinine. You might be a little malarious. I think it is well that you have taken the quinine, and I think you should continue to take it."[31] Helen's roommates returned, and Mrs. Potts met them. She left the Comstock School at 3:00 P.M. to return to Ocean Grove. That was the last time she saw her daughter alive. Later that afternoon Harris escorted Helen to his mother's home for a visit and they stayed there approximately an hour. Mrs. Harris would later recall that "Helen was radiantly happy and the boy and girl were such evident lovers" that she decided to abandon her opposition to his marrying her.[32]

That evening Helen took the final capsule and died despite the heroic efforts of Dr. Fowler and his assistants to save her. Mrs. Potts received word of her daughter's illness early Sunday morning, but she could not get a train to New York until that afternoon. She got to New York, took the ferry into Manhattan, and Harris met her as she debarked. She could tell by the expression on his face that it was serious.

"Carl, what is it, is she very ill?" Harris delayed answering until he assisted her into a carriage for the trip to the Comstock School.

"It is the very worst."

Mrs. Potts settled herself into the carriage before speaking. "Carl, is this your work?" she asked.

"My God, mother, what do you mean?"

"Have you repeated last summer's work? Have you performed another operation?" Mrs. Potts assumed that Harris killed her in a botched attempt at an abortion.

"As God is my judge, there was no need of an operation!" replied Harris. "She died of morphine poisoning."

"How can that have been?" asked Mrs. Potts.

"It was the druggist's awful mistake." Mrs. Potts was somewhat relieved at hearing this. She leaned her head against the window of the carriage door to feel the coolness of the glass against her brow, and they rode on in silence for some time. Then she thought of something.

"Carl, there is one thing we must decide before we reach Miss Day's. She is your wife, she has been the mother of your child, and she must be buried under your name." Harris was terrified by this pronouncement from Mrs. Potts.

"It cannot be!" he said. "Ask anything of me and I will do it, but the knowledge of this marriage coming at this time will destroy me!"

"Why?"

"My family will never forgive me."

"Carl, she is out of your way, and out of your family's way. How can you be so hard?"

Harris was emphatic, "I would answer just the same as if it was Queen Victoria's daughter. She cannot be buried under my name. If you have no mercy upon me, have mercy upon Miss Day's school. You have ruined her school putting your daughter there under false pretenses."

"Did I do it?" replied Mrs. Potts. "Didn't you select the school?"

"She was put there under false pretenses; it will ruin the school; if you have no mercy upon me, have mercy upon Miss Day," said Harris. "I told her even of the engagement and it almost drove her frantic. If not for my sake, do it for Miss Day's sake and say nothing about the marriage." Mrs. Potts concluded that Harris had more than one secret wife. Things just got worse and worse. The scandalmongers would have a field day. She decided to keep quiet about the marriage and bury her daughter as Helen Potts.[33]

CHAPTER THREE

A World of Concern for Harris

Shortly after noon on the day following Helen's death, Dr. George F. Peabody received a visitor in his office at 57 West thirty-Eighth Street in New York City. The visitor was a young medical student by the name of Carlyle Harris, and he had a letter of introduction from his preceptor at the medical school, Dr. Robert Abbe. Dr. Peabody knew Harris slightly because the young man had recently attended his lectures on materia medica at the college. Was Dr. Peabody aware of the death yesterday at the Comstock School? Yes, he had read about it in the papers. Harris wanted Dr. Peabody's opinion on the matter. Harris told Dr. Peabody that he had prescribed a grain of morphine and twenty-five grains of quinine to be divided into six capsules because she had suffered from insomnia and some malarial symptoms, and he thought the combination would be a good one to give her. He had signed the prescription as a medical student and had it filled at McIntyre & Son's pharmacy. Harris told Peabody about holding two capsules in reserve and then detailed the circumstances of Helen's death. Harris wanted to know if he could be held accountable for killing her.

Peabody told him that he had prescribed very stupidly; that there was no warrant for giving morphine to any young girl who was merely suffering from insomnia, as he should have known if he had listened to Peabody's lectures. Peabody went on to say that it was very bad treatment; that if Harris had attended his lectures he ought to have known it, but that if that was all the morphine she got, Peabody did not think he could be held accountable for her death. Peabody concluded by telling Harris that as a medical student, he had no right to prescribe, and he must have been aware of it at the time.[1] Harris made no reply to the scolding he received from Dr. Peabody; he left the doctor's office, and Dr. Peabody did not see him again until Harris testified at the coroner's inquest.

At the funeral on February 4, George Potts thought he saw his daughter move. He refused to allow her to be buried but ordered that she remain aboveground with a twenty-four-hour-a-day guard in case she should suddenly revive. This was, of course, impossible, as she had been embalmed. It was not until February 7 that the grieving father finally admitted that she was truly dead and gave permission for her to be buried.[2]

Harris did not attend Helen's funeral, but he did return to McIntyre & Son's pharmacy. Hearn Power, the pharmacist's assistant who compounded Harris's concoction of morphine and quinine, was on duty on February 7 when Harris came in with another prescription. "I suppose you won't put up a prescription for me?" asked Harris.

"If it is from a physician we will," replied Power. Harris showed him the prescription; it was signed by Dr. Hayden. Power agreed to fill the prescription. As he was filling the prescription, Harris asked if he had seen an account of Miss Potts's death in the newspapers. Power said that he had.

"You don't believe it, do you?" asked Harris.

"No, I believe the girl died of heart disease," said Power.

"So do I," replied Harris.[3]

During this time Harris did not see Mrs. Potts, but he kept up a correspondence with her. Finally, a few days before the coroner's inquest he came to see her in Ocean Grove. It was around 8:30 P.M., and Mrs. Potts had just received the mail for the day and was beginning to read it when Harris arrived. She had just opened a letter from Dr. Fowler when she became aware that Harris was at the door. She laid the mail on the dining room table with the opened but unread letter from Dr. Fowler on top and admitted Harris to the house. He asked that he be allowed to speak to her alone, and she escorted him through the dining room into a private room.

Harris began the conversation by saying that everyone in the park had met him very kindly and that more people had shaken hands with him than ever did so before.

"That is because I have told no one the fear that I have felt about you, Carlyle," she said.

"Mother, you will find that the coroner's inquest will exonerate me. I am innocent."

"If innocent, Carl, how did she die?" Mrs. Potts wanted to know.

"It was the druggist's mistake," said Harris.

"How could it be the druggist's mistake when you said all the capsules upon being analyzed would prove all right? The statements conflict."

Harris replied, "I will have the capsules analyzed if I have to pay for it out of my own pocket. It's Dr. Treverton. He has influenced your judgment about me."

"Dr. Treverton does not know one word of the fear I have felt of you," replied Mrs. Potts, "but he came here believing you guilty of another crime, and after I had assured him that was not the case, he went home on the night of the funeral without our ever having spoken about this fear I am feeling towards you now."

"Does Mr. Potts know it yet either?" Harris wanted to know.

"No, Mr. Potts doesn't know." At this response from Mrs. Potts, Harris laid his head on his arms and appeared to be crying. After a moment he regained his composure, raised his head, and spoke.

"Mrs. Potts, if you give me the affidavit I will forgive you every word you have said."

"You can't forgive me, Carl; there is no question of forgiveness between us, because her grave is right there; we cannot cross it."

Harris replied, "Yes, I will forgive you. I must have that affidavit. It is more valuable to me than I dare tell you."

"How will you get it?" asked Mrs. Potts. "It is not here."

"Does Miss Day know of the marriage?" asked Harris.

"Yes," replied Mrs. Potts. At this Harris turned and rushed out of the room. Mrs. Potts sat for a moment, then got up and left herself. She went into the dining room to return to reading her mail. The letter from Dr. Fowler was not there.[4]

Mrs. Potts feared that Harris had murdered her daughter, but she feared the scandal associated with a murder trial even more. She corresponded with Mrs. Harris, who feared that her son would be charged with murder. The two mothers met and discussed the situation. Mrs. Potts offered Mrs. Harris fifty dollars and urged her to use the money to help her son flee the jurisdiction.[5] When Mrs. Harris arrived back in New York she received bittersweet news—Harris had been appointed house surgeon at Charity Hospital upon his graduation from medical school.[6]

Mrs. Potts made one more effort to cover up the possibility that her daughter had been murdered. She went to Dr. Peabody and urged him to use his influence to cause the coroner's jury to return a verdict that her daughter had died of heart disease aggravated by the morphine in the capsules prescribed by Harris. Dr. Peabody told Mrs. Potts quite frankly that he suspected Helen had been murdered.[7] After hearing all the testimony, the coroner's jury brought in a verdict of death by morphine poisoning. The verdict, but not the transcript of testimony, was transmitted to the district attorney's office, where Assistant District Attorney Vernon M. Davis wrestled with what to do about the case.

Vernon M. Davis, assistant district attorney for New York County, 1885–97 (King, *Notable New Yorkers*)

Davis found himself confronted with a case in shambles. The coroner's office did not call in either the police or the district attorney to assist at the scene, and then they bungled the investigation by making repeated mistakes. They lost the pillbox; they did not perform an autopsy; they fumbled their efforts to get the capsule analyzed; and they lost the transcript of testimony before the coroner's jury. Any one of these blunders could potentially scuttle a prosecution, and all of them coming in one investigation could be expected to be fatal for any case. The police had little interest in the case,[8] and it appeared that if any further investigation was going to be done on the case, it would have to be done by the district attorney's office.

Bungling and apathy on the part of investigating agencies are well-recognized reasons for a prosecutor to refuse to file charges,[9] but there is also authority for the proposition that when an investigating agency fails to properly investigate a crime, the prosecutor has the power, and sometimes the duty, to step into the breach and do the investigation.[10] There are problems with a prosecutor's office trying to conduct an investigation. First, prosecutors' offices are not designed to investigate cases, they are designed to prosecute cases investigated by other agencies. Second, few prosecutors have either the training or the experience necessary for a competent criminal investigation. Third, although many prosecutors' offices have investigators on staff, they have too few investigators to conduct a major investigation. If a prosecutor's office becomes involved in the preindictment investigation of a case, it is of utmost importance that the prosecutor's office work in tandem with a cooperating law enforcement agency. Given the lack of interest shown by the New York police, that was not going to happen in the Carlyle Harris investigation. Given all the negative factors, Davis decided not to prosecute the case.

This decision would have brought the case to a most unsatisfactory conclusion had something remarkable not happened. On March 21, 1891, the *New York Evening World* printed an article that the *World* later modestly claimed "startled the world"[11] and led to Harris's arrest. The editors of the *World* almost broke their arms patting themselves on the back for the exemplary work they did in resurrecting the case from the dead. In the 1908 edition of the *World Almanac and Encyclopedia*, they stated:

> WORLD reporters followed the case in all its crooked turnings, and forged a chain of evidence about Harris which led to his arrest. . . . The Harris case is cited because of its publicity. The bringing of criminals to justice by THE WORLD during the past twenty-five years, when police methods and professional detective efforts had failed, have led to its recognition as the most powerful sleuth in the newspaper field.[12]

The *Brooklyn Daily Eagle* gave voice to a similar sentiment: "This is one of many instances in which legitimate, aggressive, straightforward and courageous newspaper work has provided a needful impetus to authority at the start, a salutary spur to authority all along and the disinterested aid of law and its official ministers at every stage [of a criminal prosecution]."[13]

Oddly enough, there is a kernel of truth in the *World*'s bombastic boast. In reality, the "world-startling" article was not the ultimate cause of Harris's arrest, but one event in the middle of a chain of causation that began with Dr. George L. Peabody deciding that Harris was morally unfit to be a doctor and ended with District Attorney De Lancy Nicoll deciding that Harris was a murderer. Here is how the *World* really contributed to the arrest of Harris: Despite Mrs. Potts's lobbying efforts, Dr. Peabody had grave concerns about Harris's fitness to serve as a medical doctor. He went to Dr. James W. McLane, president of the College of Physicians and Surgeons, and shared his misgivings.[14] Dr. McLane wrote to Mrs. Potts, asking her for an affidavit outlining her knowledge of Harris's involvement with Helen's death. She complied, thinking that Dr. McLane intended to use the affidavit in support of his efforts to have the faculty expel Harris from the college.[15] Dr. McLane also got an affidavit from Dr. Treverton.[16] He took these affidavits to the faculty of the college and prevailed upon them to expel Harris "in consequence of charges of a serious nature involving his moral character."[17] Then, without first talking to Mrs. Potts, Dr. McLane took the affidavits to the office of De Lancy Nicoll. When Mrs. Potts learned of McLane's action, she said, "Had I been consulted I would not have allowed the sad affair to be placed in the Prosecutor's hands."[18]

There was a rather disreputable reporter working for the *World,* a man named Dilworth Choate, who had once hidden in a jury room to eavesdrop on the jury deliberations. The jury deliberated in an empty courtroom, and Choate hid under the judge's bench to listen in. His presence was discovered after the jury agreed upon a verdict, and he was immediately taken before the judge. The trial judge made him turn over the notes he took on the jury's deliberations, but he could not get Choate to promise that he would not publish what was said during the deliberations. The next day the *World* ran an account of what was said during the jury deliberations, and the trial judge held Choate in contempt of court and lamented that he could sentence the reporter to only thirty days in jail.[19] Choate was later indicted, convicted, and fined for his misconduct in connection with his eavesdropping escapade. In light of his sentence for contempt, the judge declined to give him any more jail time.[20] Despite Choate's unsavory character, he had a close working relationship with the district attorney's office. When the affidavits came into the office, someone in the office gave Choate copies.

The very next morning Choate went to the residence of Dr. Benjamin W. McCready and interviewed Harris about the allegations. Apparently, he even showed Harris his copies of both Mrs. Potts's and Dr. Treverton's affidavits. Upon hearing the allegations, Harris's lip began to tremble, but he quickly regained his composure. He then began to talk.

"I regret exceedingly that Mrs. Potts has made public this scandal," he said. "The most charitable view I can take of Mrs. Potts's conduct is that her mind has been affected by the loss of her daughter. But what do you think my feelings have been? I have been forced to lead a double life—to mourn in secret and appear gay in public—for the Pottses and I had agreed to keep secret our relationship.

"But now that they have brought such serious charges against me I think I am justified, in self-defense, to make public my side of the story. Besides, I have nothing to conceal, and am willing to answer any and all questions.

"To begin with, Mrs. Potts intimates that I substituted capsules containing enough morphine to kill for those that I had prepared at a drug store. I prescribed the capsules for her at her own request, and gave them to her at an afternoon reception in the presence of a number of friends. She said she was suffering with malaria, headache and sleeplessness. This was January 1. Helen died February 1. It is understood that she took one of the capsules the night prior to her death.

"Of the six capsules which I originally procured, I only gave four to her. The other two I threw in a waste drawer, because I did not wish to introduce into a girls' boarding-school a dangerous amount of opium. Of the two capsules I threw away, and which I looked for at the earnest request of the Coroner, I succeeded in finding one. The giving of this capsule to the Coroner in evidence seems to be the poor mother's main reason for her dreadful suspicion.

"Now you might call me a criminal, but I am not stupid. If I had committed a crime and wanted to conceal it, I would not have produced that capsule, in fact would never have spoken of it, and would have thrown the blame on the druggist. The other capsules were never found, and I could easily have said the druggist made a mistake, as I at first believed he did. As it was, I exonerated the druggist."

Choate asked, "If the capsules were properly compounded and contained each a harmless portion of the opium, what then do you consider the cause of death?"

"I believe poor Helen took several of the capsules instead of one the night previous to her death. The amount of opium they contained is unlikely to cause death ordinarily, but in certain instances it might, and may have done so in this instance. Only a few days ago Dr. Robert Abbe of 11 West Fiftieth Street told me of the case of a man who took the same amount of morphine constituted in several capsules like I gave to Helen, and whose life was only saved after the operation of a tracheotomy was performed."

Harris then addressed some of the other allegations. "Now, as to the other statements in Mrs. Potts's affidavit: it is true that Helen and I were secretly married under assumed names, not for the purpose of invalidating the marriage but to keep it secret until we had both completed our studies, after which I was willing to have a public ceremony performed. I so stated to Mrs. Potts."

"She says that you promised in writing to have the public ceremony performed February 8 last and that February 1 Helen was dead," objected Choate.

"If Mrs. Potts has that in my handwriting, I know nothing about it. I promised verbally to have a public ceremony but fixed no time. This was last summer after our marriage, when Helen visited Homesdale and Scranton. At Scranton she stopped at the house of her uncle, Dr. Treverton. While there, Dr. Treverton sent me a threatening letter." Harris produced the letter that Treverton had written about the abortion and allowed Choate to copy it.

"On receipt of this letter, I wrote to Helen saying I would permit no operation. I submitted her uncle's letter to Lawyer Davison, of 170 Broadway, my attorney. Then I started for Scranton, and I found on my arrival there that the operation had been begun. Treverton afterwards sent me a bill for $500 for his services.

"Dr. Treverton only told Mrs. Potts part of the story he tells in his affidavit, and did all he could to disprove our marriage. Fortunately Mrs. Potts believed her daughter's word and mine, and to further assure her I took her to the office of Lawyer Davison and made the affidavit now in her possession as to the time and facts of our marriage."

Harris reiterated his statement that he was perfectly willing to enter into a public marriage with Helen, but that all parties had agreed to wait until both he and Helen had finished their studies. He concluded his statement by saying, "I deny the charge that I performed two or three criminal operations, which necessitated the fourth one spoken of by Dr. Treverton. The only operation was performed by Dr. Treverton without my consent."[21]

Harris then announced his intention to go straight to the district attorney's office and straighten things out. He recruited his aunt, Mary L. McCready, to go with him. Choate tagged along, and the trio arrived at the office of De Lancy Nicoll. Nicoll was not there, but the Harrises spoke with Assistant District Attorney Henry W. Unger. They made an immediate impression on him. He would later recall, "I saw they were persons above the ordinary class." Unger asked what he could do for them.

Harris replied, "I am Carlyle W. Harris, and this is my aunt, Miss Mc-Cready." Apparently, Harris thought the mere mention of his name would be enough for Unger to know why he had come to the district attorney's office. Unger was clueless.

"Well, what is your business, Mr. Harris?"

"I have come in answer to the publication in this morning's papers and of course desire to repudiate the insinuations contained in the newspapers and to let the District Attorney know that if any investigation of the matter is at all desirable or necessary that I want to render every possible assistance: that I assure the District Attorney that I have no object whatever in concealing any facts. I wish the District Attorney to know that I am a gentleman of some social connection and I want to know promptly if this matter calls for any serious consideration." Harris was mistaken or had been misled by Choate; nothing appeared in the papers until the evening edition of the *World* came out later that day.[22]

Unger sent for the closed-out file and looked it over.[23] "Oh, I don't think this is a matter for any concern on your part," Unger told him, "but at the same time, as long as you are here, I would advise you to wait for the District Attorney, or if you have any business to transact in this neighborhood you might attend to it and return here later. The District Attorney will be here shortly and I think he will be pleased to receive any statements that you or anybody else desires to make."

Miss McCready spoke up indignantly, saying that the charges were "of a shocking nature." She then huddled with Harris and they had a whispered conversation. After the private conversation Miss McCready returned to the fray. "My nephew and I are highly connected. I am the daughter of Dr. McCready of East Seventeenth Street, and Mr. Harris's mother is a lady of literary standing in the community." Unger assured them that there appeared to be no reason for concern, and Harris departed to consult with an attorney, saying he would return later. Choate went back to the *World* offices to write a lengthy article, which appeared in the evening edition that very day. The article contained the full text of Mrs. Potts's affidavit, a summary of Dr. Treverton's affidavit, and the full text of Dr. Treverton's letter to Harris.[24]

An hour or so went by, and Harris returned with his aunt. They were admitted to see District Attorney De Lancy Nicoll. A graduate of Princeton in 1874 and Columbia Law School in 1876, Nicoll was appointed as an assis-

tant district attorney in 1885 and served in that capac-
ity until 1888, distinguishing himself as an excellent
trial attorney with a string of brilliant prosecutions,
including the conviction of a contractor for manslaughter in the collapse of a building, the conviction of a business partner of Ulysses S. Grant
for brokerage fraud, and the prosecution of the
"Boodle" Aldermen for bribery in connection
with a streetcar franchise.[25] In 1888, although a
lifelong Democrat, Nicoll ran for district attorney as an independent to distance himself from
Tammany Hall. He lost that election, made an un-
easy peace with Tammany, and was elected district
attorney on the Tammany ticket in 1890.[26] Not long
after the conclusion of the Harris case, Nicoll tired
of having to deal with "Boss" Richard Croker of Tammany Hall and declined to run for another term.[27]
When Harris met with Nicoll, he confronted a tal-

De Lancy Nicoll, New York
County district attorney,
1891–93 (King, *Notable New
Yorkers*)

ented, experienced prosecutor and a shrewd judge of character—not an
easy man to hoodwink. Harris impressed Nicoll as a handsome chap, cool
and self-possessed, but his attitude was "gratuitously frank."[28] Harris
probably left Nicoll's office confident that he had convinced Nicoll of his
innocence, but he had no sooner left the office than Nicoll told Unger,
"There is no doubt in my mind that Harris is a guilty man." He immediately ordered that the case be reopened and reinvestigated. Harris's visit
with Nicoll proved to be more responsible than anything else for his even-
tual prosecution.[29]

Nicoll assigned his best assistant to the case. Francis L. Wellman was
a newcomer to the district attorney's office. A Harvard graduate and a
former law professor, Wellman had worked for seven years as corporate
counsel for the City of New York and had developed a reputation as a
"shrewd and searching cross-examiner,"[30] and in later years he wrote a
classic book on cross-examination, which is still in print.[31] At this point
in his career, however, Wellman had never prosecuted any sort of criminal
case. Despite Wellman's inexperience, Nicoll immediately assigned him
to the trial of the office's most important cases, and Wellman soon con-
firmed the wisdom of Nicoll's decision. It had been a decade since a jury

had found anyone guilty of first-degree arson in New York, but Wellman quickly achieved a verdict of guilty and a twelve-and-a-half-year sentence for the crime.[32] In the first three months of Nicoll's tenure as district attorney, Wellman tried three homicide cases,[33] and then he was assigned to the Harris case just four days before beginning his fourth homicide trial.[34] Over the next nine months leading up to the trial, Wellman had little time to prepare. During that time the newspapers reported him trying another ten jury cases, five of which were murders.[35] We can be sure that this number is just the tip of the iceberg of the cases he tried in that time. Only a small percentage of jury cases ever get reported in the newspapers.

With such a heavy load of trials, Wellman needed help to prepare the case against Harris, and Nicoll gave him the best helper to be found in the district attorney's office—Charles E. Simms Jr. Simms was the careful, studious type who was capable of assimilating a mass of testimony and evidence, assessing its significance, and assembling the evidence into a powerful presentation.[36] Simms went on to become a judge of the First Civil Court[37] and later served as a police magistrate.[38] Simms's skills complemented Wellman's perfectly, and the two men made an excellent team.

CHAPTER FOUR

Working Up a Case on Harris

When De Lancy Nicoll ordered Wellman and Simms to reopen the Harris case, they faced a monumental task. They had to reassemble the shattered pieces of the coroner's botched investigation and supplement it with sufficient evidence to warrant filing charges. The bare minimum of evidence necessary to bring criminal charges is "probable cause." When a criminal complaint is supported by probable cause, there can be no legal basis for criticizing the decision to prosecute.[1] In nineteenth-century New York, probable cause was defined as "a reasonable ground of suspicion, supported by circumstances sufficiently strong in themselves to warrant a cautious man in the belief, that the person accused is guilty of the offence with which he is charged."[2] With amendment to render the language gender neutral, that definition is still good. Probable cause is a very low standard of proof, and the existence of probable cause in no way guarantees a conviction. Most prosecutors want more proof of guilt than mere probable cause, and it has been long recognized that a prosecutor can properly refuse to prosecute a case despite the existence of probable cause.[3] No matter how certain a prosecutor may be of the guilt of an accused, if the chances of getting a conviction are remote, it is folly to waste time, energy, effort, and limited resources trying a case that is a lost cause. It is problematic when the case falls on or near the borderline between prosecutable and unprosecutable.

As things stood on the morning of Harris's visit to the district attorney, even with the affidavits of Mrs. Potts and Dr. Treverton, the case fell outside that borderline. The evidence gave rise to a strong suspicion of guilt, but the necessary proof was lacking. Herculean effort might have resurrected the case or further investigation might have simply become a black hole draining time and resources from more worthy cases to no purpose. What could impel De Lancy Nicoll to opt in favor of taking a chance on expending all that effort? The appearance on his doorstep of a brash young murderer so supremely confident of his ability to bamboozle an audience that he thought he could breeze into the district attorney's office and talk him out of filing charges. At least that is the way Nicoll saw things. Nicoll believed, as do most experienced prosecutors, that he had a finely tuned blarney detector and he wasn't going to let anyone con him.

Thus we see that the *World*'s primary contribution to the Harris case was to send the young man scampering to the district attorney's office in a failed effort to convince Nicoll of his innocence. If Harris had just stayed home after Choate had interviewed him, the scandal would have eventually blown over and he would have escaped prosecution. That did not, however, end the *World*'s contribution to the prosecution of Carlyle Harris. The police were apathetic toward the case, the district attorney's office didn't have the manpower to fully investigate the case, and Dilworth Choate was a diligent but somewhat unsavory bloodhound. The district attorney's office enlisted Choate as an ally, and he unearthed a massive amount of salacious information, which he shared with both the district attorney and the *World*'s reading public. Harris complained bitterly about Choate's activities on the district attorney's behalf, accusing him of unethical conduct and calling him "Sneak" Choate.[4] In the book that Mrs. Harris published after the trial, she wrote about Choate with such vitriol that he sued her publisher for libel.[5]

The refusal of the coroner's office to call in the police at the outset, its bungling of the investigation, and the resulting lack of police involvement were all serious blows to the prosecution. Had the police become involved, Nicoll's case could have escaped the taint of using the disreputable Choate as a legman. It could also have profited by the participation of the greatest police detective of the Gilded Age—Insp. Thomas F. Byrnes.

Byrnes, an Irish immigrant who grew up in the Five Points, was a Civil War veteran who fought with Company B, 11th New York Volunteer Infantry, better known as Ellsworth's Fire Zouaves, at the Battle of First Manassas. Declining to "re-up" after his enlistment expired, Byrnes returned to New York City and joined the police force shortly before the New York Draft Riots. Byrnes distinguished himself during the Draft Riots, being credited with single-handedly standing off a mob bent on burning the Colored Orphan Asylum on Fifth Avenue between Forty-Second and Forty-Third Streets. Although he was unable to prevent the asylum from being burned to the ground, he successfully oversaw the safe evacuation of more than two hundred children.[6] He rose rapidly through the ranks, and in 1892 he was chief inspector overseeing the most modern and efficient detective bureau in the nation. During his tenure as chief of detectives, his bureau was responsible for the conviction of thousands of criminals, resulting in an aggregate prison sentence of over ten thousand years.[7] Although an innovator in the use of modern methods of crime detection, he was also credited with pioneering the "third degree" interrogation method, which was a forerunner of today's "enhanced interrogation" technique.[8]

Deprived of Byrnes's assistance, Nicoll made do with Choate. Not content to rely solely upon the affidavits of Mrs. Potts and Dr. Treverton, Nicoll summoned them both to his office for interviews. Choate, being an "ally" of the investigation, was naturally privy to the decision and publicized it.[9] The result was that Mrs. Potts and Dr. Treverton gave several statements to different newspapers before they ever got to Nicoll's office.[10] Aching for a scoop, and not as well connected with the district attorney's office as Dilworth Choate, an anonymous reporter for the *Sun* reported: "Little doubt was entertained yesterday that the investigation into the death of Harris's young wife, Helen Potts Harris, will result in nothing. There is no evidence, an attaché of the District Attorney's office said yesterday, that her death resulted from any one's fault, and, even if proof should be produced that young Harris committed malpractice, the offence was committed in New Jersey six months before Mrs. Harris's death."[11]

It is difficult to credit that an attaché of the district attorney's office would have led a reporter so far astray. On the issue of whether a charge will or will not be filed against a suspect, prosecutors are most reluctant to make any public pronouncements until after the suspect has been arrested or at least charged. The reporter probably got misled in the following manner. Harris went to the district attorney's office ostensibly to inform Nicoll that he was about to leave Manhattan to spend a few days at his mother's home in Brooklyn. His real mission was more likely to try to determine what progress was being made in the investigation against him. The attaché of the district attorney's office felt no compunction about lying to Harris and told him that the investigation was going nowhere. Jubilant, Harris made a beeline for the *Sun* reporter and gave him the good news.

Charles Edward Simms Jr.,
assistant district attorney,
New York County (King,
Notable New Yorkers)

Wellman and Simms confronted three problems of proof. Two of the problems had to be solved or no case could be made. The third problem did not necessarily need to be solved, but failure to solve it would substantially weaken the case. First, they had to prove that someone poisoned Helen. Second, they had to prove that the poisoner was Carlyle Harris. Third, they had to prove that Carlyle Harris had a reason to kill Helen. For the first problem they had the opinions of the three attending physicians, all of whom stood ready to testify that Helen died of morphine poisoning; they had the coroner and deputy coroner, both medical doctors, who would testify to the same conclusion; and they could recruit any number of other experts to give the same opinion in response to hypothetical questions. Was that enough? Probably not. There is an old saying among trial lawyers that for every expert there is an equal and opposite expert. The defense could, and eventually did, summon a host of experts to criticize the procedures employed by the attending physicians and to give alternative opinions based on hypothetical questions. Wellman and Simms needed some evidence that there was a large quantity of morphine in Helen's system when she died. They needed an autopsy.

The ideal time to perform an autopsy is shortly after death and before the body is embalmed and buried. Helen's body had been embalmed and buried, and over a month had passed since she died. Wellman and Simms had two choices—exhume the body and perform a belated autopsy or quit the case. They chose the first option. On March 25, 1891,[12] without notifying Mrs. Potts, undertaker James H. Sexton exhumed Helen's body and turned it over to Dr. Allan McLane Hamilton, a grandson of Founding Father Alexander Hamilton, to perform the autopsy.[13] Hamilton had testified at the trials of presidential assassins Charles J. Guiteau and Leon Frank Czolgosz and would go on to testify in over one hundred murder trials during the course of his career. Hamilton was a member of the Royal Society of Edinburgh and the author of numerous books, including *A Manual of Medical Jurisprudence* and *The Intimate Life of Alexander Hamilton*—a biography of his famous ancestor.[14] Despite his credentials, Hamilton may not have been the best choice to perform the autopsy. He was an alienist—what we would today call a forensic psychiatrist—not a pathologist.[15]

Hamilton found the body to be extremely well preserved because it had been embalmed and placed in a brick vault surrounded by dry, gravelly soil.[16] Upon first looking at her, Hamilton thought Helen a pitiful sight.[17] He later recalled that she was "a beautiful young girl who, notwithstanding the fact that she had been buried several months, looked almost lifelike in her simple grey dress embroidered with silver and her tiny slippers."[18] Assisted by Dr. George D. Smith,[19] he began the autopsy.

Dr. Allan McLane Hamilton, professor of mental diseases, Cornell University (King, *Notable New Yorkers*)

Dr. Hamilton reported that the body was that of a "remarkably well developed, strong, muscular young woman, apparently about twenty years of age."[20] Upon opening Helen's skull and inspecting her brain, Hamilton found symptoms of morphine poisoning.[21] In addition to the congestion of the brain consistent with morphine poisoning, Hamilton noted that there were no lesions on the pons Varolii,[22] a condition that could cause death with symptoms similar to those exhibited by Helen.[23] He also found Helen's kidneys to be healthy and normal,[24] which ruled out death by uremia, another condition that could have produced symptoms similar to Helen's.[25] Everything from the autopsy indicated morphine poisoning, but there was one more investigation that needed to be made. Was there any morphine or quinine in Helen's body?

Hamilton and Smith removed Helen's internal organs and placed them in jars for delivery to the laboratory of Dr. Rudolph Witthaus for toxicological examination.[26] Dr. Witthaus obtained from the embalmer, William Vannett, a sample of embalming fluid from the same lot as the fluid used to embalm Helen.[27] He then subjected Helen's internal organs to a series of examinations, which lasted several weeks.

Nicoll was impatient to go ahead and have Harris arrested. On April 1 Nicoll went before Judge James Fitzgerald in the Court of General Sessions and personally swore to an affidavit for the arrest of Carlyle Harris on a charge of murder in the first degree.[28] One might criticize Nicoll for jumping the gun on charging Harris. The autopsy would not be fully complete until Dr. Witthaus had completed his toxicological examination of Helen's internal organs. This caused some problems as shall be seen later, but first we must finish discussing the problems of proof that Wellman and Simms confronted.

Eventually Witthaus concluded his examination. His bottom-line opinion: There was a small quantity of morphine in her body and absolutely no quinine. Given the length of time between ingestion and death, he estimated that she had taken a fatal dose of three to five grains of morphine.[29]

Wellman and Simms could be satisfied that they had sufficient proof of the cause of Helen's death, but what about the manner? Of the four manners of death, they had ruled out only natural causes. They needed to rule out accident and suicide as well. On the issue of suicide, Wellman asked the question "Did Helen Potts commit suicide?" and resolved the question by asking and answering two additional questions. The first question: "Had she any cause to commit suicide?" Wellman ticked off the evidence: she was well; she was in love with Harris; her roommates believed her to be happy and content; her mother observed her to be very happy the afternoon before she died; Miss Day saw that she was well and happy when she bade her good night on the evening of her death. She had no cause to commit suicide. Wellman's second question: "Had she any means of committing suicide?" No sign of any drug of any kind was found in her room except the empty box marked "C. W. H."[30] Wellman concluded that Helen had neither the motive nor the means to commit suicide. Wellman then asked and answered the question of accident: "Was it the 'druggist's awful mistake'?" The analysis of one of the two capsules that Harris had unwisely kept out for his own protection provided the best possible evidence that the druggist had not made a mistake.[31]

Ruling out accident, suicide, and natural causes solved the first problem of proof—it was a homicide. And solving the first problem of proof also resolved the second problem of proof—that Harris was the killer. As Sherlock Holmes was wont to say, when you rule out the impossible, then whatever is left, however improbable, is what happened. The chain of reasoning proceeded like this: The druggist put a nonlethal dose of morphine in each capsule; Harris gave Helen the capsules, but the morphine in one of the capsules killed Helen; therefore, Harris reloaded one of the capsules with a lethal dose of morphine. If Harris reloaded one of the capsules with a lethal dose of morphine before giving it to Helen, he meant to kill her. If he meant to kill her, then he was guilty of premeditated murder, a capital offense.

Wellman and Simms may have had logical proof that Harris was the killer, but they were probably short of satisfactory proof to sustain a criminal charge. In a criminal case it is not sufficient to prove that the defendant might have done it; it is not sufficient to prove that the defendant probably did it; it is not even sufficient to show that the defendant most likely did it. The defendant must be proven to have done it beyond and to the exclusion of every reasonable doubt. Where did he get the morphine? It may have been enough to argue that she was dead, so he must have gotten it from somewhere, but it was much better to be able to prove where he got it.

One way to do this might be to show the ease with which one could obtain morphine during the Gilded Age, and the prosecution would attempt such proof in the upcoming trial. Dr. Peabody, however, could suggest an even better answer to the question of where Harris got the morphine. Back when Harris and Mrs. Potts were trading letters over the issue of the secret marriage, Harris was attending a series of lectures on materia medica, or clinical pharmacology, taught by Dr. Peabody. During that series of lectures Dr. Peabody spoke extensively on the topic of poisons,[32] including morphine. One of Dr. Peabody's lectures bore the title "Morphine—Its Uses as a Medicine and Its Poisonous Effects in Large Quantities."[33] During that lecture he passed around open containers of morphine among his students and allowed them to remove the morphine from the containers so that they could closely examine it.[34] This did not constitute proof that Harris actually took some of Peabody's morphine, but it was proof that he had easy access to a large quantity of morphine just before Helen died and at a time when Mrs. Potts was pressuring him to marry Helen properly.

As for the third problem of proof—motive—here was where the prosecution came up short. Under the law, motive is not an element of the crime of murder, but reasonable doubts can easily arise without proof of motive. On the surface it seemed that Harris had no real reason to kill Helen. He and Helen were apparently in love, and the only source of friction seemed to be a disagreement between Harris and Mrs. Potts about when to make the marriage public. When Harris received his diploma and the marriage became public knowledge, Mrs. Potts was going to pay for the couple to go to Europe. Harris did seem to have issues with fidelity, but unfaithfulness on its own is small reason for murder. An investigation of motive was something that Dilworth Choate would excel at, and in the weeks and months leading up to the trial, all sorts of salacious gossip was printed characterizing Carlyle Harris as a cad, a bounder, and a despoiler of innocent girls. Some of it was even true, and an even smaller percentage of it actually made its way into evidence at the trial.

In Gilded Age New York the traditional series of proceedings in a murder prosecution began with a coroner's inquest before a coroner's jury. The coroner's jury would return a verdict finding an unlawful homicide and naming the perpetrator if he could be identified. In New York at the time of the Harris case, the coroner had the testimony before the coroner's jury transcribed, and if the coroner didn't lose the transcript, the district attorney got a copy. Then a warrant would be issued for the arrest of the killer and he would be placed in jail. Next came an examination before a committing magistrate who would take evidence to determine whether probable cause existed for the continued detention of the defendant for the crime charged. Unlike the coroner's inquest, the examination was a full-blown adversarial proceeding where the prosecution presented evidence, the defense cross-examined, and the defense could present evidence. The testimony at this proceeding could be transcribed also. The next step in the process was the grand jury, another nonadversarial proceeding, which was held in secret. The defendant could not attend the grand jury hearing, nor could his attorney, and normally the defense had no opportunity to see the transcript of testimony before the grand jury. This lack of access to the testimony before the grand jury was not much of a disadvantage because at trial the defense team had the transcripts of the coroner's inquest and the examination.

The proceedings against Harris had advanced to the warrant stage, and the next step was to arrest him.[35] Two officers were dispatched to take him into custody—Detectives Von Gerichten and Trainer. They first went to Mrs. Harris's home. She informed the officers that her son was not at home, that they could find him at the office of his lawyer, Charles E. Davison. They then went to Davison's office at 170 Broadway. There they detained a young man who bore a striking resemblance to Harris. They asked his name, but he refused to identify himself. When they put hands on him to take him into custody, he told them they had no right to arrest him. "Sure," they said, "we've heard that story before and we're too old in the business to be fooled by it."

They hauled the young man back to the Court of General Sessions before Judge Fitzgerald at 1:00 P.M., and Assistant District Attorney Vernon M. Davis appeared for the prosecution. Davis moved that the prisoner be remanded to custody to await the action of a grand jury. As Judge Fitzgerald pronounced the commitment to custody, the young man asked Davis, "I beg your pardon, Mr. District Attorney, but will you tell me where I am to be committed to?"[36]

"To the Tombs," replied Davis. No jail is a pleasant place to stay, but the Tombs was particularly uncomfortable.

"There is a serious mistake," the young man answered, "I am not Carlyle W. Harris. I am his brother, Robert McCready Harris." This threw the proceedings into disarray. Davis suggested committing McCready to the Tombs until his identity could be substantiated, but the judge thought that then and there was the time and place to substantiate his identity.

The Tombs, the prison where Harris was held pending trial (Courtesy of the Library of Congress)

They began to take the testimony of Detective Sergeant Von Gerichten about the circumstances of McCready's arrest, and before Von Gerichten could finish his testimony, Davis received a summons to the district attorney's office to take an urgent telephone call.

After a brief period, Davis came back to court and informed Judge Fitzgerald that Carlyle W. Harris had turned himself in at City Hall and that he was in the custody of Detective Reilly. Harris had arrived at his lawyer's office and learned of his brother's arrest. He had immediately telephoned the police and arranged to meet Reilly at City Hall to surrender to the authorities. Reilly first took Harris to the district attorney's office and then brought him before Judge Fitzgerald. By 6:15 that evening, McCready was on his way home and Carlyle was on his way to the Tombs.

It was now that Nicoll's haste to arrest caused the problems. The next stage of the proceeding was the examination, which today would be called a preliminary hearing. Examinations should be held as soon as possible after the arrest, but Nicoll feared that the judge would release Harris from custody if he could not hear the results of Dr. Witthaus's toxicological examination. Nicoll asked for and obtained delays of the examination for almost a month while waiting for Witthaus's report,[37] and when he got it, he bypassed the examination and went straight to the grand jury.[38] He called five witnesses before the grand jury—Dr. Fowler, Dr. Witthaus, Mrs. Potts, Hearn Powers, and Assistant District Attorney Unger—and the grand jury returned an indictment for murder in the first degree, charging that Harris gave Helen five grains of morphine with malice aforethought.[39]

Going to the jury without first holding an examination caused more problems. Remember that a murder defendant could expect to go to trial with a transcript of the examination and a transcript of the coroner's inquest in hand. Having these transcripts was of supreme importance because grand jury testimony was confidential and usually inaccessible to the defense. In the nineteenth century a criminal defendant had no right to "discover" the prosecution's evidence until he or she heard it from the witness stand during trial, and even today there is no constitutional right to discovery.[40] The only way that the defense could learn of the evidence against Harris (aside from reading Choate's articles in the *World*) was to read the transcripts of the coroner's inquest and the examination. In Harris's case the coroner's transcript was lost, and there was no transcript of an examination. What was the defense to do?

The defense moved the court to order disclosure of the grand jury testimony, but they didn't state the real reason they wanted the testimony. Saying "We want the grand jury testimony because we want to know something about the evidence against us" is defeated by the answer "You have no right to know what the evidence is against you." They took a roundabout approach. They argued that a prosecution cannot go forward unless there is probable cause to believe that the defendant committed the crime charged. The coroner's verdict found probable cause to believe that Helen died of morphine poisoning and nothing more. It did not name her killer. A public examination would have established probable cause when the witnesses were called, examined, and cross-examined, and a committing magistrate made a judicial finding of probable cause, but that didn't happen. The grand jury's indictment is a finding of probable cause, but how can we be sure that they didn't err? The defendant has a right to contest the issue of probable cause for his detention, but he has been robbed of that right by the loss of the coroner's transcript and the denial of the examination. The only way to remedy that injustice is to give the defendant access to the grand jury testimony and give him an opportunity to contest the existence of probable cause to support the indictment.

On June 27, 1891, the defense motion for inspection of the grand jury testimony was heard before Judge Rufus B. Cowing in the Court of General Sessions. William Travers Jerome, a former assistant district attorney, argued for the disclosure on behalf of Harris. Assistant District Attorney Davis opposed the motion, and Judge Cowling reserved ruling.[41] On June 30, Judge Cowling held that "In my judgment, the defendant, under the circumstances disclosed in this motion, is fairly entitled to inspect the evidence given by the People's witnesses before the Grand Jury, and I fail to see how the people will suffer any prejudice by allowing such inspection." Harris's case became one of the first in a long line of New York cases that held "A defendant who seeks inspection of the grand jury minutes on the sole plea that he has been deprived of a preliminary examination should have the ear of the court."[42]

Harris's defense team, consisting of Charles E. Davison, William Travers Jerome, and John A. Taylor, managed to delay the trial until the end of the year. During that time Choate published as much dirt on Harris as possible.[43] In one article Choate advised the *World*'s readers that "Harris's record has been looked up and it is not a very creditable one. A Swedish serving girl in his father's house, charges him with fathership of her child. He was mixed up in a scandal with the Neptune Club of Asbury Park, and altogether his character is unsavory."[44]

The case finally came up for trial on December 7, 1891, in the Court of Oyer and Terminer, but Assistant District Attorney Wellman asked for a continuance. Mae Schofield, who now lived in Michigan, had been stricken with apoplexy during her journey to New York and it would be impossible for her to be in court for at least two weeks. Jerome complained that Harris had been in the Tombs for eight months and insisted that the trial go ahead.[45] The case got reset for December 16, and on that day Wellman was ready to go to trial but Jerome wasn't. He was too ill to proceed. This caused a scheduling problem. The trial would be a lengthy one, and any more delays would cause the trial to run past the scheduled end of the session of Oyer and Terminer. Justice Charles H. Van Brunt solved the problem by transferring the case back to the Court of General Sessions.[46] Miss Schofield was in New York now but was too ill to come to court. Wellman talked Taylor into agreeing to take Schofield's deposition.[47] It looked as though the case would finally get to trial at the beginning of the next year.

CHAPTER FIVE

Wellman States His Case
against Harris

The trial finally got under way on Thursday, January 14, in the Court of General Sessions before Recorder Frederick Smyth,[1] one of the most experienced judges on the New York bench. He not only presided over more jury trials than any of his contemporaries,[2] he tried almost all the most sensational cases in New York City during the closing years of the nineteenth century. In addition to Carlyle Harris, he tried the Robert Buchanan murder by poisoning case; the Henry C. F. Meyer murder by poisoning case; Ben Ali, the "American Jack the Ripper"; the Frank "Biff" Ellison assault case; and the Charles W. Gardner extortion case.[3] Smyth was born in County Galway, Ireland, and immigrated to America in 1849. Upon his arrival, he took a job as a law clerk, and he was admitted to the bar in 1855. As an appointed assistant US attorney, he gained international fame prosecuting William Walker, the "Grey-Eyed Man of Destiny," who was recognized as the "King of the Filibusters." Although a lifelong Democrat, he did not ally himself with Tammany Hall until after the ouster of the infamous "Boss" Tweed and the Tweed Ring. Smyth served one fourteen-year term as recorder of New York City[4] and was later elected to a fourteen-year term as a justice of the Supreme Court.[5] He had a cordial relationship with trial lawyers, and he would invite them to join him in chambers to await jury verdicts. Smyth would drink water, eat raw apples, and regale the lawyers with "war stories" of incidents from long-ago trials—but he would never talk directly about the case being tried.[6]

John A. Taylor, whose field was municipal corporations,[7] served as lead counsel for the defense. Taylor appeared on behalf of Harris "due . . . to long association with the kindred of the defendant."[8] Francis Wellman publicly praised Taylor. "The thing I most dread in him is his perfect fairness. He apparently scorns to tell the jury anything that he does not believe himself."[9] Privately Wellman had his doubts. Although Wellman recognized that Taylor was a prominent, talented lawyer, he believed that Taylor knew next to nothing about trying a murder case. Wellman thought it would have been much better for Harris if the position of lead counsel for the defense had been entrusted to Taylor's assistant, William Travers Jerome, who had just left the district attorney's office to go into private practice and who "knew every nook and corner of a murder trial."[10] As lead counsel, Taylor decided the trial strategy, made the jury speeches, and made the legal arguments. Jerome cross-examined all the prosecution witnesses and presented all the defense witnesses. The third member of the defense team, Charles E. Davison, did not speak before the jury.

William Travers Jerome was a colorful character, an athletic amateur boxer with boundless energy who proved to be the almost-tireless workhorse of the defense team. After the Harris trial, Jerome would go on to serve as associate counsel to the Lexow Committee's investigation of corruption in the New York Police Department,[11] as a justice of the Court of General Sessions, and later as one of New York City's most famous elected district attorneys. His most notorious prosecution was the trial of playboy Harry K. Thaw for the murder of the prominent New York architect Stanford White—the first "Trial of the [Twentieth] Century."[12] A staunch foe of Tammany Hall, Jerome gained election as district attorney on the reform ticket and became famous for personally leading police raids on gambling houses. When leading raids, Jerome carried a Bible in his hip pocket so that he could use it to swear witnesses on the spot.[13]

Jury selection took three grueling days, and the final juror was seated on the afternoon of Monday, January 18. Recorder Smyth recessed court upon the selection of the last juror and announced that opening statements would begin on the morning of January 19.[14] On the morning the trial commenced, Harris came to court well groomed, neatly dressed, and seemingly unstressed.[15] The *Tribune* described his demeanor as one of "careless good nature,"[16] while the *Herald* said he appeared "calm, strong, self-possessed, and alert."[17] He maintained that demeanor through most of Wellman's opening statement, although he did give way to emotion on two occasions. How agitated he became is open to question. The *Brooklyn Daily Eagle* reported that he "burst into tears during the address and became visibly nervous,"[18] but the *Herald* had a different interpretation: "It is true that for a few moments he appeared to be weeping when his girl wife's death was mentioned. But then he carefully removed his glasses and hid his face in his hands. No trace of tears was apparent on his well shaven cheeks." The *Herald* then went on to praise Harris, something that the newspapers would continue to do over the years while his case wended its way through the labyrinth of capital litigation. The *Herald* said, "His conduct was a model for all young widowers. It could not fail to make a good impression on the jury."[19]

Wellman began his speech by assuring the jury of his uncompromising desire to be fair to Harris:

> May it please the Court, Mr. Foreman and Gentlemen of the Jury—The duty you are called upon to perform is the most solemn which anyone can possibly discharge—to sit in judgment on a fellow human being charged with the greatest of crimes. In such a case, I need not ask your earnest attention. Its circumstances have given it a profound interest to our entire community, and it is hard to find anyone, who does not know something about its details, and hasn't formed some opinion as to the guilt or innocence of this defendant. As the public prosecutor in this case, as a minister of justice, I must caution you not to allow anything of prejudice or preconceived opinion to weigh against this prisoner. It is your duty to try this case on the evidence and on nothing else. If that evidence satisfies you of the guilt of the prisoner, you will discharge your duty by fearlessly declaring your verdict accordingly. But if the evidence fails to satisfy your minds of the guilt of the defendant, God forbid that the scales of justice should weigh against him by any prejudice or preconceived opinion.
>
> My duty in this case is simple. It is to lay before you the facts. They are necessarily somewhat complicated, and they extend over a considerable period of time, so that it will be necessary to prove not only facts immediately surrounding this accusation, but prior facts as well. I must ask your patient attention, but I will not prove a single fact which is not important to this case.[20]

Having established his bona fides as an honorable, honest guide through the thicket of evidence that would confront the jury, Wellman then gave a brief biography of Harris and described the courtship that ended in Harris's secret marriage to Helen. He then moved quickly to the tragic events surrounding the botched abortion. Wellman briefly described Schofield's talk with Harris, the botched abortion, Helen's illness, and her visit to her uncle, Dr. Treverton. It was at this point that Wellman said some things that belied his initial claims to scrupulous fairness:

> The scene now changes to Scranton, Pennsylvania. After Helen had arrived at her uncle's, he noticed she was not well; she was pale and listless, and one morning she was nauseated at the breakfast table. He went to her room and spoke with her. I would not be justified in repeating the conversation, as it would not be allowed in evidence in this case. Anything that Helen said in the absence of the defendant cannot be given in testimony. This rule necessarily keeps a great deal of important information from the jury. I am sorry, because it would illustrate the beautiful character of this young girl, but the testimony will bristle with evidences of the loving, devoted, Christian nature of this sweet young woman just entering upon her nineteenth year.[21]

In his work *Language and the Law,* Frederick A. Philbrick astutely observed that Wellman was very good at suggesting facts that were inadmissible.[22] This was perhaps the most egregious example of what Philbrick was talking about. If evidence cannot be set before the jury, then it cannot be mentioned in the opening statement. Wellman should never have told the jurors that they were not going to hear a lot of inculpatory information because of those nasty rules of evidence, and he certainly shouldn't have told them that the evidence they weren't going to hear would convince them of the loving, devoted, Christian nature of this sweet young woman just entering upon her nineteenth year.

Wellman then described how Treverton summoned Harris to Scranton, and he outlined the grisly details of the operation that saved Helen's life. He told how Mrs. Potts rushed to her daughter's side and how Helen spent several weeks in Scranton recuperating. Suddenly he moved his attention from Helen to Harris:

> It may be interesting at this juncture to pause for a moment and see what has become of Carlyle. Where is Harris at this time, while his secret wife is convalescing from her serious illness at Scranton? Is he at Ocean Grove? No. He has been there; but he has gone. Is he in New York? We cannot find

him there anywhere. Where is Harris? Can that be he at Canandaigua, at the Webster Hotel? No, surely not; that is Carl Graham. But it looks like Harris. Carl Graham, according to the register; but Carlyle W. Harris according to the mail claimed by him. Who is it that is with him? Who is that young lady? Are they married? She is very young—she is very beautiful. They are together all day, all the evening; plainly they are lovers. Are they married? Who is she? Let us inquire at the hotel how they came. They came together; she was to visit some friends, Mr. and Mrs. Latham, who had asked her to visit them. They are respectable people and considered her a respectable girl. Harris came with her, as a Mr. Graham, and gave out the story that they met by chance on the railroad. Mr. and Mrs. Latham's suspicions are aroused; they notice the intimacy between this young couple. Perceiving that they are lovers, they watch them, and one night upon going to the lady's room late at night Harris is found in her bed, and now Mr. Latham tells him: "It is time for you to leave this place." Harris packs his gripsack and we find him again back in Ocean Grove writing to Mrs. Potts, who has just returned from her daughter, after discovering the secret marriage. He tells her of his penitence; that he loves her daughter; he will be a good husband to her, and will she not forgive him? He will win her respect. After this we do not find Harris in Ocean Grove any more. Why? I don't feel entitled to tell you at this stage of the case. It may come out in the testimony, but I don't feel justified in telling you now. But we do not find Harris at Ocean Grove any more that summer. He has changed his quarters to New York. It may be an interesting inquiry for you, perhaps, later in the case.[23]

Wellman was, of course, referring to evidence of Harris's refusal to go back to New Jersey to answer charges of keeping a disorderly house, which he correctly believed was going to be held inadmissible by Recorder Smyth. If he had doubts about its admissibility, he should never have mentioned it in opening statement. Wellman then described Helen's enrollment in the Comstock School, Harris's waning interest in her, and Mrs. Potts's waxing pressure on him to enter into a proper marriage with her daughter. Wellman then told of Harris's agreement to a proper marriage, provided no other way could be found to satisfy Mrs. Potts's scruples, Helen's sick headaches, Harris's prescribing quinine and morphine, Helen's death, and the aftermath. Wellman ended his recitation of the facts of the case with a description of Mrs. Potts's last interview with Harris.

A few days [after the funeral] Harris himself went down to Ocean Grove to see Mrs. Potts. "I want that affidavit and I want the marriage certificate," he said, and the grief-stricken mother, replied, "Well, Carlyle, you cannot have it. There is a grave between us and you are responsible for that grave; neither of us shall ever cross it. Other people may not know and suspect you as I do. I will not injure you. At one time you suggested cutting all and going West. I tell you, as your friend, now is the time for you to do it. I will even pay your expenses; but we never can speak together again." Harris left without the papers.[24]

At this point in his speech, Wellman had painted a sordid picture of Harris as a self-centered cad and a despoiler of innocent youth, but he had said nothing that directly incriminated Harris of murder. He then began to put the pieces of the jigsaw puzzle of circumstantial evidence together for the jury.

Now, gentlemen, it is claimed by the prosecution in this case that for mo-tives which will become patent to you as you hear the evidence the pris-oner at the bar, having become tired of his wife, and knowing that within eight days he would have to declare her as his lawful wife and submit to a ministerial marriage, Harris prepared this medicine for her as a remedy for her sick headaches; that he took out two of the capsules in order to protect himself if any suspicion attached to him afterwards; the remaining four capsules he took home with him and retained in his possession for thirty-six hours after having them compounded. One of these capsules he unloaded and substituted five grains of morphine for the quinine therein and then gave them to his girl-wife. She was directed to take one each night on retiring. She took one and did not like its effects, and he persuaded her to take more, not knowing which one of the four was the fatal dose, for they looked precisely alike. Harris went away immediately to Old Point Com-fort, not knowing which night Helen would take the morphine, apparently wishing to be out of town when she took the fatal dose.[25]

Wellman had stated a reasonable inference to be drawn from the circum-stantial evidence he had outlined, but other reasonable inferences could be drawn from the evidence consistent with a theory that Harris was innocent. In order to insure a conviction, Wellman was going to have to negate each and every reasonable inference consistent with innocence. The law of New York was clear on this point:

> Where the case depends . . . on circumstantial evidence, . . . those circumstances shall be of such a persuasive or satisfactory character as to leave no rational ground of doubt as to the defendant's guilt before he may be convicted. In other words, the circumstances are required to be of so forcible a nature as to exclude every other reasonable supposition or hypothesis or theory than that of the defendant's guilt, before a conviction can be reached by force of evidence of this description.[26]

Before Wellman turned to the task of making guilt the only reasonable inference, he made an argument that he hoped would help to turn the jury's dislike for Harris, which he had so carefully cultivated up to this point, into utter disdain. It was an argument calculated to make the jury eager to find Harris guilty.

> In a case of death by willful poisoning a jury must expect to find as defendant a cunning, shrewd, clever, calculating man, one who weighs circumstances and prepares for them. Such a man does not use a knife or pistol. He does not strike in passion or in public. He lays his plans carefully and discounts in advance possible failures in his calculations. Such a one was Carlyle Harris. He was a medical student. It is fair to presume that if he gave this morphine in the manner described, he knew just what the effects would be and he knew the difficulty of detection in a postmortem examination, because all the medical authorities agree that morphine is so quickly absorbed into the system that it frequently happens that, when very large doses are taken, only traces can be found in the stomach after death, and having given a trace, a sixth of a grain of morphine, who could discover or prove that he had given her more than that amount. Had not these roommates of hers gone to the concert that night, had they gone to bed as ordinarily with her, had they not come in late and awakened her, the first sleep produced by the drug would have been the sleep of death. Had this plan succeeded there would have been no talk about the druggist, no investigation into the matter to prove the druggist had made no mistake or had not properly compounded the prescription; it would have been said she died from natural causes; no symptoms could have been

testified to by the doctors and Harris would have gone to his wife's funeral an object of sympathy to all her friends and relatives. But the plans of the shedder of human blood always fail. So this one failed. Murder will out, because God wills it so![27]

Wellman was now ready to share some facts that he had thus far withheld. He spoke of Harris's threat to kill Helen, which was heard by Mae Schofield: "Before I would have anybody know of the secret marriage, I would kill her and kill myself, too. I wish that she were dead, and I well out of this."[28] He told the jury about Harris's strange visit to the pharmacist after Helen died:

In listening to this testimony, I beg of you to contrast in your minds the conduct of the prisoner with that of a man who really loved his wife and who discovered that a harmless prescription he had himself given her had suddenly caused her death. Dr. Fowler told him "There is some trouble, some mistake here; four and a half grains of morphine have been taken by this patient. Go to the druggist and find out who has made the mistake." One would expect an innocent man to run to the druggist, and demand: "What have you put in those pills? The lady I gave them to is dying!" What did he do? He walked round the corner and returned, saying there had been no mistake, although he had not been near the druggist's. After Helen died, and when advised to get possession of the original prescription, he then walked into the store and said calmly, "I had some capsules put up here ten days ago. Won't you kindly look in the book and tell me what was in the prescription?" The clerk turned to the book, and read it off to him; he wrote it down in his own notebook, said "Ever so much obliged," and left. That was all! And that is after his lovely wife was dead, and when he had been informed by Dr. Fowler that she had taken a large overdose of morphine.[29]

Wellman recounted the ominous words Harris included in his reply to Mrs. Potts's ultimatum concerning the sacred marriage:

Go back a little with me. The 20th day of January, 1891, was the day this prescription was put up. Do you remember that it was on the 20th day of January that he wrote Mrs. Potts, "I will concede to all your wishes. It shall be just as you say about this marriage *if no other means can be found of satis-fying your scruples.*"[30]

Wellman explained that when Harris got Helen's prescription filled, he well knew that a medical student had no authority to write any sort of prescription:

Well, the morning that he wrote that note he was calling on a physician, a friend of his. Dr. Hayden was a professor at the medical college and was treating Harris at that time for some malady. Sitting in Dr. Hayden's office, on that 20th day of January, he used these words: "Do you know, doctor, you have been giving me prescriptions now for the last five or six weeks, but I have never handed one of them into Ewen McIntyre's." "What," says the doctor; "never handed any prescription in? Why is that?" And Harris replied, "I always go there and repeat them myself by word of mouth, and they put them up for me." "Don't you know it is against the law? You are a medical student and you have no right to have prescriptions put up as a student. That is against the law. You are not a practicing doctor; you are not a recorded physician. You will be sure to get in trouble if you write pre-scriptions of your own." Not ten minutes after that conversation he goes into Ewen McIntyre's store, which is on the corner, right near the doctor's office, and asks the clerk, "How long will it take you to put up thirty cap-sules of sandalwood?" And the clerk answered, "It will take an hour." He said, "I cannot wait. Put me up six capsules of sandalwood, and I have a prescription here I would like to have you put up for me." He took out of his pocket a prescription carefully written by himself, signed "C. W. H." with "student" under it underscored, and the clerk said, "It will take ten minutes to put up this prescription," and Harris said, "All right, I will wait; put me up six capsules of sandalwood and that prescription, and I will come back tomorrow morning for the other twenty-four capsules of san-dalwood, but I want the prescription put up now." That was eleven o'clock on the 20th. He was to see Helen on the afternoon of the 21st, when there was to be a reception at the school, and yet he could not wait for these cap-sules. He says, "I will call tomorrow morning for the other twenty-four of my own capsules, but put me up this prescription, I want that now." Two or three times while he was waiting, he asked if it was ready. Finally he got it and took it home with him, and I ask you, during this testimony, to ask yourselves the question why he needed these six capsules for thirty-six hours before they were to be delivered to his wife? Why was he willing to call the next morning for his own capsules, but could not call for this prescription at the same time, although he was not to see Helen until the afternoon following at a reception given at Miss Day's school? Why did he have six capsules put up if he was to give the girl only four? Why did he keep out two unless he wanted them in case of an emergency? Ask yourselves these questions? Did he want to take them home in order to unload one of them and reload it again? It is the very simplest thing in the world to do. You may have seen this new form of capsules which are now commonly used. Any novice could load and unload one of them in a moment. All one has to do is to take them apart, empty out the powder of quinine and put in the powder of morphine; they are alike in appearance, and then you can put the two parts of the capsule together again, and nobody could detect which contains the poison and which the quinine. Harris could buy the poison, as a student, at any of the wholesale drug stores, and I will show you where he came in contact with it if you will bear with me for a moment. He was with Dr. Hayden on the 20th day of January, asking the doctor to prescribe for himself. Did he ask Dr. Hayden what would be good for a wife who had headaches? He gets a physician's prescriptions for himself, but who prescribed for his wife?[31]

Wellman then recounted Harris's lie about Helen's death being the result of the druggist's error:

You will remember that it has been said it was the druggist's awful mistake. Harris told Mrs. Potts in the carriage that Helen died of morphine poisoning. Why, five days after this he goes into Ewen McIntyre's place and seeing the clerk who put up the prescription for him, said to him, "None of you around here blame me, do you, for the newspaper stories?" And the clerk replied to him, "Well, I don't know any reason why we should blame you." He said, "Why, no, the girl died of heart disease; it is plain to everybody she died of heart disease." Five days before he had said it was the druggist's awful mistake, and here we find him talking with the very man who put up the prescription, and not a word is said about the mistake; he declares it was a case of heart disease. The following day, the 7th of February, he goes back to Dr. Hayden to get another prescription for himself, and Dr. Hayden says, "Well, young man, I told you not to write prescriptions in your own name but a few days ago, and I told you you would get into trouble, and now here you are in a peck of trouble." Harris replies, "Oh, no, doctor, I am all right. The two capsules I saved out will let me out of that." Don't forget that, gentlemen, "The two capsules I saved will prevent any jury from finding me liable in this case." Was it the druggist's awful mistake? Ewen McIntyre is one of the most respectable chemists in this town; he has been president of the College of Pharmacy for thirteen years, and so careful is he in his prescription department that he never allows morphine to be sold in his store unless it is checked while being weighed by a second clerk in his employ. The clerk behind the counter remembers in this case going over and looking at the scales and seeing that it was one grain of morphine that was weighed out for these six capsules. Furthermore, the capsule which the Coroner took from this young man has been analyzed and has been found to contain just one sixth of a grain of morphine less a fraction, so that it is proved absolutely that the prescription was correctly compounded, because the capsule produced by this defendant turns out to be the means of his detection; it turns out to be the very thing which completely lets the druggist out of this case.[32]

Wellman then told of Harris's boastful remarks about his amorous conquests to Charles Oliver at Scranton and of his access to morphine through Dr. Peabody's lectures, and he was ready to give them one last damning fact before he closed: "When Harris was overheard talking with the girl he had with him at Canandaigua, in whose bed he was found, he was speaking on the subject of getting married. He told the girl that he personally hadn't any money, and that the best thing for her to do would be to marry some rich old man. She asked, 'How will that help you if I get married?' and he replied, 'Oh, that will be all right; I can easily fix that. I'll mix him a pill and get him out of the way at short notice.'"[33]

Wellman told the jury of how Helen's body was exhumed and autopsied and of the results of Dr. Witthaus's chemical examinations, then he concluded:

The questions you must bear in mind are these: Did Helen Potts commit suicide? Why, she was happy; she was in love with this prisoner; she was well; her mother will tell you that she was very happy that day, and had been all along; her roommates will tell you she was both happy and contented; Miss Day, who spent the last evening with her, will tell you that she was well, happy, in a peaceful frame of mind and contented. Had she any cause to commit suicide? Had she the means of committing suicide? Was there any drug found in her bedroom but this one box marked "C. W. H."?

Was it the "druggist's awful mistake?" The analysis of the remaining capsule, the care with which it was compounded and its having been checked by a second clerk when the morphine was first weighed out—all will bear you evidence that it was not the druggist's mistake.

What did Helen die of? Natural causes or disease? The autopsy shows a perfectly healthy body. All the doctors agree morphine caused the death, and that three grains had been taken.

The last and important question is: Who administered the poison? I ask you, who had a motive to do it? Who said he "would kill her before the marriage should be made public?" Was the marriage about to be consummated by a Church marriage? Was Harris tired of his secret wife? Had he neglected her? Was he faithful to her, or did he want to get rid of her? Did he, as he said to Miss Schofield, "wish she were dead," and he "were well out of it," or, as he wrote to Mrs. Potts, had he "found some other means of satisfying her scruples"?

Those, gentlemen, are the questions that you are to keep constantly before you in this case. If, in the end, nothing succeeds in convincing you of this man's guilt, in God's name let not the innocent suffer; but if, on the other hand, all the facts and all the circumstances satisfy your minds of his guilt, then the best interests of society demand his conviction.[34]

The *Herald* pronounced Wellman's opening statement the best he had ever delivered, given without oratory, arraying the facts simply but eloquently. The jury listened to him with rapt attention during the hour and a half of his speech. So did Harris, staring fixedly at Wellman and looking away only to jot down notes on the prosecutor's statements.[35] The *Tribune* declared that Wellman's "brilliant qualities . . . were never so strongly manifested as in the case which he is now trying. . . . His opening argument to the jury was a model of clearness and accuracy, and for hours he told, without a single note, a story involving a great mass of detail, remarkably well arranged in his retentive memory."[36]

Francis L. Wellman, assistant district attorney, New York County, 1891–95 (Wellman and Simms, *The Trial of Carlyle W. Harris*)

Wellman's opening statement had completely erased any good impression Harris might have made upon the jury with his cool demeanor and decorous show of grief. It was incumbent upon the defense to do something immediately to offset the huge advantage Wellman had gained by his masterful opening statement. The best antidote to a compelling opening statement by the prosecution is for the jury to immediately hear a compelling answer from the defense. This did not happen. At the time of Harris's trial, under New York law, defense counsel had the right to defer giving their opening statement until after the prosecution had rested.[37] This is a good tactic if the prosecution has a strong case and the defense really doesn't have an answer. The defense attorney listens to the prosecution case unfold, identifies the weaknesses in the case, and then gives an opening statement designed to take advantage of the flaws in the prosecution case.

If there is a defense, however, and the defense attorney is going to use cross-examination of the prosecution witnesses to help build that defense, then the jury ought to be introduced to the defense as early as possible. Otherwise they might miss the significance of much of the cross-examination. In this case the defense had two good reasons to go ahead and make an opening statement: something had to be done to neutralize the force of the prosecution's opening statement, and they had a defense that they were going to try to lay the groundwork for with the cross-examination of prosecution witnesses. It was all the more important that they immediately make their opening statement because the defense was not a simple one. It was a complex scientific defense, and the jury's understanding would undoubtedly have been enhanced if they had immediately made their opening. The defense thus began the first day of testimony in a hole, and it was going to take some excellent lawyering to be able to climb out.

CHAPTER SIX

⌒✳⌒

The Prosecution Case—Week One

Immediately upon finishing his opening statement, Wellman began calling witnesses. His first group of witnesses consisted of Miss Lydia Day, the headmistress of the Comstock School, and two of Helen's roommates, Frances D. Carson and Rachel M. Cookson. They rehearsed the now-familiar story of how Helen stayed at the school on the evening of January 31 while her roommates went to a concert; how she read in the sitting room with Miss Day before retiring; how her roommates came back and found her in distress; how Miss Day was summoned and Dr. Fowler called in. The one pertinent witness whom Wellman wanted very much to call was Miss Reed, the housekeeper, who had been told by Helen, "My young doctor friend has given me a prescription to cure my malaria. He says that I must take it just before going to bed and that I must not be awakened. If I wake up, he says, the medicine won't do any good. I wish you would warn my roommates not to wake me tonight when they come home from the concert." Wellman and Simms spent many fruitless hours poring over law books trying to find an exception to the hearsay rule, which would render the statement admissible in evidence, but they had finally decided that it was impossible.[1] Today New York law would likely allow the statement into evidence under the state of mind exception to the hearsay rule. It would arguably be relevant to show Helen's state of mind toward her killer and to show that she acted in accordance with her expressed intent.[2] Although this evidence played no part in the actual trial itself, it took on great importance in the aftermath.

Things ran rather smoothly until Wellman called Dr. Fowler to testify about Helen's death. He asked the preliminary questions about Fowler's profession and experience, asked if Fowler had been called to the Comstock School on the night of January 31, and then began to ask about Fowler's treatment of Helen on the night of her death. Jerome objected to the testimony and asked, "Now, will your Honor allow me two preliminary questions?"[3] When Recorder Smyth said yes, Jerome, in true lawyerly fashion, asked four questions. He established that the doctor was called to attend Helen in her illness, that he was acting as Helen's physician, and that everything he knew about Helen's illness he learned as her physician.

Jerome then turned to Recorder Smyth and said, "Now, we object to the testimony as inadmissible, without an express waiver of the personal representative."

"Who is the personal representative?" asked Smyth.

Taylor interjected, "I suppose under the statute her husband would be the representative, the one qualified to waive the question."

This objection caught Wellman utterly off guard. The doctor-patient privilege was apparently something that had not occurred to him and he had no ready answer. The best he could do was to say, "If your Honor wishes me to do so, I will withdraw this witness till to-morrow morning."

"Yes," responded Smyth. "Give me an opportunity to look at this question. It is a very important question in this case, although I confess my present opinion about it is that the doctor is a competent witness. However, I will give the District Attorney an opportunity to look at this matter, and you may withdraw this witness and call another."[4] Wellman and Simms would have a busy evening researching the question of doctor-patient privilege.

Trial lawyers must be resilient. Wellman had hit a roadblock, but he could not allow it to stop his progress. Having successfully postponed the argument on the admissibility of Fowler's testimony, Wellman immediately turned to the next witness and soldiered on through the rest of the day without any further difficulties. Mrs. Cynthia Potts, Helen's mother, took the stand next, and Wellman had not concluded her direct examination when the time came to recess court for the day. The next morning, January 20, Wellman hit another snag. It was time to continue with Mrs. Potts's testimony and she was nowhere to be found. The weather was stormy, and Wellman suggested to the judge that her transportation into the city may have been delayed because of inclement weather. There was nothing to do but return to Dr. Fowler's testimony.

Before Fowler testified, the lawyers argued the issue of doctor-patient privilege. Over the evening both sides had provided Recorder Smyth with citations to cases that they believed would support their position. The prosecution relied heavily on the case of *Pierson v. People,* an 1880 decision of the New York Court of Appeals, which held that the doctor-patient privilege could not be used as a shield by a husband who had killed his wife.[5] Simms argued the case on behalf of the prosecution, and Taylor handled the argument for the defense. At the end of the argument Recorder Smyth ruled. He engaged in a lengthy discussion of the statute and the cases interpreting it, holding that the statute clearly allowed a doctor to testify about the physical or mental condition of a deceased patient and that only things told by the patient to the doctor in confi-

Dr. Edward P. Fowler, a founder of the New York Homeopathic Medical College (King, *Notable New Yorkers*)

dence were privileged. Although he did not specifically say so, Smyth's ruling was grounded on a finding that *Pierson* did not apply to the Harris case. Dr. Fowler never had any confidential communications with Helen because she was unconscious the whole time he was with her. Smyth concluded by saying, "Entertaining the views I do, I will have to overrule the objection and of course give you an exception."[6] Under the archaic nineteenth-century rules of procedure, it was important that the lawyer "except" to a judge's adverse ruling and that the judge allow the exception. If this was not done, the lawyer would not be able to appeal the judge's ruling on that particular point of law.

Jerome apparently did not listen to Smyth's ruling. When Wellman recalled Dr. Fowler, Jerome renewed his objection. "We object to the question of the District Attorney on this ground: Your honor has evidently construed this statute on this principle, that [a] man cannot shield himself from crime by using or by invoking this statute."[7] Jerome went on to argue that the *Pierson* case had carved out an exception to the statute and therefore the state had to prove the exception applied. In other words, he argued that the state had to prove Harris was guilty of murder before they could use Fowler's testimony. Jerome was trying to put Wellman in a Catch-22

William Travers Jerome, assistant district attorney, New York County, 1888–90; district attorney, New York County, 1902–9 (King, *Notable New Yorkers*)

situation. He was arguing that before Wellman could use Dr. Fowler to prove Helen was poisoned, Wellman would have to prove that Harris poisoned her. It would have been an inspired argument if Smyth had made the ruling Jerome thought he did. But Smyth hadn't ruled that Harris's case was an exception to the privilege. He had ruled that in Harris's case there was no privilege. Smyth was laconic, "I don't think it is necessary for me to add anything more to what I have said in reference to this objection. The objection will be overruled." Jerome excepted to the ruling.[8]

With the objection resolved, Wellman then led Fowler through a description of Helen's symptoms and the lifesaving measures taken. Dr. Fowler testified that he found Helen in a deep coma. Her skin was cold, pale, and blue, and she was taking about two breaths per minute. There was a perceptible pause between respiration and expiration of the breath. Her pupils were contracted to pinpoints. Despite the fact that her skin was cold, she was perspiring profusely. Fowler decided that he had a very serious case of morphine poisoning and needed help, so he sent for Dr. Baner, asking him to bring his electric battery and other appliances. Baner came in about fifteen minutes, and meanwhile Fowler gave Helen an enema of between one and two pints of strong black coffee as an antidote to the morphine. He also tried artificial respiration. During the night he and Dr. Baner injected Helen with atropine, caffeine, and digitalis. The atropine was intended to counteract the morphine poisoning. They used digitalis to promote the action of the heart—a remedy commonly used in that day when the heart was deadened by poisoning. The caffeine was meant to act as a stimulant. The doctors also used electricity as a stimulant, but they did not use the stomach pump because they decided she was breathing so slowly that if they suspended artificial respiration to use the pump, she would suffocate.[9]

Fowler described his discovery of the pillbox and how he summoned Harris to Helen's bedside. He testified that Harris's contribution to the lifesaving efforts was to stand by and repeatedly ask if he would be held responsible for Helen's death. Wellman pressed for detail as to anything

Harris did to help save Helen's life: "I think he held one of the poles—if I remember, he held one of the poles [of the battery]." Did he do anything else? "I don't remember any other aid." Dr. Fowler recalled one unhelpful suggestion Harris made—that they perform a tracheotomy. Fowler, believing that such a procedure would kill Helen, rejected the suggestion.[10] An awful silence fell over the courtroom at Fowler's words. Harris seemed the least affected of anyone in the courtroom. "For all the effect the testimony had upon him," reported the *Herald*, "he might have been deaf."[11] His demeanor mirrored Fowler's description of his demeanor at Helen's bedside. Fowler testified that he was surprised by Harris's general lack of interest.[12]

Jerome objected, and this initiated a wrangle with Wellman over whether Fowler could be allowed to testify that Harris seemed uninterested in his wife's death struggle. Taylor joined the fray, asking Smyth to instruct Fowler that he could not characterize Harris's acts. Smyth ruled that it was proper for Fowler to say that Harris appeared disinterested in his wife's well-being, but Fowler could not say that Harris's lack of interest surprised him.[13] Wellman pushed his advantage.

Wellman was now ready to ask his most important line of questions, those concerning the cause of Helen's death. "What was the cause of Helen Potts's death?"

Dr. Fowler replied, "An overdose of morphine it must have been, because it has been proven." Fowler explained that his opinion rested on the aggregate of symptoms: the condition of the skin, the condition of the respiration, the condition of the pulse, the condition of the pupils of the eyes, the manner in which the pupils of the eyes dilated later. Fowler stated that the whole condition from beginning to end was a picture of morphine or morphine poisoning and a picture of nothing else. No other cause that he knew of could have produced it. Fowler estimated that the minimum dose of morphine required to cause such symptoms would have been from three to four grains.[14]

Jerome made a manful effort to neutralize Fowler's testimony on cross-examination, and he showed himself to be well prepared. Jerome began his cross-examination behind a stack of medical books and journals heaped onto counsel table.[15] Keeping the books close at hand, he bounded to his feet to begin questioning. Chroniclers of the trial report that Jerome began his questioning with an apology for his small library, telling Dr. Fowler that he did not want to appear "smart," and reminding Dr. Fowler that Fowler had treated him when he was a child.[16] If Jerome made these comments, the court reporter did not see fit to include them in the transcript of the trial.[17] This is the first of many places where the newspapers give details that the court reporter saw fit to omit from the official transcript.

Jerome's cross-examination seemed to have a four-pronged strategy: He tried to establish that Helen could have died from some disease other than morphine poisoning—possibly uremia, epilepsy, or apoplexy; that Helen could have died from a dose of morphine as small as one-sixth of a grain; that on the night Helen died Dr. Fowler jumped to the conclusion that she suffered from morphine poisoning and refused to consider any other possibility; and that the doctors Jerome intended to call as defense witnesses were eminent scientific and medical authorities.

To achieve his first objective, Jerome had Fowler describe the symptoms of uremia, a form of kidney disease, and admit that they were similar to the symptoms of morphine poisoning.[18] He then quoted from page 275 of *Blythe on Poisons*: "Deaths by apoplexy will only simulate opium poisoning during life. A post-mortem examination will at once reveal the true nature of the malady. In epilepsy, however, it is different, and more than once an epileptic fit has occurred and been followed by coma—a coma which certainly cannot be distinguished from that produced by narcotic poisoning." Did Fowler agree with Blythe? "That may be so,"[19] admitted Fowler. Jerome also got Fowler to admit that patients suffering from undiagnosed kidney disease were highly susceptible to poisoning by morphine or other morphines to the extent that a dose of morphine as small as one-sixth of a grain could kill.[20]

In pursuit of his second objective Jerome sought to show that even absent kidney disease, a small dose of morphine could kill. He did this by asking a rapid-fire series of questions about whether Fowler knew of various cases where a patient was either killed or nearly killed by doses of morphine as small as one-twelfth of a grain. In this series of questions he cited volume and page from a number of medical references, including the *Boston Medical and Surgical Journal,* the *Cincinnati Lancet and Clinic,* and the *Chicago Medical Record and Examiner.*[21]

Jerome pursued his third objective by questioning Fowler's competence and then suggesting that he had made a snap decision about Helen's condition and was now unwilling to retreat from it. Jerome questioned Fowler on the amount of atropine administered to Helen; Fowler said he didn't know, that Dr. Baner could answer that question because he was the one who had administered the drug to Helen. When Jerome insisted on an answer from Fowler, Wellman interjected, "we are going to show by [Dr. Baner] the amount he used of all these things." Jerome replied, probably sarcastically, "I don't doubt it."[22] Jerome continued to hammer away at Dr. Fowler's lack of knowledge as to the amount of atropine used, indignant that Fowler did not know the quantity of what Jerome characterized as one of the deadliest drugs known to the pharmacopeia.[23] An old maxim of cross-examination says, "When you strike oil, stop boring." Jerome had scored his point on Fowler, and it was time to move on to another subject, but he couldn't resist driving his point home with just one more question, trying to make it plain that Fowler had no idea how much atropine had been used.

Fowler said, "I am aware of the amount in totality."

Jerome stood on the brink of undoing his entire line of questioning. "How much?" he asked.

"A seventeenth of a grain,"[24] replied Fowler. Jerome had asked the infamous "one question too many."

Jerome then asked a line of questions that emphasized that Fowler quickly diagnosed Helen as suffering from morphine poisoning and that he did not use available diagnostic tools to rule out uremia. He ended the series with an argumentative summary question: "You jumped at once to the conclusion that it was morphine poisoning, and you did nothing to make a differential diagnosis; isn't that true?" Jerome had again asked one question too many. He should have saved this last question for final argument. Recorder Smyth, thinking the question unfair, interjected, "He did not say he jumped at once to the conclusion."

Smyth had undercut Jerome's argument, but Jerome soldiered on trying to reinforce the argument that Fowler had jumped to conclusions: "Inside of five minutes you had ordered coffee?"

Fowler fired back, "I think if you lay in the same condition you would want someone to jump at a conclusion."[25]

Jerome easily established the fourth objective of bolstering the credibility of witnesses he intended to call. He first got Fowler to say that he knew of Prof. Horatio C. Wood, and to endorse him as one of the foremost writers on the subject of therapeutics in the country. Jerome read passages from Wood's book, *Therapeutics: Its Principles of Practice,* and tried to get Fowler to agree with them. Fowler refused. Jerome then ran into trouble by trying to paraphrase a statement from Wood's book. "Do you remember a case reported by Professor Wood in that same book where one-sixth of a grain of morphine caused death?"

Wellman showed that he had done his homework by correcting Jerome and pointing out that Wood was repeating something he had read in the newspaper. It should have embarrassed Jerome that he had to amend his question to accurately state what Wood wrote in the book.

"Do you remember a case reported by Professor Wood, as follows: 'In regard to the amount of opium which will cause death, the smallest fatal dose is one-sixth of a grain in an adult, reported by Dr. Buskirk, in the *Washington Post* January 12, 1878?'" Fowler refused to endorse a hearsay report from a newspaper.[26]

Jerome would have been better off if he had omitted questioning on the one-sixth grain dose reported in Wood's book. He came off looking as though he might be capable of stretching the truth, and all he got was disagreement from Fowler. He should have waited until he called Wood to prove the point.

Jerome got Fowler to admit that another defense witness, Prof. Theodore Wormley, was an eminent authority on toxicology. He then read several passages from Wormley's book, *The Micro-chemistry of Poisons,* and asked Fowler to agree with them. Fowler was somewhat more obliging with the quotes from Wormley's book than he had been with Wood's book, but he stopped short of wholehearted endorsement of Wormley's statements.[27]

Only one juror, Joseph Bell, paid any attention to Jerome's cross of Fowler. He seemed quite interested in Fowler's description of the similarities between uremia and morphine poisoning.[28] Although Bell was only one juror, one juror was all the defense needed to prevent a conviction. It may be that the other jurors were more interested in Harris's nonchalant disregard of the testimony. While Jerome worked manfully to undermine Fowler's opinion, Harris engaged in a whispered conversation with his mother. Whatever they were talking about, it seemed to amuse them both.[29] The attitude that Harris displayed before the jury during Fowler's testimony certainly did nothing to advance his case with the other eleven jurors.

Mrs. Potts retook the witness stand wearing a black dress on her slim figure and a sad expression on her kindly face. She refused to look at Harris, but he and his mother only had eyes for her as she testified.[30] Although she was obviously grief-stricken, she held up fairly well until she came to tell of how Harris had broken the news of Helen's death to her. She broke down in tears during the middle of her description and asked for a glass of water. At this point Harris looked at her "with polite curiosity."[31] There is no record of how the jurors looked at Harris.

The *Evening World* initially adjudged Mrs. Potts a very bad witness, saying that she sometimes evaded questions and sometimes had too ready an answer,[32] but by the conclusion of her testimony, the paper had changed its tune: "The hardest blow that Harris has received was dealt by the gentlest, tenderest of hands—those of Mrs. Cynthia Potts, who mourns with a pathetic sadness the daughter lost, but has no room in her wounded mother's heart for thoughts of vengeance. She told her story tearfully and with no suggestion of anger or hate for Carlyle W. Harris, although she confessed that she had suspected him from the first."[33]

The *St. Louis Republic* gave a less melodramatic assessment: "Mrs. Potts' testimony . . . unless shaken by the defense later on, must militate greatly against Harris." The *Republic* recounted her testimony about Harris's many selfish acts and concluded that "The cold-blooded manner in which he went about the killing of his own unborn child was also brought out."[34]

Jerome's two-hour cross-examination of Mrs. Potts was courteous and deferential.[35] Any other type of cross-examination would have been suicidal. He concentrated on showing that Helen was a beautiful, talented young lady who would have made an ideal wife.[36] Jerome obviously wanted to show that any young man would have been proud to have Helen as his wife, and certainly no young man would want to kill her. The testimony could prove a two-edged sword, however. Instead of making the jury think it impossible that Harris could have killed Helen, the testimony was just as likely to make the jury think that Harris was that much more a villain for having killed such a fine young lady. Jerome made the best of a bad situation in cross-examining Mrs. Potts, but something he did during her direct examination was a blunder of the first magnitude. Wellman had directed Mrs. Potts's attention to her final conversation with Helen and was trying to get her to describe what Helen did with the pillbox. Mrs. Potts began to describe what Helen both did and said. Wellman stopped her, cautioning Mrs. Potts not to repeat any of Helen's statements, but Jerome interjected, "We don't object to what she said at that time."[37]

Wellman had quite properly cautioned Mrs. Potts not to testify to anything Helen had said about the capsules—it was hearsay—and Jerome had thrown the door open to allow testimony about anything and everything

Helen had told her mother concerning Harris giving her the fatal capsules. Wellman didn't need a second invitation. He stepped through the open door. "What did she say about it?"

"She said that she had been taking some capsules that Carl brought her and that they made her feel ill and she disliked to take them, but I assured her," Mrs. Potts replied. "She said that she had no doubt they had helped her, but she was tempted to toss it out of the window rather than take it." Wellman then had her describe how she argued against Helen's objections to taking the last capsule and persuaded her to take it.

Wellman concluded his line of questioning, "When was the next time you saw her?"

"When she was dead," replied the grieving mother.[38]

Objectively this testimony didn't hurt Harris because there was ample admissible evidence that he had given the capsules to Helen, but the pathos of Helen's mother describing how her blind trust in Harris led her to encourage Helen to take that last fatal capsule could do little to help Harris in the eyes of the jury.

It was during the examination of Mrs. Potts that friction began to build between Wellman and Jerome. The spark of animosity was ignited when Wellman asked Jerome to turn over a portion of a letter that Harris had written Mrs. Potts. McCready Harris had requested that portion of the letter because Carlyle had made derogatory comments about him, and Mrs. Potts had obliged McCready by giving him that portion of the letter. The *Herald* reported that when Wellman made the request, Jerome smiled sardonically and replied, "When you acquire a legal right to it you may have it."[39] Jerome may well have said this, but the transcript tells a different story. According to the transcript, Jerome first said he didn't know whether he had the letter,[40] but he eventually gave it up after a lengthy wrangle.[41] Then another wrangle developed over whether Jerome had the letter from Dr. Fowler to Mrs. Potts, which had disappeared on the day Harris made his last visit to Mrs. Potts. Wellman contended that Jerome had read from it when he cross-examined Dr. Fowler, and Jerome contended, "We have stolen no letters and have no such letters in our possession."[42] The animosity between the two continued to fester throughout the course of the trial.

Wellman concluded Mrs. Potts's testimony on the morning of January 21. Next came Dr. Treverton to tell of Helen's illness in Scranton, his delivery of Harris's stillborn child, Harris's nonchalant attitude toward the whole affair, and Harris's scandalous statements about his relationship to Helen and his debauching of other women. Wellman's direct of Treverton emphasized that he treated Helen with quarter-grain doses of morphine every three hours for pain.[43] The *Herald* took note of this testimony and remarked that Treverton's giving such a dose of morphine to Helen every three hours for four days was certainly inconsistent with Jerome's suggestion that four one-sixth grain doses given every twenty-four hours killed her.[44] Harris lost his usual cool demeanor and appeared nervous during Treverton's direct examination.[45]

Jerome was not gentle with Treverton. Adopting a fierce, confrontational air, Jerome began by cross-questioning Treverton on his qualifications, phrasing his questions in such a way as to suggest that he had little respect for Treverton's medical expertise.[46] He then questioned Treverton's ethics by suggesting that Treverton had improperly divulged the circumstances of Helen's treatment to a Scranton newspaper.[47] Then he approached very close to Treverton on the witness stand. Putting his face as close to Treverton's as possible, he asked, "When Helen Potts returned from Scranton with her mother, did you ever learn what she told [her] mother in reference to you?"

"I don't know anything about it,"[48] replied Treverton.

None of the jurors knew anything about it, either. Mrs. Potts hadn't been asked any questions concerning the matter, and Smyth would have ruled the testimony inadmissible hearsay if she had. Jerome was obviously trying to suggest to the jury that Helen had told her mother something derogatory about Treverton in hopes of rousing the jury's anger against him. If Jerome hoped to rouse any emotion in Treverton with the question, he failed miserably. Treverton seemed completely unperturbed.

By this time in the trial, after hearing Wellman's opening statement and Mrs. Potts's testimony, the jury had to be angry with Harris, and upcoming testimony should make them even angrier. Anger, of course, was no reason to convict Harris, but anger certainly made it easier for the jurors to dismiss doubts raised by the defense as unreasonable. Jerome had to deflect some of that anger off onto someone else, and he felt Treverton provided an easy target. Jerome's inability to fluster Treverton was only a minor defeat; he had still planted the seed of suspicion in the jurors' minds that Treverton might not be the kind of doctor they would want to consult. Having softened his target with suggestions that he was underqualified, unethical, and unkind toward Helen, Jerome was ready to hit him with what he hoped would be the coup de grâce.

Jerome brandished Treverton's letter to Harris, asking if Treverton wrote it. Treverton acknowledged that he had written the letter. Treverton offered to read the letter, but Jerome preferred to read it himself. He probably felt that he could give a much more dramatic reading than Treverton. He marked the letter into evidence and then read it to the jury. The obvious point Jerome was trying to make was that Treverton cared little or nothing about Helen but cared everything about money and extorting a fee out of Harris. Jerome might have tarred Treverton with the brush of low character, but he could do nothing with the facts to which Treverton testified.

Dr. David B. Hand, who had assisted Treverton with Helen's treatment, followed Treverton onto the stand and corroborated him in every detail. Jerome tried the same tactic of questioning Hand's ethics by asking him about the fact that he had spoken to the local paper about Helen's treatment, but it backfired when he concluded his line of questioning by asking if Dr. Hand thought such a disclosure was honorable for a doctor. Hand replied he thought it the honorable thing to do under the circumstances.[49] Jerome didn't ask what those circumstances might have been, but Wellman jumped at the opportunity.

On redirect examination, Wellman asked Dr. Hand, "What do you mean by 'under the circumstances'?"

Hand replied, "The case was generally known; the friends wished to protect the girl's good name as far as they could; therefore I considered it not only right but more than right."

Hand went on to say that someone had been spreading false statements impugning Helen's character and that he and Dr. Treverton had made the statements to correct the falsehoods and protect her reputation as much as possible.[50]

The defense took a completely different approach to Wellman's next witness, Dr. James R. Hayden, who was a faculty member at the College of Physicians and Surgeons and also Harris's personal physician. Wellman tried to establish by Hayden that Harris knew full well that he should not be writing prescriptions and that he was lying when he said his preceptor had told him it was proper for students to write prescriptions. Lead defense attorney Taylor's argument against the admissibility of this testimony stood on three legs: Hayden was a physician; Harris was his patient; the physician-patient privilege applied to any discussions Hayden and Harris had about any matters whatsoever.[51] Smyth had little patience for Taylor's argument, despite the fact that Taylor assured him, "I shall make no proposition to your Honor which I do not really believe myself."[52] Although Taylor made repeated, vehement, and vociferous objections, Smyth allowed the testimony that Hayden had repeatedly warned Harris against writing prescriptions and that he had warned him against doing so on the very day that Harris got the six capsules from McIntyre & Son's pharmacy. Taylor won a minor victory when he persuaded the judge to exclude Harris's statements to Hayden about what he did with the prescriptions Hayden had given him.

Wellman then moved to a conversation Hayden had with Harris shortly after Helen's death, and Smyth allowed the testimony despite a renewed torrent of objections. Hayden testified: "I said 'You see what a foolish thing it is for you to have written those prescriptions? They may get you into a great deal of trouble. You are not a graduate of medicine.' And he said that these capsules would not hurt anyone; and 'No jury would convict me because I have two capsules which can be analyzed and found to contain the correct dose.'"[53]

Wellman never seems to have remarked on the fact that this statement came almost a week after Harris had told Deputy Coroner Weston that he had lost one of the capsules. It suggests that Harris held back one capsule from Weston, lied about keeping the capsule in reserve, and held it against contingencies so that he could "discover" it and have it analyzed should the need arise at a later date. When the coroner's analysis showed the surrendered capsule to be harmless, he had no need for the second capsule held in reserve.

At the conclusion of Wellman's direct examination, Jerome conducted a three-question cross-examination designed to underline the fact that Hayden had a physician-patient relationship with Harris. Jerome's failure to challenge Hayden's testimony was a tacit admission that Hayden spoke the truth when he said Harris knew he shouldn't have written the prescription. This gave rise to an inference that Harris was lying when he said his preceptor had told him he could write prescriptions and was evidence of guilt—but guilt of writing prescriptions without a license, not necessarily of murder.

Hearn J. Power next took the witness stand and testified about filling Harris's two prescriptions on January 20, one for sandalwood and one for a mixture of quinine and morphine. Wellman took pains to have Power testify about how impatient Harris was to have the prescriptions filled. When he was told that it would take time to prepare thirty capsules of sandalwood, Harris said to just prepare six immediately and he would come back later for the others. While Power was compounding the six capsules of sandalwood and the six capsules of the quinine-morphine mixture, Harris repeatedly asked if the prescriptions were ready yet. Upon receiving the prescriptions, Harris left, saying he would be back for the remainder of the sandalwood.[54] Power did not see Harris again until after Helen's death,[55] when Harris came in with a prescription from Dr. Hayden. Harris asked Power if he had seen the paper and Power said he had. Harris asked Power if he believed what he had seen in the paper. Power testified that he told Harris, "No, I believe the girl died by heart disease," to which Harris replied, "So do I."[56]

Wellman had Power perform a number of demonstrations for the jury, one of which was to show the jury how quickly a capsule could be emptied and refilled. A reporter timed the demonstration, and the whole operation took eighteen seconds.[57] Another demonstration showed how it was near impossible to tell the difference between a capsule filled with quinine and a capsule filled with pure morphine.[58] These demonstrations were conducted despite a barrage of objections from Jerome and Taylor.

One objection that gained traction came when Wellman had Power testify that he went to a wholesale druggist where he was not known and bought an ounce of morphine with no questions asked. Jerome moved to strike that testimony and Smyth granted the motion without argument. When Wellman asked if he could argue the motion, Smyth replied, "No sir; I don't care about hearing any argument on this subject." He went on to say that he had allowed a number of demonstrations with capsules over the objection of the defense and concluded by saying, "That is about as far as you can go." Wellman argued that the testimony was relevant to show how easy it was for anyone to purchase morphine. Smyth was firm, "I don't propose to allow any such evidence."[59]

Jerome's cross-examination tangled up Power on several points. He grilled Power about the differences between powdered and crystalized forms of morphine and quinine and exposed Power as being somewhat ignorant about the differences in weight of the two drugs. He produced some capsules and challenged Power to identify their size in relation to the size of the capsules Power used to fill Harris's prescription. He cross-examined Power on perceived differences between his current testimony and his testimony before the coroner and the grand jury. He showed Power the facsimile box that Coroner Schultze had made to replace the one he lost, and Power said he couldn't tell whether it was the box he made for Harris's prescription or the facsimile box. Power became so defensive that when Jerome produced a set of scales and challenged Power to weigh out a quantity of drugs, Power demurred, saying the scales were German and he didn't know how to operate German scales.[60] This seemed patently ridiculous. It was a balance-beam scale, which differed from an American balance-beam scale only in that it bore German writing and metric weights rather than English writing and avoirdupois weights.

In addition to making Power look foolish, Jerome scored two points on the witness. First, he established that Power knew he was breaking the law by filling a prescription for Harris,[61] and second, he established that Power knew he would be responsible for Helen's death if he improperly mixed the quinine and morphine.[62] Jerome lost some ground, however, when he established that Power had filled many prescriptions for Harris but only one prescription actually written by Harris.[63] No matter how bad Jerome made Power look, he could not refute the most important point of Power's testimony—Helen's medicine was properly compounded. Wellman immediately followed Power with the testimony of George Manson, the pharmacist's clerk who double-checked Power's work. Manson assured the court that Power had properly compounded the medication.[64] And then there was the capsule Harris had saved and turned over to the coroner—it had unquestionably been properly compounded.

When he cross-examined Manson, Jerome tried to repair some of the damage he had done by getting Manson to testify that the fatal prescription for Helen was not the only prescription Harris had ever written. He began a line of questioning on the subject, which ended with a disastrous exchange that established that Manson knew of no other prescription signed "student," that Manson never put up a prescription for a student, and that he knew of no other student ever having had a prescription put up.[65]

Ex-Deputy Coroner Weston took the stand next and testified concerning his investigation and Harris's statements. On cross-examination Jerome tried to read an excerpt from a written statement Weston took from Miss Day. Wellman objected that the statement was hearsay, and Jerome said that the statement was made in the presence of the defendant and therefore an exception to the hearsay rule. There is no such exception to the hearsay rule, although many old-time lawyers thought that there was. In Florida the purported hearsay exception even had a name—the Duval County Rule.[66] Jerome withdrew his offer of the statement upon learning that Harris was not present when the statement was made.[67] The only real point that Jerome scored on cross-examination was to have Weston testify that Jerome had once been an assistant district attorney and that Weston had worked on many cases with him. Wellman objected, and Smyth cut off Jerome's questioning by saying, "It will be conceded, I suppose, that you were an Assistant District Attorney, Mr. Jerome, that you tried many cases during the time you were in office, and that you tried them well; I am satisfied of that."[68]

Wellman called Coroner Schultze next. Given Schultze's bungling of the investigation, Wellman would probably have preferred not to put the coroner on the stand, but Schultze was an essential witness in the chain of custody on the capsule Harris turned over to Weston. Weston had given the capsule to Schultze, and Schultze had given the capsule to Gustave Pfingsten, the chemist who analyzed its contents. In order to prove that Pfingsten analyzed the capsule given by Harris to Weston, Wellman had to call Schultze. Jerome butchered Schultze on cross-examination, walking him through the loss of the transcript of testimony from the coroner's inquest and the loss of the pillbox. Schultze didn't help matters any by trying to blame the loss of the transcript on the district attorney. He was only made to look worse when he was forced to admit that he had never even seen the transcript of testimony, much less delivered it to the district attorney.[69]

More sparks flew between Wellman and Jerome when Jerome demanded that Wellman turn over a copy of the transcript of testimony before the coroner's jury and Simms replied that the district attorney's office had never gotten a transcript, and the only record of the coroner's inquest that they had was a copy of the minutes, which they had received from Jerome.[70]

Things didn't get any better when Wellman called Pfingsten to the stand and tried to have him testify to the results of his testing. Taylor objected that the chain of custody on the capsule was insufficiently proven—Wellman

Dr. Gustave Pfingsten, prosecution toxicologist (Wellman and Simms, *The Trial of
Carlyle W. Harris*)

had neglected to ask Weston and Schultze whether they had altered the
contents of the capsule in any way.[71] Wellman had to excuse Pfingsten
and recall Schultze to testify that he had not tampered with the contents
of the capsule. He could not recall Weston because Weston had already
left the courthouse, but Smyth allowed Pfingsten to state his opinion on
the basis of Schultze's testimony alone.[72]

Pfingsten, speaking with a heavy German accent, described in detail the
tests he performed to determine the contents of the capsule and voiced his
opinion: "The contents of that capsule was four and five-eighths of quinine
and one-sixth of a grain of morphine, less one-thirtieth; that is as near as I
can give it."[73] On cross-examination Jerome asked about many other sub-
stances that might give a similar reaction to the tests performed by Pfingsten. The courtroom erupted in laughter when Jerome asked, "Mustard
seed gives a pretty good reaction when combined with nitric acid, doesn't
it?" and Pfingsten replied, "I ain't eggquainted mit the chentleman."[74]

Dr. George White testified next. He told the jury that he was a classmate of Harris's at the time of Helen's death and that Harris had spoken to
him concerning the incident. Wellman asked him to relate the conversations. White replied that Harris told him he had given Helen some quinine
and morphine sulfate pills for a headache, that she had taken those pills,

and that she had died from the effects of them. Harris claimed he did not know whether the druggist had made a mistake or whether there was an idiosyncrasy on her part by which a small dose of morphine would affect her. Harris then told White he thought there was an idiosyncrasy probably produced by a brain tumor. Harris said that Helen had had headaches that resembled those headaches common in brain tumors, and he believed that she had a brain tumor, which accounted for the fact that one-sixth of a grain of morphine killed her.[75]

Wellman also tried to get White to testify about some statements Harris had made concerning one of his sexual conquests, but Jerome objected, and Smyth had White step to the bench to whisper the statement to him. After hearing the statement, Smyth ruled, "I do not think I will allow it."[76] Wellman protested that the statement involved Dr. Treverton; but upon further questioning White denied knowing the name of the doctor involved. Smyth ruled the statement inadmissible. The trial transcript merely says that White was privately examined by the Court[77] without giving the details, but enough was said in the presence of the jury for them to understand that Harris had told White that he had gotten a girl pregnant and procured a doctor to perform an abortion on her.

Jerome didn't challenge White's testimony on cross-examination. Instead he concentrated on some anticipatory rebuttal of Dr. Peabody's testimony about Harris attending his lectures on morphine poisoning. He asked if White had been a classmate of Harris's and whether they both attended Dr. Peabody's lectures. When White affirmed both questions, Jerome asked if he had read Harris's notes on the lectures. Yes, White had read the notes. They were typewritten, and White could remember reading no mention of morphine in the notes. On redirect Wellman established that White could remember attending classes with Harris where Peabody lectured on morphine.[78]

Wellman next put on *New York Times* reporter George B. Taylor to testify about Harris's disavowing any romantic involvement with Helen,[79] and then he was ready to turn to the sordid story of Harris's romantic tryst in Canandaigua while his wife recovered from the delivery of his stillborn child. Wellman first called John F. Latham, a young man who was obviously quite full of himself. The *Herald* declared him to be "pompous and given to ponderous declamation," comparing him to Mr. Podsnap from the Charles Dickens novel *Our Mutual Friend*. When asked whether he knew Harris, Latham answered with a gesture of his right arm that was so melodramatic the courtroom erupted in laughter. Harris himself laughed so hard that his glasses almost fell off.[80] When Latham got to the heart of his testimony, Harris had nothing to laugh about.

Latham began by describing how he and his wife were boarding at the Webster House, a hotel with a connection to one of the darkest times in American history. John Harrison Surratt Jr., one of the suspected co-conspirators in the Lincoln assassination, spent the night at the hotel as he fled to Canada after the president's death.[81] Latham told how Harris had arrived at the Webster House in the company of a beautiful young lady; how the two were obviously a romantic couple; how he registered at the hotel as C. W. Graham; and how C. W. Graham received mail at the Webster House addressed to Carlyle W. Harris. Latham went on to tell how he went to the young lady's room one evening to ask her to come minister to his sick wife and found Harris in her bed, and how he evicted Harris from the hotel on that account. After describing these events, Latham told how Harris had boasted to him about his sexual exploits. Harris listened to this portion of Latham's testimony intently.[82] Latham's most damning testimony came when he recounted a conversation he overheard between Harris and the young lady:

> He said to the young lady: "You had better marry some old gentleman with lots of 'mun,'" she answered, "Where will I find him?" He replied, "Oh, you can do that," and she responded, "Well, what if I do? What about the old gentleman?" "Oh," he says, "we can put him out of the way." She says, "What!" He says, "We can get the old gentleman out of the way." And she says, "How would you do it?" He says, "You find the old gentleman and we will give him a pill. I can fix that." the subject of conversation then ended.[83]

Wellman didn't ask the lady's name, but he did establish that it wasn't Helen Potts. It may appear that Wellman had a sense of decorum in not asking the young lady's name, but it was more likely a sense of showmanship. He wanted to conceal the woman's name until the very last moment when he had Latham identify the woman as not being Helen Potts. Wellman had his very next witness, Lizzie Latham, identify the woman as Queen Drew, a friend of Lizzie's whom she had invited to Canandaigua for a visit.[84] Mrs. Latham also testified that after his eviction, Harris wrote a letter to Miss Drew care of Mrs. Latham. Mrs. Latham produced the letter and it was introduced into evidence.[85] The letter read:

Dear Queenie:

I will enclose $10 and send this registered to-morrow, Monday morning. You will get it in ample time to leave Tuesday night. I would send more, but it is nearly every cent I have been able to get. Write either at once or as soon as you reach the city, where we can meet and when. Wednesday or Thursday afternoon at the Eighteenth street station might answer very well. And say, little girl, we must get you something to do, for my relatives are dead leery of me and will keep me dreadfully short. They kick now on my smoking cigars and say I should give up smoking until I am earning something. I will be ever so glad to see you, Dolly, so hurry back home and meet me as soon as you can.

Aff., C.[86]

Jerome conducted a perfunctory cross-examination of the Lathams, not really challenging their testimony at all.[87]

The first week of the trial was rapidly drawing to a close, but Wellman had four more blows to strike at Harris before court recessed on Friday. He intended to call Charles Oliver to testify about Harris's statements concerning his sexual conquests; to read Mae Schofield's deposition that she heard Harris threaten to kill Helen; to call Dr. Charles Krom to testify that he heard Harris say how easy it was to get away with murder; and to call Dr. John Elwyn Cochran to testify that he heard Harris say it was easy to put someone out of the way without anybody knowing it.

Oliver testified first, and his testimony came off fairly well despite a barrage of objections by Jerome. When Oliver was tendered for cross-examination, the best that Jerome could do was to establish that Oliver had talked with Dr. Treverton about the case before he took the witness stand.[88]

Then Wellman hit a snag. When he proposed to read Schofield's deposition into evidence, Jerome objected on the grounds that the court that entered the order for the deposition lacked jurisdiction to enter such an order. The written order was entered on December 28, 1891, by Justice Van Brunt, sitting as a judge of the Court of Oyer and Terminer. The deposition, to which the defense had agreed, was held on December 31. The indictment, however, was date stamped as being transferred to the Court of General Sessions on December 18. If Justice Van Brunt transferred the case to General Sessions on December 18, he would have been without jurisdiction to order the deposition on December 28. In response to Wellman and Simms's protestations that Jerome knew the case wasn't transferred until December 28 and, furthermore, that Taylor had agreed to the deposition, Jerome merely said, "I go by the record." Smyth said that he could not allow the reading of the deposition on the state of the record currently before him, and Wellman withdrew the offer of the deposition, saying he would go back and procure the records of the Court of Oyer and Terminer to show that he was correct about the dates.[89]

Dr. Charles Krom next took the stand and testified concerning a conversation he had with Harris when they were medical students. The topic was arsenic poisoning. Harris had expounded on the fact that it was perfectly possible that a person could be killed by use of poison and no one would find it out.[90] Jerome asked six questions on cross-examination, none of them doing anything to blunt the force of Krom's testimony.[91]

Wellman's last witness of the week was Dr. John Elwyn Cochran, who testified that when he was a fellow student of Harris's, he once had a conversation with him about arsenic poisoning and heard Harris say he thought that it was easy enough to put anyone out of the way without anyone knowing about it. The only thing that Jerome accomplished on cross-examination was to establish that this was the same statement heard by Dr. Krom.[92]

All things considered, it had been a good week for the prosecution. Wellman had delivered a powerful opening statement; he had gotten almost everything into evidence that he needed to get in; Jerome had scored some minor points on cross-examination, but the case was holding together quite well; and Wellman had gotten through twenty-one witnesses, some of whom had given highly technical testimony. Wellman had painted a picture of Harris as a self-centered cad with an insatiable sex drive and no concern for his wife, and as a man who considered murder by poison to be a safe method of solving problems. He had failed, however, to show through Mae Schofield's deposition that Harris had contemplated using murder to solve the problem of Helen Potts.

Despite the speed with which the testimony was going, Recorder Smyth expressed frustration with the pace of the trial and announced that he was going to hold night sessions the following week. He then recessed the case until Monday morning at 11:00 A.M.[93] It seems to have escaped Smyth's notice that one method of speeding the trial process would have been to start the trial earlier in the morning.

CHAPTER SEVEN

The Prosecution Case—Week Two

Wellman began the second week with the testimony of Dr. Byron P. Tompkins, Helen's personal physician, who testified, over objection, that he had examined Helen on December 14, 1889, and her heart was perfectly healthy. Jerome did not ask a single question on cross-examination,[1] virtually conceding that Helen did not die from an idiosyncrasy of the heart that heightened her sensitivity to morphine. This virtual admission became even more harmful in light of the very next witness Wellman called, Dr. James J. Mapes, another of Harris's classmates. Mapes testified that Harris laid the blame for Helen's death at the feet of Mrs. Potts. Harris said Mrs. Potts was the only person who knew Helen had a heart disease, and she did not tell him. If Mrs. Potts had only told Harris about Helen's heart condition, he would never have given her the dose of morphine that killed her.[2]

Again, Jerome failed to ask a single question on cross-examination; again, Jerome virtually admitted that Harris made the statement. Coupling the admission that Harris made the statement with the admission that Helen's heart was sound, we arguably have an admission that Harris was lying about the cause of Helen's death. That leads us to the following chain of reasoning: If he was lying when he said the death from morphine was accidental, then he knew the death from morphine was a homicide. If the death from morphine was a homicide, and if Harris was the one who gave Helen the morphine, then he is Helen's murderer. Of course, this chain of reasoning does not conclusively show Harris to be a murderer, but it certainly makes it easier for the jury to believe him a murderer.

Just to make sure that the jury believed Harris was lying to Mapes rather than simply mistaken, Wellman followed Mapes with Ewen McIntyre Jr., who co-owned the pharmacy where Harris had the capsules compounded. McIntyre testified to a conversation he had with Harris while waiting to testify at the coroner's inquest. McIntyre testified, "I remarked—I was introduced to Mr. Harris there at the Coroner's Inquest, and I remarked that it was very bad that our names should appear in connection with this case in the paper, and he remarked that it did not affect his professional standing any; that he had simply lost a friend and that was all."[3]

Jerome ignored Harris's statement, and instead undertook a lengthy cross-examination about different sizes of capsules, how much they could hold, the difference between morphine and sulfate of morphine, the difference between quinine and sulfate of quinine, and the difference between powdered and crystalized preparations of the two drugs.[4] He had a three-pronged strategy for the cross. First, he was attempting to show that it was impossible to get five grains of morphine into the capsules used to fill the prescription. This was important because the indictment charged that Harris had poisoned Helen with five grains of morphine. Jerome succeeded admirably in showing that it was impossible to get five grains of crystalized morphine into the capsule, but powdered morphine would fit. Power had testified that he used powdered morphine. The second prong of Jerome's strategy was to prove that the prescription had been improperly filled. A line of questions of the "have you ever made a mistake" variety seemingly made no headway, but a second line of questions scored. Jerome established that there was a difference between "morphine" and "sulfate of morphine." He further established that Harris's prescription called for "morphine," but Power had filled it with "sulfate of morphine." McIntyre Jr. responded that for practical purposes, there was no difference between the two and they customarily filled prescriptions for "morphine" with "sulfate of morphine." Jerome's third strategy was to blunt McIntyre's damning direct testimony by burying it under an avalanche of collateral cross-questions.

McIntyre Jr. weathered the storm of cross-examination with his credibility intact, but Wellman immediately undermined it by calling his father as a witness. Wellman's sole reason for calling the elder McIntyre was to refute Jerome's "have you ever made a mistake" line of questioning with McIntyre Jr. This was a mistake on two levels. It did immediate harm when on cross-examination McIntyre Sr. testified that if he got a prescription for "morphine" he wouldn't fill it with "sulfate of morphine" without first inquiring of the doctor who wrote the prescription.[5] It did long-term harm because Jerome had evidence to show that the senior McIntyre most certainly had made a mistake and been sued because of it. Proof of this mistake would have to wait for the defense's turn to put on evidence, but it would come.

In having the elder McIntyre differentiate between "morphine" and "sulfate of morphine," Jerome asked a series of questions that displayed his scientific knowledge of the factual differences between the two, but whose potential for final argument the defense team seems to have missed. Jerome had Mr. McIntyre testify that sulfate of morphine would dissolve in water much more quickly than morphine.[6] This gave the defense team a platform for arguing that if Helen had been given a proper dose of morphine rather than sulfate of morphine, her body would have absorbed it far more slowly and its toxic effects would have been greatly diminished. This would open up the possibility that Helen's death was "the druggist's awful mistake" after all. For whatever reason, the defense did not make that argument to the jury.

Wellman then called a number of witnesses to shore up testimony from the previous week: Richard Jones corroborated Charles Tuerke's testimony that Harris had not come into the pharmacy before 11:00 A.M. on February 1, 1891;[7] Albert Weston retook the stand to shore up the chain of custody

Jerome cross-examines Dr. Kerr (*New York Herald*, January 26, 1892)

on the capsule examined by Gustave Pfingsten;[8] Adolph Tscheppe testified that he had assisted Pfingsten in the analysis of the capsule;[9] and Dr. William Baner[10] and Dr. George Kerr[11] testified about how they assisted Dr. Fowler's lifesaving efforts and about Harris's lackadaisical attitude toward those efforts. Both Baner[12] and Kerr[13] testified unequivocally that the cause of Helen's death was morphine poisoning and none of the other causes suggested by Jerome. Jerome engaged in a lively cross-examination of each witness, but he didn't score any major points. During Jerome's cross of Dr. Kerr, Wellman smiled and whispered something to Jerome. Jerome reacted angrily. "I am requested by the District Attorney," he said, "to 'blow off' my technical knowledge upon someone else. I think that is an indecorous remark—an indecent remark." Recorder Smyth lost some of his usual composure and replied sharply, "It is certainly improper!"[14] Relations would continue to worsen between Jerome and Wellman.

Wellman now had the opinions of three medical doctors that Helen died from morphine poisoning, but they were all subject to the criticism that they had made hurried decisions on the scene with limited diagnostics and were now unwilling to admit they had made a mistake. He needed to close the door on this criticism, and the best way to do that was with the belated autopsy.

Before he could offer proof of Helen's autopsy, Wellman had to prove that her body had been buried and exhumed. He began the burial process with undertaker William P. Vannett, who testified that he pumped three to four quarts of Meade's Embalming Fluid into Helen's arms and legs, torso, and head.[15] Then came undertaker James H. Sexton, who testified that he buried Helen on February 9, 1891, and exhumed her body on March 25, 1891, in the presence of Dr. Allan McLane Hamilton, Dr. George D. Smith, and Dr. Rudolph A. Witthaus. Sexton affirmed that he had known Helen during her lifetime, and he was certain that it was Helen whom he had buried and Helen whom he had exhumed. He further testified that he had not tampered with Helen's body in any way while it was in his custody and that she looked to be in an excellent state of preservation.[16] With the preliminaries out of the way, Wellman was now ready to proceed with evidence of the autopsy itself.

Dr. Allan McLane Hamilton took the witness stand and gave a lengthy recital of his qualifications. Wellman wanted a thorough catalog of Hamilton's accomplishments because the doctor had worldwide fame as a

scientist and medical man.[17] Once Wellman established Hamilton's qualifications, he went into a minute description of the procedures used in
dissecting Helen's body. At the conclusion of Hamilton's graphic description of the autopsy, Wellman asked a series of questions designed to show
that each and every major organ in Helen's body was sound, healthy, and
normal. The only remarkable abnormality Hamilton found was a congestion of the brain consistent with narcotic poisoning.[18] At this point Jerome interjected that Wellman had led him to believe he would be given
advance notice of the calling of an expert witness so that Jerome could
prepare the cross. Jerome complained that he needed an opportunity to
prepare for cross-examination. Smyth replied, "Yes; and I will give you an
opportunity. It is now five o'clock, and we will adjourn for the day." Smyth
adjourned court until Tuesday, January 26, at 10:00 A.M.

The next morning Wellman concluded his direct examination. When he
turned Hamilton over to Jerome for cross-questioning, his direct had a gap-
ing hole in it—he had neglected to ask Hamilton the cause of Helen's death.
Jerome hammered away at the witness, reading to him from various medical treatises, without making much headway. He did score one point on
cross-examination. He got Hamilton to disagree with Fowler's treatment
of Helen. Hamilton testified that he would have used a gastric siphon to
try to remove some of the morphine from Helen's stomach.[19] On redirect
examination Wellman plugged the hole he had left on direct with a hypothetical question. He gave Dr. Hamilton a recitation of the circumstances
surrounding Helen's death, asked him to add to that the findings from his
autopsy, and asked him to render an opinion on the cause of her death. Jerome strenuously objected to the question, but Smyth allowed the answer.
Hamilton replied, "I should say that the subject died of opium poisoning."[20]
Jerome's attempts to soften the blow on re-cross-examination proved only
somewhat helpful: "Taking brother Wellman's hypothetical question and
leaving out what you observed at the autopsy, would you be willing to swear
that Helen Potts died of morphine poisoning?" Dr. Hamilton declined to diagnose opium poisoning on the symptoms alone, but he qualified his statement by saying, "I should suspect it very strongly."

Here was where Jerome should have stopped his line of questioning. He
had subtracted out the autopsy findings and gotten the witness to admit
that he could not say solely on the symptoms that morphine caused Helen's
death. The most eminently qualified doctor to testify so far had called into

question the testimony of the previous three doctors; Jerome was later going to offer evidence that an autopsy on a body dead for fifty-three days was worthless; he had grounds to argue reasonable doubt. Like a moth drawn to a flame, however, Jerome fell prey to the lawyerly temptation to ask one question too many. "But as a scientific man, you would not be willing to swear that she died of morphine poisoning would you?" Dr. Hamilton wouldn't go so far as to say it was opium poisoning, but "I would say it was a case of narcotic poisoning." Jerome asked if the doctor were certain. Dr. Hamilton said the symptoms ruled out any disease of the brain and any poisoning from uremia, leaving only narcotic poisoning.[21]

Jerome had not stopped while he was ahead, and he lost his point when Hamilton testified he could rule out all the alternative possible causes being offered by the defense and say that, while it may not be morphine poisoning, it was poisoning from a drug of some kind. This leads to the conclusion that since morphine was the only poisonous drug Helen took, she died of morphine poisoning.

Wellman called Dr. George Smith, who assisted Hamilton with the autopsy, and had Smith testify that Helen died from opium poisoning.[22] He was then ready to call Dr. Rudolph Witthaus, who had examined Helen's internal organs and found them to contain a trace of morphine and no quinine at all, but he had neglected to fully pave the way for Witthaus's testimony. Witthaus had worked with the organs from a body that had been embalmed, and it was important that he have a sample of the embalming fluid so that he could separate it from the other chemicals found in the organs. Wellman had forgotten to ask Vannett if he had given a sample of his embalming fluid to Witthaus. He had to recall Vannett to testify that he had not only given Witthaus a sample of the fluid, he had given him a sample from the same container of fluid as the fluid used to embalm Helen.[23]

Ill feelings between Wellman and Jerome almost came to a boil over an exchange that Jerome had with Vannett. Vannett had previously said that he didn't remember whether he gave Witthaus embalming fluid or not. Jerome suspected that Wellman had coached Vannett to say the words necessary to lay the foundation for Witthaus's testimony and he wanted to prove it.

"You saw me at the District Attorney's Office one morning didn't you?" he asked. "When you were leaving Mr. Wellman?"

Vannett temporized: "Yes, sir; I think so, though I am not sure."

Jerome was ready to set up the killing question: "Now, when you left Mr. Wellman on the morning to which I have called your attention, in the District Attorney's office, as you were going out Mr. Wellman made a loud remark, did he not?"

Vannett couldn't remember. Wellman interjected that he was in the habit of making a good many loud remarks. Jerome soldiered on.

"Didn't I step right out behind you and repeat Mr. Wellman's remark, and was not the remark this: 'Remember the importance of it and work it'?" Vannett didn't remember. Jerome continued with several more questions attempting to get Vannett to admit the remark, but Vannett steadfastly refused to remember it. Jerome concluded with a question: "But your memory is very good in the point that you gave Professor Witthaus a sample of the embalming fluid . . . , isn't it?"[24]

It was an embarrassing line of questions for both Wellman and Vannett, and a series of questions that Jerome should not have asked unless he was willing to abandon his role as defense attorney and become a witness to testify to the facts he alleged in his question. It is a well-established rule of professional conduct that a lawyer should not "in trial, allude to any matter . . . that will not be supported by admissible evidence, [or] assert personal knowledge of facts in issue except when testifying as a witness."[25] Jerome thought Wellman had behaved improperly by coaching Vannett to give the needed testimony and his response was to behave improperly by asserting facts that he could not prove.

There is nothing wrong with refreshing a witness's recollection, nor is there anything wrong with impressing upon a witness how important it is that the witness remember a particular fact. Assuming Jerome heard what he said he did, he had no grounds to accuse Wellman of doing anything more than refreshing Vannett's recollection and impressing upon him the importance of remembering that he had given Witthaus the embalming fluid. Both Jerome and Wellman were falling into the trap of fighting each other and not trying their case. When trying a case, the objective is not to defeat, disgrace, or disparage the lawyer on the other side; it is to persuade the jury that they should return a verdict in your client's favor.

Dr. Witthaus took the stand and gave one hundred pages of highly technical testimony describing a number of scientific experiments and analyses that he performed on Helen's internal organs, and then he weathered a vigorous cross-examination by Jerome. In his masterwork, *The Art of*

Dr. Rudolph Witthaus, prosecution toxicologist (Wellman and Simms, *The Trial of
Carlyle W. Harris*)

Cross-Examination, Wellman wrote: "Mr. Jerome's cross-examination of
Professor Witthaus, the leading chemist for the prosecution, was an extremely able piece of work, and during its eight hours disclosed an amount
of technical information and research such as is seldom seen in our courts.
Had it not been for the witness's impregnable position, he certainly would
have succumbed before the attack."[26] Jerome's cross-examination didn't
last for eight hours as Wellman remembered, but it was such an able performance that it probably seemed that long to Wellman.

Cutting through the technical testimony, Witthaus's bottom line
was clear. There was morphine in Helen's body. There was no quinine
in Helen's body. If Helen had taken quinine and morphine in the proportions specified in the prescription, there should have been quinine in
her body.[27] Wellman was not content with this testimony. The amount
of morphine Witthaus found in Helen's body was small. Witthaus had
said that the residue in Helen's body meant she had consumed five grains
of morphine; the indictment read that Harris gave Helen five grains of
morphine; Wellman wanted Witthaus to say that Helen had consumed
five grains of morphine. He asked Witthaus, "Had five grains of morphine
been taken and the patient kept alive by artificial respiration and other
means for thirteen hours and then embalmed as described here by the

witness, and buried for fifty-five days, and then analyzed by you, would you expect to find in the intestines or in the stomach more morphine than you did find?" Jerome objected and Wellman withdrew the question. Try as he might, the best Wellman could do was to show the speed with which morphine dissipated in the body and the length of time that the doctors kept Helen alive, giving rise to the inference that Helen had been given a large quantity of morphine.[28]

Wellman made his point, but Jerome's well-timed objections insured that he did not make it nearly as strongly as he wished. Wellman also used Dr. Witthaus's testimony to attempt to show that doctors hired by the defense, who had gone to Witthaus's laboratory to examine his work, had stolen the valves of Helen's heart. The testimony was rather weak, simply that Witthaus had noticed that the valves were missing after the doctors left. Witthaus really didn't know whether they might have gone missing before the visit of the defense experts.[29] Wellman's maneuver understandably angered Jerome.

Wellman and Jerome were going at each other like two boxers intent on fouling each other, but skilled enough to never commit a foul so egregious as to receive anything more than a warning from the referee. This sort of thing is a commonplace in boxing, and sadly a commonplace in the trial of criminal cases as well. The problem with such activity, over and above the fact that it is wrong, is that each time a minor foul is perpetrated, the combatant who is fouled becomes angry and responds in kind. With boxers this sometimes leads to an escalation in the seriousness of fouling until someone is disqualified or injured. With trial lawyers an escalating tit-for-tat of fouls leads to mistrials, reversals of convictions, bar discipline, and sometimes even black eyes and bloodied noses. The war between Wellman and Jerome would continue to escalate.

Dr. John Rogers took the stand next and told of a conversation he had with his classmate Carlyle Harris the day after reading reports of Helen's death in the newspaper. Harris told Rogers how sorry he was that the incident had occurred, what a ticklish situation it had put him in, and how glad he was that he had signed the prescription as a medical student. Rogers had no recollection of Harris saying anything about any sympathy toward or feelings for the deceased girl.[30] Rogers also testified over objection that he assisted Professor Peabody in his lectures on morphine.

Rogers recalled that Harris was in class for those lectures and that Rogers had passed around open containers of morphine so the students could take out the morphine and examine it more closely.[31]

Dr. William H. Thomson, professor of materia medica and therapeutics in the Medical Department of the University of New York,[32] took the stand next. Thomson had been in practice for thirty-three years and had been a professor of materia medica for twenty-five of those years. Thomson testified that in connection with his job on staff at Bellevue and Roosevelt Hospitals, he had seen some five to ten cases of uremia per day, nine months per year, for the past twenty-five years.[33] Wellman should have stopped Thomson at this point and done the math to show that Thomson was talking about a minimum of 22,500 and a maximum of 45,000 cases of uremia that he had seen in his twenty-five-year practice in the hospitals.

Wellman was now ready to ask Thomson his opinion as to the cause of Helen's death. Since Thomson had not attended Helen, had not been a party to the autopsy, and had no direct knowledge of the facts of Helen's death, Wellman had to do this in the form of a "hypothetical" question. There was nothing hypothetical about Wellman's hypothetical question. It had to include only facts that were already in evidence. Wellman had written the question out in advance and read it to the doctor. It was 633 words long and included every important detail of Helen's death and autopsy. When he finished reading it, Jerome objected and Smyth overruled him. The witness answered, "The symptoms are those of death from opium poisoning."[34]

Wellman repeated the question, omitting all the facts relating to the autopsy, which reduced the question's word count to 484. Jerome again objected, and Smyth again overruled the objection. Thomson answered, "The symptoms are those of death from opium poisoning."[35]

Wellman then tried to hammer home the fact that the death was not due to uremic poisoning, but Jerome objected, Recorder Smyth sustained, and Wellman's attempt to get Dr. Thomson to rule out uremic poisoning was stymied.[36] Jerome had objected to the question on the grounds that there was no evidence of uremic poisoning, but he won his victory at the cost of admitting before the jury that there was no evidence of uremic poisoning. Taking his cue from the proverb "If you can't go over or under, go around," Wellman went at the proof he wanted from another direction and got it.

He asked how Thomson knew that Helen died of morphine poisoning and from no other cause. Jerome objected, Smyth overruled, and Thomson gave a lengthy explanation of why death was not caused by uremic poisoning.[37]

Wellman had one more point to make before he turned Thomson over for cross-examination. "How much morphine would be necessary to cause the symptoms and the complete coma, as described in the hypothetical question that I put to you?"

"Three grains as a minimum," came the reply.[38]

Jerome worked hard on cross-examination to minimize the number of cases of uremia that Thomson saw in a year and got the number down from as many as ten per week to the lower estimate of five per week. Then he made the mistake of doing the math and announced that the number was 22,500 cases seen over the course of Thomson's career. From the vantage point of the defense, this was a number the jury didn't need to hear. Thomson then interjected that the number of uremia cases he saw outside the hospital in his private practice weren't counted. When Thomson added the private practice cases to the hospital cases, his total grew to 30,000 cases seen over the course of his career.[39] Jerome went after Thomson hammer and tongs for quite some time, but he failed to shake the doctor's testimony.

Wellman's next significant witness was Dr. George Peabody, who testified about his lectures on materia medica in general and morphine poisoning in particular. He also testified about his conversations with Harris shortly after Helen's death. He told of how Harris had come to him and described his prescription for Helen's insomnia, and how Harris had asked if he could be held responsible. When asked what he told Harris, Peabody said, "I told him that he had prescribed very stupidly; that there was no warrant for giving morphine, as he knew from my teachings, if he listened to my lectures, to any young girl who was merely suffering from insomnia."

Wellman wanted to drive the point home: "You told him that?"

"Yes, sir," Peabody replied, "I told him that it was very bad treatment; that if he had attended my lectures he ought to have known it, but that if that was all the morphine that she got, I could not see how he could be considered accountable for her death if his prescription had been properly filled and administered as he said."[40] Peabody added that he told Harris a student had no right to write prescriptions,[41] and Wellman moved on to other topics.

Jerome examines a
witness, early 1900s
(Courtesy of the Library
of Congress)

Wellman established that Peabody had performed some two thousand
autopsies and then asked him the same hypothetical question he asked
Thomson. Peabody said that the cause of death was opium poisoning and
nothing else and that the minimum dose that could have caused death
was two grains of morphine.[42] Wellman then had Peabody describe how
death by any of the other means suggested by the defense would have
been different and easily distinguished from opium poisoning. Wellman
weathered a storm of objections by Jerome while he covered this aspect
of Peabody's testimony, but he finally got everything into evidence and
turned Peabody over for cross-examination.[43]

Jerome attacked Peabody's testimony vigorously but failed to make
much headway. The only real point he scored on cross-examination was to
bring out the fact that when Harris came to Peabody after Helen's death,
Harris had a letter of recommendation from Dr. Robert Abbe, who said

Harris was a "fine fellow, straight as a string."[44] The biggest problem Jerome had with refuting the finding of death by morphine poisoning was the symmetrical contraction of Helen's pupils. No other known form of toxicity would produce such a contraction. Jerome worked with Peabody trying to get Peabody to admit the possibility that symmetrical contraction could have come from something else. Jerome established that there were two nerves leading into the pons Varolii, which controlled the pupils of the eyes. He then suggested that there might be two lesions pressing symmetrically on each of the nerves. Wouldn't that cause the pupils to contract symmetrically? Peabody replied, "That is a theoretical possibility which could not be proven by any demonstration that I am aware of." Jerome pressed, trying to get Peabody to admit that if there were symmetrical lesions on the nerves, one-sixth of a grain of morphine could produce symmetrical contraction of the pupils. Peabody replied, "I think that medical science would be largely in the realms of fancy in indulging in such things."[45]

For all practical purposes, Wellman was through with his presentation after Peabody testified, but he still had to get Mae Schofield's deposition into evidence. He called Mae's mother and attending physician to testify to how ill she was and how she was unable to attend the trial, and although Jerome combated the testimony with a barrage of objections, he had no questions to ask either one of them on cross-examination. Wellman called the clerk of the court to clear up the discrepancy with the date that the case was transferred, and he easily showed that the date stamped on the indictment was erroneous, the court had jurisdiction to order the deposition, the defense agreed to the deposition, and the deposition was taken before the file was transferred to the Court of General Sessions.[46] Jerome made eleven separate technical objections to the admission of the deposition, each of which was overruled. Smyth then invited Jerome to make as many more objections as he wished. Jerome took a moment to compose his thoughts and made thirteen more technical objections. Smyth overruled each one of them.[47]

Wellman then read Mae Schofield's deposition into evidence, and the effect on Harris was devastating. Wellman merely had a few housekeeping matters left, and he began recalling witnesses to quickly plug minor holes in the proof that he should have covered the first time he called them. It would have been far, far better if he had covered the matters the first time the witnesses testified. It would have been not as good, but still much better, if he had called them before he read Mae Schofield's deposition into evidence. Jerome had ammunition he could use against some of the witnesses, and that meant that the next-to-last day of the prosecution case ended in a pothole rather than on a summit.

The McIntyres returned to the stand, and Jerome was able to get them to admit that they really had made a serious mistake in compounding a prescription and had to pay $1,000 to settle a claim by a patient who had been injured by the medicine.[48] The prosecution case reached a low point with the last witness of the day. William P. Vannett had to be recalled to flesh out details of the chain of custody of Helen's body, and Jerome took the opportunity to pounce back on the issue of the embalming fluid.

Jerome asked whether Vannett could now recall Wellman telling him to "Remember the importance of it and work it," and that Jerome followed him out of the office and repeated Wellman's words verbatim.

"No, sir; I do not." Vannett was emphatic.

At this point Jerome lost his composure, exclaiming, "I was with Mr. Simms and I heard it!"

Wellman interjected, "I never use the term 'work it;' never used it in my life; it is not in my vocabulary."[49]

According to the trial transcript, the exchange stopped with Wellman's interjection, but the New York Times reported a verbal scuffle the court reporter saw fit to exclude.

Wellman angrily told Jerome, "You were hiding in the District Attorney's Office, evidently, when you allege you overheard such a conversation. You know the office so well you could hide most anywhere there, I suppose."

Jerome replied, "I am not a sneak."

"You are proving yourself to be one,"[50] Wellman shot back.

At this point the recorder adjourned court, but the lawyers weren't through. While Recorder Smyth sat on the bench chatting with another judge, Wellman and Jerome confronted each other in the well of the court. The Herald reported their confrontation:

"If I couldn't try a case without playing the sneak I wouldn't try it at all," sneered Wellman as he shook a pencil under Jerome's nose. Jerome maintained his composure.

"I heard you say it," he replied.

"That's a God damned lie," said Wellman, "and I will take pleasure in telling you so again out of this court if you will come."

"Oh," replied Jerome, his voice icy cold, "If only you were a gentleman!" Although he kept his voice under control, Jerome's right hand clasped repeatedly into a fist. Then, his restraint evaporating, Jerome began to unleash a verbal torrent upon Wellman. "If you only were a gentleman! You talk about sneaking! You, who dare not, cannot associate with—" What Wellman dared not associate with is lost to history because at this time Recorder Smyth intervened.

"Gentlemen," he said without a hint of anger, "I hardly think it shows proper respect to the Court to go at this sort of thing while I am within the room." With that said, Smyth got up and beat a hasty retreat into his chambers, leaving the two lawyers confronting each other in the courtroom. This word of warning from Smyth seems to have doused the fire of anger in both men. Neither one showed any disposition to resume the confrontation.

After describing the flare-up, the *Herald* then assessed the physical prowess of the two men, saying that Wellman was short, fat, and out of shape. Jerome was younger, taller, had a longer reach, and was a talented boxer. The reporters assembled in the courtroom that evening amused themselves by taking bets on the likelihood and possible outcome of fisticuffs between the two lawyers,[51] but as is usually the case when lawyers come to the brink of exchanging blows, the tension was released and they got along tolerably well for the remainder of the trial.

CHAPTER EIGHT

The Defense Case—Day One

It was Friday, January 29, Wellman had one final inconsequential witness to tie up loose ends, and it was now time for Taylor to do something that he should have done two weeks ago—deliver the defense opening statement. Before giving his opening, Taylor announced that the defense would call fifteen witnesses and the presentation of their testimony would take another ten days.[1] This was a mistake. He led the jury to expect a sustained defense. They must have believed that the defense had fizzled when Jerome called only nine witnesses and the trial lasted only two more days. Having stumbled before he spoke a word in opening, Taylor had another negative to overcome—he gave his opening statement with the backdrop of Mrs. Potts sitting on a sofa next to Recorder Smyth's bench and weeping onto her husband's shoulder. Mrs. Harris, not to be outdone, sat weeping next to her son. Harris held up fairly well, but he did succumb to tears on one occasion, wilting onto his mother's shoulder.[2]

Taylor began his speech with an ardent plea for sympathy. He reminded the jury that Harris had been in jail for nine months, subjected to all the degrading influences of life behind bars, that he had been cut off from the outside world and allowed contact only with his family and counsel. Nonetheless, Taylor asserted, Harris retained his self-respect, his dignity, and was able to look the jurors steadfastly in the eye with confidence that could come only from innocence.[3] Harris's demeanor had radiated more arrogance than innocence, but Taylor was putting the best face he could on the situation.

Taylor said that despite the whole case having been born of a "monstrous suspicion" in the heart of Mrs. Potts, he was not going to say anything bad against her. Taylor said that Mrs. Potts's suspicion had been fanned by

John Taylor, lead trial counsel
for Harris (Wellman and
Simms, *The Trial of Carlyle W.
Harris*)

the flames of envy and fed by the maneuverings of unnamed enemies to the point that it had overwhelmed Harris and permanently disgraced his honorable family. It was still, however, no more than a suspicion, as the defense would prove.[4] "This indictment, is born of a monstrous suspicion; a suspicion which, taking its lodgment in the heart of a woman, concerning whom I shall have nothing but words of praise to say, fanned by the flames of envy, supplied by the machinations of possible enemies, has developed into a consuming fire which threatens to overwhelm its unhappy victim, and to compass the lasting disgrace of his family. I shall hope, before this case is done, gentlemen, to demonstrate to your entire satisfaction that there is nothing more or less in the case of the prosecution than such a suspicion." Taylor was becoming somewhat counterfactual, as the evidence had clearly shown that Dr. Peabody and Dr. McLane were the moving forces behind the resurrection of Harris's case.

Taylor then said something remarkable: "I shall purposely reserve to my final consideration of this case those elements which seem to point to me conclusively to the innocence of my client."[5] And why would he do such a thing? Now was the time for the defense to outline the proof of Harris's innocence and explain precisely how they intended to prove it—if they could.

Instead of talking about the defense's proof of Harris's innocence, Taylor talked about the prosecution's proof of Harris's bad character.

Taylor couldn't very well deny the record of Harris's misdeeds, so he tried to put as nice a face upon them as possible. The district attorney had spent months hunting for dirt on Harris. Could anyone's character withstand such scrutiny? After all, young men will sow their wild oats, and the harvest of those oats is bound to be embarrassing. And while the prosecution, with its great wealth, was ransacking the highways and byways looking for some unseemly act to bring before the jury, poor Harris was behind bars and denied any such opportunity. Even the press had joined in the quest to assassinate Harris's character.[6]

Taylor told the jury that the one thing that had sustained Harris through this lengthy ordeal was the expectation that he would eventually face a jury who would suspend judgment on his character and fairly decide the case based on the evidence and the instructions of Recorder Smyth. Of the hundreds of thousands of men eligible for jury service, Taylor asserted, the defense had chosen this jury because the defense believed them to be "men of intelligence, of intellectual equipoise, and men calculated to sit in cool, calm and unbiased judgment upon this young man." This jury, Taylor said, was the antidote to the machinations of the prosecution, the calumny of the press, and the cancer of prejudice.[7]

Taylor's melodramatic, emotional appeal may or may not have touched the jury, but it moved Harris to break into tears.[8] Satisfied that he had sufficiently flattered the jury, Taylor now turned to matters that were at least arguably relevant. Taylor outlined Harris's pedigree and the high social standing of both his mother and grandfather and described how she stood by him when fair-weather friends abandoned him. His point? "Gentlemen, out of such planting the upas tree of murder does not grow."[9] Taylor painted a picture of an industrious student living at home who had taken the first prize in the competition for the hospital appointment, and had made Mrs. Potts's generous offer to send him and Helen abroad to Germany unnecessary.[10] Taylor then praised Helen as the ideal mate for Harris, a beautiful, intelligent, refined, and charming young woman who would make any man proud to call his wife. As a warrant of their love for each other, the last words upon her lips were the name of her husband, "Carl."[11] Taylor neglected to mention that her last words concerning Carl were to ask whether he might have poisoned her.

Taylor next set out the central fact in issue in the case—whether Helen died of morphine poisoning—and said that the proof of morphine poisoning failed to meet the reasonable doubt standard because the testimony of the state's experts was too uncertain, and the testimony of the defense experts would show that it was impossible to say. We have just stated the central fact in issue using 48 words. It took Taylor 263 to say the same thing.[12] Since classical times it has been an article of faith that a forensic speech must be "lucid, brief, and [worthy] of belief."[13] Taylor's statement of the central fact in issue had none of these qualities.

Taylor next attempted to raise the prosecution's burden of proof by saying that the prosecution claimed to have proven beyond "a shadow of a doubt" that Helen died of morphine poisoning. Taylor named the witnesses the defense would call to testify that, based on an autopsy done fifty-three days after Helen died, it could not be proven what Helen died from.[14] Finally, Taylor had gotten around to talking about the evidence that the defense intended to present. He mentioned one more witness, a Professor Wormley, and gave a convoluted description of Wormley's findings concerning whether there was any morphine at all in Helen's body. Then he concluded his speech by calling on the jury not to be seduced by "scientific possibilities," but to keep their deliberations in the "plain domain of common sense."[15]

The *Brooklyn Daily Eagle* was enthralled with Taylor's speech, saying, "The opening words for the defense on Friday by Mr. Taylor were a model of thoughtfulness, sincerity, eloquence, and high forensic skill. They were so utterly at variance with the conventional pettifogging too often heard at the criminal bar as to be a cause for pleasure and even delight to lovers of the noble literature of the law."[16] The English barrister and judge Frederick A. Philbrick, who wrote *Language and the Law: The Semantics of Forensic English*, was less charitable. He characterized Taylor's opening as an attempt to "divert the attention of the jury from the facts of the case by producing irrelevant feelings in their minds,"[17] persuade the jury that Harris's mother was "so admirable a woman that no one could believe her son to be a murderer,"[18] and get the jury to disregard the medical evidence "by a covert appeal to the ignorance of the jury [by suggesting] that scientific experiments might be good enough for the witnesses but would never convince plain men."[19] Comparing Wellman's opening statement with Taylor's calls to mind the words of Charles Caleb Colton: "When the

Romans [heard] Cicero, they departed [saying,] 'What a splendid speech our orator has made.' But when the Athenians heard Demosthenes [they left] exclaiming, 'Let us go and fight against Philip.'"[20]

In keeping with the proverb that you should always strive to put your best foot forward, trial lawyers try to begin their evidence with a strong witness. To borrow a phrase from the celebrated Gilded Age attorney L. P. Stryker, in the field of trial practice, as in the field of pugilism, a knockdown blow scored at the very outset often determines the contest.[21] Taylor and Jerome had lined up a witness who seemed able to deliver that first-round knockout—a medical man with an international reputation, a distinguished author on the subject of poisons, and an esteemed educator. Dr. Horatio Wood, of University Hospital in Philadelphia, took the stand as the first witness for the defense, and he bore the entire weight of the defense upon his shoulders.

Dr. Wood hardly needed an introduction to the jury. Jerome had referred to him and his work no fewer than sixteen times when cross-examining the state's experts, and they all had expressed admiration for him and his textbook, *Therapeutics*.[22] Wood was a true polymath, having begun his education at boarding school at the age of four and graduated with an MD from the Medical Department of the University of Pennsylvania in 1862 at the age of twenty-one. Upon receiving his medical degree, he immediately enlisted in the US Army and served until the end of the Civil War. After the war he went back to the University of Pennsylvania, where he taught medicine, chemistry, and botany. Recognized as an expert in the fields of botany, entomology, pharmacology, physiology, pathology, and medical jurisprudence, he authored almost three hundred scientific papers and six books.[23]

Wood gave excellent testimony on direct examination. The *Tribune* said that it "appeared that no one could be more competent than Dr. Wood to testify as to the effects of morphine."[24] Wood began by declaring that it was impossible to diagnose morphine poisoning from the symptoms alone.[25] He gave as an example a case of apoplexy in which a misdiagnosis of morphine poisoning had been disproven by autopsy. He said if the patient had been first embalmed, there would have been no way to rule out morphine poisoning. He further declared that the internal organs of the body cannot be declared to be healthy unless they have been examined under a microscope.[26] Furthermore, microscopic examination of the internal organs of the body would be impossible if a body had been embalmed and then buried for fifty-three days.[27] Sometimes, he said, the cause of death just cannot be determined by an autopsy.[28] He testified that upon finding a patient in the condition that Dr. Fowler found Helen in, he would have thrown her on the floor and rendered vigorous artificial respiration until her breathing was steady enough to pump her stomach.[29] Furthermore, small doses of morphine could kill a patient suffering from uremia.[30] The jury seemed deeply impressed by this testimony.[31] Jerome ended his examination by reading Wellman's hypothetical question to Wood, minus the autopsy findings, and asking Wood, "can you state or can medical science state, from what the girl died?"

"I should be unable to state, sir," replied Wood. "My own belief is that in the present state of medical science no accurate opinion could be passed upon it. The symptoms are compatible with various conditions."[32] Wood did not elaborate on what other conditions might have caused the death, and Jerome did not ask. This was an oversight that would cost the defense dearly on cross-examination. When he turned Wood over to Wellman for cross-examination, Jerome had to be optimistic—he had struck a blow with Wood's testimony and the blow had been a hard one. It was time for Wellman to counterpunch, and the counterpunch had better be a good one.

The ability to plan ahead is essential to a good cross-examination, but just as important is the ability to respond to a rapidly changing tactical situation. Wellman proved that he was not only an excellent planner, he could think on his feet with the best of them. Wellman began his cross-examination by challenging Wood to make a definitive statement that Helen had not died of morphine poisoning.

Q: Do I understand you to swear that Miss Helen Potts did not die of morphine poisoning?
A: I don't know, sir, what you understand; I don't swear that.
Q: Do you swear what she died of?
A: I don't swear what she died of.[33]

Wellman then tried to pin Wood down on a definitive statement that morphine poisoning could not be diagnosed on the symptoms alone. He phrased his questions loosely and gave Wood an opening to temporize.

Wood played cat-and-mouse with him, repeatedly objecting to the form of the question until Wellman finally phrased the question in a way that Wood approved.

Q: What do you intend to say [on] the subject of diagnosing a case of morphine poisoning from the symptoms alone?
A: I don't think it can be done with positiveness.[34]

Wellman was incredulous. He launched off on a series of questions with the general tenor "Do you mean to tell me you've never diagnosed a patient as having morphine poisoning without an autopsy?" Wood became defensive, and Jerome objected, trying to help Wood as much as possible. Smyth would have none of the objection. Wood then said the question could not be answered categorically "because the word 'diagnosed' is used with two different meanings."[35] This was where the oversight on direct examination came back to haunt the defense. Wood had testified that other conditions could cause the symptoms exhibited by Helen, but he didn't elaborate that morphine poisoning would be the most obvious cause and that the other conditions would usually be turned up on autopsy. In their attempt to discredit Fowler's diagnosis, they oversold their case by not distinguishing between two types of diagnoses on direct examination. Now, on cross-examination, Wood looked like he was being evasive.

When Wood testified that morphine poisoning couldn't be diagnosed on the symptoms alone, he was talking about a "definitive diagnosis"—a diagnosis that is made after all the evidence is in.[36] Unfortunately, given the current state of medical science in the 1890s, in the case of morphine poisoning, all the evidence wasn't in until the patient was dead. Any physician confronted with Helen's symptoms would come to the "working diagnosis" that Helen had been poisoned, probably by some sort of opiate, and begin treating for opium poisoning.[37] If the patient survived, then the working diagnosis became a definitive diagnosis. If the patient died, then an autopsy would be relied on to get a definitive diagnosis.

Jerome should have had Wood testify that the attending physicians made the correct working diagnosis, but assert that a definitive diagnosis could only be made on autopsy. Had Wood made such a distinction on direct examination, it would have given the defense a platform for arguing that "A working diagnosis of morphine poisoning is fine for treating someone to try to save their life; but you must demand a definitive diagnosis of morphine poisoning before you decide to take someone's life with a first-degree murder verdict."

Wellman went after Wood and his two meanings of diagnosis, but Wood never made the distinction clear. He just continued to look evasive. He did, however, admit that he had once made a false working diagnosis of opium poisoning that had been proven wrong by an autopsy.[38] This admission was not something that would instill confidence in the jury that he was a bona fide poison expert. Their confidence was about to be shaken even more.

Wellman became interested in precisely how many cases of opium poisoning Wood had ever seen. Wood answered evasively, but Wellman finally corkscrewed the information out of the reluctant witness. The last case of opium poisoning Wood had seen was eight to ten years ago. The case before that was fifteen years ago. His third and final case of opium poisoning was twenty years ago.[39] Of the two more recent cases of opium poisoning, only one was morphine poisoning; the other case involved poisoning from Dover's Powder.[40] In the past fifteen years, Dr. Wood had seen only one case of morphine poisoning.

> Q: And will you come here and state, from Philadelphia, that the doctors who have gone on the stand and who attended this patient, and who said they had seventy-five cases . . . and stated as a matter of fact that this was morphine poisoning, they who had seen the patient and treated her, will you—with only one experience in twenty years come here and say that you don't believe that they can tell what she died of? [The *Philadelphia Inquirer* reported, "It is impossible to describe the amount of sneering Mr. Wellman put into the words 'from Philadelphia.'"][41]
>
> A: Yes, sir; only I deny part of the statement. . . .
>
> Q: That was your best opinion upon your reading and upon your own experience; your own experience in twenty years is confined to one case; is your reading confined to your own book?
>
> A: No, sir.
>
> Mr. JEROME—That I object to as involving two or three statements and half a dozen questions.
>
> Q: Is your reading confined to your own book?
>
> A: No, I say no.

Q: But I suppose you embodied in your book the results of your reading, didn't you?

A: I tried to, sir.

Q: Allow me to read to you from page 166.

The COURT—Of what?

Mr. WELLMAN—Of his own book on *Therapeutics and its Practice* (Reading) "I have thought that inequality of the pupils is proof that a case is not one of narcotism; but Professor Taylor has recorded an instance of opium-poisoning in which it occurred."

Q: So that until you heard of the case that Professor Taylor had reported in which it occurred, your opinion before that was that it never had occurred, symmetrical contraction of the eyes, besides, morphine poisoning?

A: No, sir.

Q: Now, did you inquire and did you inform yourself that the case of which Professor Taylor spoke, was a case where a man had one eye?[42]

At this point, two things happened almost simultaneously. The audience roared with laughter at Wood's embarrassment,[43] and Jerome sprang to his feet to object.

Mr. JEROME—Now, if your Honor please, I have Professor Taylor's book here, and I object to that question because that case is not stated in Professor Taylor's book.

The COURT—We have evidence by one of the witnesses that it has been looked up, and I prefer, with due respect to you, to take Dr. Hamilton's opinion.

Hamilton had mentioned the case of the one-eyed poison victim on January 26 in a single answer to a single question.[44] That Smyth could remember Hamilton's answer on January 29 is a testament to the judge's mental powers.

Q: Before you made the statement in your book that the case Professor [Taylor] had cited, did you look it up and find that it had one eye? Yes or no?

A: Not according to my remembrance.[45]

Mr. WELLMAN—Well, that has proven to be the case here. You may go back to Philadelphia, sir.[46]

Dr. Horatio Wood, professor at University Hospital in Philadelphia (Wood,
Reminiscences)

Jerome tried to repair the damage on redirect examination, but his task
was somewhat akin to rearranging deck chairs on the *Titanic*. From that
point forward in the trial, the specter of doom lurked over Harris as the
case slipped relentlessly toward a guilty verdict. The defense tried manfully, and they scored some minor victories, but it would take a miracle to
snatch victory from the jaws of defeat. The defense's last best hope at this
point was that Wellman might overplay his hand and snatch defeat from
the jaws of victory—overzealous prosecutors frequently make this mistake.

The *Herald* reported that when Jerome dismissed Wood from the witness stand, the doctor "hurried away from the witness stand with that
pained expression sometimes visible on the face of a picnicker who has
sat on an anthill."[47] Upon Wood's return to Philadelphia, he remarked that
he had "gone to New York only to make a fool of himself."[48] The *Herald*,
in a show of sympathy for Wood, reported that Wellman cross-examined
the doctor "cruelly,"[49] but the *Tribune* said, "The cross-examination of
Dr. H. C. Wood, the expert for the defense by Assistant District Attorney
Wellman was a remarkable proof of the power of a few searching questions. The examination lasted only a few minutes, but was as effective as
the long cross-questioning often employed by counsel in such cases."[50]

Wellman had a reputation among the bench and bar of New York City
as a deadly cross-examiner. The cross-examination of Dr. Horatio Wood

propelled Wellman to national celebrity as a cross-examiner and formed the foundation for his lasting fame as one of the premier cross-examiners of any age. Wellman left the district attorney's office just a few years after the Harris trial and went on to a long and prosperous career as a trial lawyer and an author of books on trial advocacy, and he attributed the successful launching of his private practice to his cross-examination of Dr. Wood.[51] Wellman wrote accounts of the cross-examination in three of his books,[52] and the cross-examination was more devastating in Wellman's memory than in actual fact. Wellman later reported in *The Art of Cross-Examination* that he said "one glass eye" rather than "one eye,"[53] but both the trial transcript and the book Wellman published immediately after the trial record the wording as "one eye," which is less dramatic but just as effective.

In his books, Wellman made the point that his destruction of Wood strongly supported the proposition that if the cross-examination of a witness is properly conducted, far more time is spent outside the courtroom preparing for the examination than is spent inside the courtroom conducting it. Wellman claimed that in preparation for the cross he and Simms had reviewed five to six thousand cases of morphine poisoning.[54]

Wellman saw the symmetrical contraction of the pupils to be crucial to proof that Helen was poisoned. According to the then current medical knowledge, opium poisoning and nothing else caused the symmetrical contraction of the pupils to the degree that they became pinpoints. Wellman later wrote that "If Jerome could succeed in discovering a single authentic case where the pupils were not symmetrically contracted and where death had resulted from an overdose of morphine, the defense he had constructed with such diligence and skill would win his case."[55]

Wellman got a copy of Wood's book, *Therapeutics: Its Principles and Practice*. As he studied it, he found Wood's reference to the patient with the asymmetrically contracted pupils.[56] Wellman believed that if Wood testified to this from the witness stand, it could be the death knell of the case against Harris. What should Wellman do? Wood was not reporting from his own experience; he was citing the report of another physician in Taylor's *Treatise on Medical Jurisprudence*—technically hearsay evidence, but the type of evidence experts are allowed to rely upon. The sensible thing to do was to check Wood's references. On checking the reference in Taylor's *Treatise on Medical Jurisprudence*, Wellman found a hearsay reference to another case.[57] Could that case be tracked down to see if the facts were as Taylor described? Dr. Allan Hamilton knew about the case. Hamilton had read the same report in Taylor's book and disbelieved it. He checked it out and found that the case originated in Washington, DC, and that it had been reported in the newspapers. Hamilton's research revealed that the reason only one pupil had contracted was that the man had only one eye. The other pupil did not contract because it was the pupil of a glass eye![58]

Wellman was ready for Wood. When Wood testified that the symmetrical contraction of the eyes was not definitive evidence of morphine poisoning because of the case reported by Taylor, Wellman would pounce on him with the devastating information that the victim had only one eye. But he was disappointed. Jerome did not ask Wood about Taylor's case of asymmetrical contraction, probably because Hamilton had testified about tracking down the glass eye when Jerome cross-examined him as a state witness.[59] Wellman still used the mistake to impeach Wood, but he had to bring the matter up on cross-examination.

There is another point about Wellman's case analysis that we should discuss before moving on. Wellman thought that if the defense could show one case of morphine poisoning with asymmetrically contracted pupils, it would destroy his case. He had it backwards. A single case of morphine poisoning with asymmetrically contracted pupils would simply be an interesting anomaly for which he could have had a ready answer: "One case of asymmetrical contraction doesn't invalidate morphine poisoning in all the cases of symmetrical contraction. Show me a case where the pupils symmetrically contracted and it wasn't morphine poisoning—that would mean something!"

Although Wellman missed this point, Jerome certainly didn't. That is why he worked so hard with Dr. Peabody trying to get him to say that hemorrhages on both sides of the pons Varolii could result in symmetrical contraction of the pupils. Dr. Peabody had refused to cooperate, dismissing such an idea as "indulging in the realm of fantasy."[60] Jerome was on the right track, and he had done his homework, but by the most unfortunate of accidents he missed the evidence he needed. Professor Taylor indeed could give evidence of cases where the pupils were symmetrically contracted and the patient was not suffering from opium poisoning. Jerome just looked in the wrong book. Taylor's *Manual of Medical Jurisprudence*, a single-volume work, did not mention the cases, but his multivolume *Principles and Practice of Medical Jurisprudence* reported two such cases:

The contracted state of the pupils has been hitherto considered to furnish a valuable distinctive sign of poisoning by opium or the salts of morphia. In relying upon it, it is necessary to bear in mind the fact pointed out by Wilks, that, in apoplexy which is seated in the Pons Varolii, the pupils are also contracted. He describes two cases of this form of apoplexy which were mistaken for poisoning by opium in consequence of this state of the pupils ('Med. Times and Gaz.' 1863, 1, 214).[61]

This, again is hearsay, but upon checking the *Medical Times and Gazette* we find firsthand reports of patients who were diagnosed with morphine poisoning due to symmetrically contracted pupils but found to be drug-free and suffering from hemorrhages in the pons Varolii on autopsy.[62] We also find in that same volume a report of a misdiagnosis of morphine poisoning due to symmetrically contracted pupils that was refuted by autopsy findings of a fracture at the base of the patient's skull.[63] If Jerome had only found those references and given them to Dr. Wood, the poor doctor might not have looked quite so foolish. Jerome would certainly have had something to conjure with when cross-examining Dr. Peabody. Peabody would have had to come out of the "realm of fantasy" and admit that hemorrhage in the pons Varolii could produce symmetrically contracted pupils.

Jerome cannot be faulted for overlooking these references. He did an excellent job of preparing the defense that had been decided upon. He did not have the luxury of the internet, Google Books, and the Internet Archive in his search for references. He had to do his research the old-fashioned way, going to physical libraries, searching card catalogs, and reading actual books. Even with today's highly sophisticated computerized research and document retrieval, evidence of this type gets overlooked.

In his book *Success in Court*, Wellman gives us further evidence of a faulty memory when he describes what happened after Wood left the stand. Wellman reports that "Jerome nearly collapsed, along with his defense. He fairly begged the recorder to adjourn the court and give him an opportunity to investigate further (but really to get his second wind). It was no use. He tried hard the next morning with some new doctors, but his ambition to be known as a great trial lawyer and his client's liberty had gone out the window the afternoon before."[64]

There is a kernel of truth in Wellman's recollection. Jerome didn't nearly collapse. He collapsed. But his collapse did not come immediately on the heels of Wood's testimony. It came in the middle of the direct examination of his next witness. Jerome got his early recess, but he didn't try hard the next morning with some new doctors because the next morning was a Saturday. Wellman's account of how court recessed that day is not the only inaccurate account. Reading the transcript of the trial, you will find no hint that Jerome collapsed. The court reporter once again chose to omit a portion of the trial that could reflect badly on the lawyers involved.[65] The newspapers, however, were not reticent to air every possible detail of the trial, and the reporter for the *New York Times* took down every word.

As Wood retreated from the courtroom, Jerome announced that he had run out of witnesses and needed a recess until another witness arrived. Recorder Smyth was not amused. He lectured Jerome on the need for efficiency in the marshaling of the evidence and admonished him not to let his witnesses cause any further delay.[66] None of this exchange was taken down by the court reporter.[67] Smyth had no choice but to recess court until after lunch.

Over the lunch hour, Jerome rounded up a witness—Dr. Herman M. Biggs, a practicing pathologist who had performed over two thousand autopsies.[68] Biggs had graduated Cornell University in 1882 and immediately entered Bellevue Hospital Medical College, where he completed the entire course of study and graduated with an MD in one year. Biggs interned for a year at Bellevue and then went to Germany, where he spent two years in Berlin and Greifswald doing postgraduate study. Upon his return to New York he was placed in charge of the Carnegie Laboratory at Bellevue Medical College, where he served as a professor of pathology, materia medica, and therapeutics.[69] Biggs was certainly more qualified to perform an autopsy than Dr. Hamilton, and he had little regard for Dr. Hamilton's procedures. Jerome put Biggs on the stand immediately after the lunch hour and walked him through a point-by-point critique of the autopsy, and it appeared that he was working toward getting the doctor to voice a climactic opinion that Hamilton and Witthaus didn't know what they were talking about when they said Helen died of morphine poisoning. Jerome seemed to be in full stride and doing quite well when he asked Biggs, "Q: Now, in regard to people who have died from kidney trouble, does it frequently happen that there may be a condition of disease of the kidneys—does it happen that there may be a disease of the kidneys that—which, on an examination such as I have narrated to you, may, the only microscopical examination being made upon one kidney, the large kidney, and that in October following—October or November following—the death, when the death was on February 1—"

Jerome stopped in mid-sentence and put his hand to his head. He then said, "I can't go on with this case, and I won't go on while I cannot ask questions and think connectedly. I cannot think. I—" Jerome sank into his seat and began to cry.

"I certainly have not done anything to cause such a remark as that," said Recorder Smyth, quite likely concerned that his dressing-down of Jerome that morning had contributed to the collapse that afternoon.

"You have been very kind to me," replied Jerome.

"If you are in such a physical condition that you feel that you cannot go on, I will adjourn this trial, of course," said the recorder. "I do not wish you to continue if you are not able. You have had the laboring oar so far in this case and are obviously in no condition to proceed. Do you want the case laid over?"

"If your Honor will," Jerome whispered. Smyth adjourned the court until the following Monday morning at 11:00.[70]

CHAPTER NINE

The Defense Case—Day Two

Although Harris began the trial with a somewhat arrogant, self-assured demeanor, the two weeks of the prosecution's case wore him down. The *Herald* reported that "Even his marvelous assurance is beginning to fail under the great strain that has been put upon it."[1] His eyes became red, his cheeks and lips pale, and his confidence seemed to wilt in the face of the evidence. By the first day of the defense case, he sat with his head on his mother's shoulder as she wrapped her arm about his neck. From that position he looked appealingly toward the jury, but the jurors kept their attention full on the witnesses, only occasionally glancing at the tableaux of son and mother at counsel table.[2] The mother's demeanor probably did not help Harris. She laughed at the prosecution witnesses whenever Jerome seemed to be getting the better of them, and she frowned and shook her head whenever the testimony seemed to tell against her son.[3]

When jury selection began, Jerome had not fully recovered from his December illness, and his health steadily deteriorated over the course of the trial. The decline hit a low point with his meltdown on the direct examination of Dr. Biggs.[4] Jerome made it out of the courthouse under his own power that afternoon, telling reporters that he was merely suffering from intense overwork and would be ready to resume the trial on Monday.[5]

Bright and early Saturday morning a crowd of reporters gathered on the doorstep of the home belonging to Jerome's mother. Jerome did not come out to speak to them, but his brother Lovell did. "Travers is all right," he maintained. "He is asleep at this moment. He was simply tired out and needed rest for mind and body. He has worked till late at night preparing his opposition to the expert [witnesses for the] prosecution. He is extremely nervous anyway, and the work keyed him up to such a point that sleep refused its comfort to him.

"He simply broke down, like a man in a six-day race, who has walked himself to a standstill. All he needs is rest. He dined at the Union Club, for a change, last night, and played pool all the evening at the Club. Then he came home and has had a night of restful sleep. He will surely be in fighting trim Monday."[6]

Some eagle-eyed reporters spotted Jerome taking a walk in the park later that morning. When they accosted him, Jerome told them, "I shall walk all I can today and tomorrow, and I am sure that I shall be in good condition Monday morning. Until then I shall try to forget the case."[7]

Taylor went to the Tombs to confer with Harris and ran into a flock of reporters. They had one burning question: "Is Harris going to testify?" Taylor put them off with a noncommittal answer,[8] but the speculation ran rampant that despite Harris's express desire to testify, his lawyers would keep him off the stand. The *Tribune* predicted that Harris would never see the witness stand: "If he is called to testify many facts about his life will be brought out which will hardly have a favorable effect on the jury. Among these is that Harris became engaged to marry a minister's daughter in Brooklyn after Helen Potts was his wife."[9]

Although it was doubtful whether Harris would proclaim his innocence from the witness stand, he certainly did so from the Tombs, where he was safe from cross-examination. It seems that reporters were allowed almost unlimited access to the prisoners in the Tombs, and that Saturday morning Harris held forth at length for them:

> It was an awful strain upon [Lawyer Jerome]. I had feared the result. I was much more worried over that than the outcome of the trial. Knowing my own innocence I have never doubted the result.
>
> I desire to go on the witness stand. I have promised not to talk, but I must say that I was less eager for this scientific combat and more desirous of meeting and refuting the absurd testimony regarding my alleged remarks about women. They are absurd!
>
> [Mrs. Potts] is a most magnificent woman. She adored my wife and she thought much of me. She thought more of my wife and myself than of all the rest of the world. Poor woman!
>
> As to my mother—she is a brave little mother! God bless her! She stands the strain well.
>
> I'm glad the prosecution did not see fit to place great stress on the fact that I, as a student, presumed to prescribe. All students prescribe. So does

everybody else prescribe. If you sneeze, every friend you meet prescribes a remedy for it, and anyone can buy drugs at any drugstore.

I don't deny that Canandaigua affair, but it is absurd as a motive for murder! Why I never met that young woman till the day before and I've never seen her since. Like most college boys I have sown wild oats. I am not worse than other young men.

I am much depressed today, but not from fear. You know tomorrow is the anniversary of my wife's death. And I have been locked up here ten months, charged with killing her. Is it wonderful that I am pale?

I shall see my good mother today. She comes every day. She is my comfort.[10]

Harris, whose eyes had moistened when he mentioned Helen, then smiled pleasantly, bade the reporters good day, and returned to his cell. The next day, before a new batch of reporters, Harris held forth again:

Why, I cannot—and I have tried—I cannot believe myself in danger. I have gone over the testimony carefully, over and over again, and I cannot see how anyone not prejudiced can find me guilty upon it.

Of course I know that the stories told by some of the witnesses about my alleged loose talk regarding women have hurt me. But I can't see how such stories can be believed. They are not true. Anyway, I do not see how that can stand as proof that I committed murder.

I can see now how foolish, how flimsy, all of my plans were of a year ago. But they looked grand to me. I was at the head of my class. It was a grand thing to be at the head of the class. My prospects looked so bright, and I thought they were paramount to all else. Helen—my wife—never suggested otherwise. She believed in me, and kept our marriage secret. Oh, how foolish it all looks now! But I have no fear. I believe that I shall go free at the end of this trial.[11]

At this moment Jerome appeared at the Tombs to confer with Harris. The reporters lost interest in Harris's self-serving monologue and began to question Jerome. He told them, "I am in first-class fighting trim today and I will have no further trouble. I have not looked at the case since Friday. I have simply ate and slept and played."[12]

Harris was still in a good mood when he arrived in court the following morning. When Smyth called the courtroom to order, Dr. Biggs returned to the stand and resumed his direct examination. Biggs flatly contradicted the testimony of Dr. Hamilton concerning Helen's autopsy. His testimony made three points: Fifty-three days was too long to wait for an autopsy. Helen's internal organs were too decomposed to make any kind of a meaningful examination. The stated weight of Helen's heart, six and one-eighth ounces, was far below that of a normal, healthy heart. Jerome tried to make a fourth point, but Wellman shut him down with objections.

Jerome tried to get Biggs to testify that he had performed an autopsy for Dr. Herman Haubold in 1889 and examined the pons Varolii of a patient who had initially been treated by Dr. Peabody, but whose treatment had been transferred to Haubold before he died. Wellman objected. Jerome explained that Dr. Peabody had treated the patient and misdiagnosed his malady as morphine poisoning, but Dr. Biggs's autopsy showed it was something else. Recorder Smyth was adamant: "I won't let it in; we will never get to the end of this case if you are going to try all the doctors in town."[13] Jerome wasn't through trying to impeach Peabody with the misdiagnosis of Dr. Haubold's patient, but he would have to wait for the arrival of another witness to try again.

The *St. Louis Republic* offered the opinion that Dr. Biggs made a good witness.[14] Biggs, however, had said something that came back to haunt him. Although he and Jerome made much of how a heart weighing six and one-eighth ounces was abnormally small and most certainly unhealthy, in another portion of his testimony Biggs read the notes he had taken when he inspected the heart in Dr. Witthaus's laboratory. The notes said: "The heart mutilated, blood stained; it is in some part black and dried to a board-like hardness—the remaining portions being more or less decomposed; the great arteries given off from the heart are entirely wanting, the walls and valves mutilated; the *size of the organ apparently about normal,* certainly not enlarged."[15]

One of the best things a lawyer can do on cross-examination is listen carefully to the direct examination. Wellman had listened carefully to the Biggs's direct, and he immediately pounced on the discrepancy in his cross-examination.

"Dr. Biggs," he began, "on Friday [Mr. Jerome asked you] whether the weight given by Dr. Hamilton of this heart as six ounces and a little over was a normal heart or not and you answered 'No.' It now appears that you did examine that very heart yourself and found it was a normal heart; did you intend on Friday to deceive the jury by that?"

Biggs was nonplussed. He began to offer a lengthy explanation, but Wellman cut him off, "I said—Q: Did you or did you not intend to deceive the jury on Friday?" Biggs swore that he did not.[16]

Wellman challenged Biggs. "Are you prepared to tell this jury that this heart that you examined at Professor Witthaus's was not a normal heart?" Biggs was not. Wellman pressed his advantage. "It was normal in size?" Biggs admitted it was.[17] Wellman had emulated L. P. Stryker and scored a knockdown blow at the outset of his cross-examination.

Wellman moved to Biggs's educational background and established that Biggs spent only one year in medical school as opposed to the normal three years. Biggs became nervous and defensive.[18] He explained that he studied medicine in undergraduate classes, but he appeared evasive in doing so.[19] Wellman caused him further discomfort by getting him to admit that he had been a professor for only a few months. Wellman then asked Biggs if he were the one who stole the valves of Helen's heart. Biggs said that "as far as my remembrance goes," he didn't take the valves. "Did you take the valves?" Wellman pressed. Biggs said he had given the best answer he could. Wellman then tried to get Biggs to say that he did not deny taking the valves, but Smyth stopped him "You have his answer,"[20] Smyth ruled, and Wellman moved on to other topics.

Biggs suffered damage but escaped the total destruction Wellman visited upon Dr. Wood. Jerome needed to do something to climb out of the deep hole that Wood had dug for the defense, and Biggs had done a little, but not much, to alleviate the damage. In his effort to regain lost ground, Jerome next called Dr. Witthaus back to the witness stand to ask him two series of questions, one that he should have already asked and one that he had no business asking at all. Jerome began with the improper series of questions. He asked Witthaus if Witthaus had seen Professor Ogden Doremus in court on the day he testified. Witthaus said, "Yes, sir." He asked if Doremus was an esteemed toxicologist who had testified in a number of important cases and Witthaus confessed that Doremus was in fact well respected. He then asked if certain of the chemical tests that Witthaus had performed were dependent on the distinguishing of colors. Witthaus agreed. Then Jerome asked the question he had been working toward: "And when you went to Professor Doremus after making this examination, did not Professor Ogden Doremus say to you, 'Witthaus, you have made a mistake; no man should perform such an analysis alone in a case of such seriousness; he should have another man with him to check his results;' didn't he substantially say that to you?"

Wellman didn't even have to object. Smyth stopped the questioning dead in its tracks. "I will exclude that question until you call Dr. Doremus."[21]

What Doremus may or may not have said was hearsay. If Jerome wanted an expert opinion from Dr. Doremus, the proper way to go about it was to pay the good doctor an expert witness fee, place him on the witness stand subject to cross-examination, and ask him his opinion. Jerome argued with Smyth over the ruling, but to no avail. When he failed to get Smyth to change his ruling, Jerome next moved on to asking Witthaus whether he had someone backing him up on the recognition of the colors that were produced by the chemical tests performed. Witthaus said no, he had no assistance.

Jerome then turned to the fourteen chemical tests that Witthaus performed in order to determine the presence of morphine. He asked if some of those tests might give a positive reaction for morphine if certain ptomaines were present. Witthaus said yes, some of the tests would react to chemicals other than morphine. Jerome started to ask about each test, and Witthaus stopped him, saying that the first four tests could be laid aside, the only significant tests were tests five through fourteen. Jerome got Witthaus to admit that for tests 6, 7, 11, 12, and 13, certain types of ptomaines would give the same reaction as morphine. For tests 5, 8, 9, 10, and 14, however, nothing but morphine would give the positive reaction.[22] Wellman's cross-examination was brief and to the point. "Mr. Jerome has asked you about ptomaines. Is there any known ptomaine that will give all the reactions obtained by you?"

"No, sir," Witthaus replied.[23]

When he finished with Witthaus, Jerome was ready to make another attempt at proving that Dr. Peabody had misdiagnosed morphine poisoning in Dr. Haubold's deceased patient. He called a Dr. Herman Haubold to testify that a patient came into St. Vincent's Hospital with symmetrically contracted pupils. He then asked Dr. Haubold what Dr. Peabody had told him about the patient. Wellman objected to the statement as hearsay, and Smyth ruled that unless the statement could be qualified as a prior inconsistent statement by Peabody, he would rule it inadmissible. Jerome explained that he was trying to prove Dr. Peabody had misdiagnosed the patient as suffering from morphine poisoning because of symmetrical contraction of the pupils, but an autopsy had shown the patient died from a brain hemorrhage. Smyth still wasn't going to allow the testimony, and Wellman got the recorder to strike all Dr. Haubold's testimony from the record.[24]

Jerome was trying to get this evidence in to impeach Peabody's expertise, and he was going about it wrong. He had not laid a foundation for the testimony. In order to make this evidence admissible, Jerome should have asked Peabody about the case, whether he made a working diagnosis of morphine poisoning due to the symmetrical contraction of the pupils, and whether it was later proven wrong by autopsy. If Peabody admitted it, he'd made his point. If Peabody denied it, then Jerome could have called Biggs and Haubold to prove the misdiagnosis.

A second and possibly better way to render the testimony admissible was to omit any reference to Dr. Peabody at all and offer proof that Dr. Haubold had a patient die of brain hemorrhage when he was diagnosed as a case of morphine poisoning because of symmetrically contracted pupils. This would give Jerome grounds to argue that "All the prosecution witnesses have testified that symmetrical contraction of the pupils is evidence of opiate poisoning and opiate poisoning alone. Here is a case that proves them wrong. Here is a case that proves the point I'm trying to make—hemorrhage of the pons could have caused Helen's death."

Stymied, Jerome released Dr. Haubold and called Dr. Theodore Wormley, an eminently qualified toxicologist. Wormley had studied medicine two years under a preceptor before entering the Philadelphia College of Medicine, which conferred upon him the degree of MD in 1849. Wormley served as professor of toxicology at Capital University and Starling Medical College, both located in Columbus, Ohio, and in 1867 he published *Micro-chemistry of Poisons,* which became an instant classic and went through multiple editions. The success of his book would not have been possible without the assistance of his wife, Ann Eliza, who drew the illustrations for the book. When it was discovered that steel engravings of the illustrations would cost too much, Mrs. Wormley learned the art of engraving and made the engravings herself. In 1877 Wormley accepted the chair of the departments of chemistry and toxicology at the University of Pennsylvania Medical School, a position he held until his death in 1897. A true Renaissance man, Wormley was an amateur botanist, an expert on fishes, and an accomplished concert musician.[25]

Dr. Theodore Wormley, defense
toxicologist (Wellman and Simms,
The Trial of Carlyle W. Harris)

One of the first things that a lawyer should do when calling an expert
witness is to demonstrate for the jury that the witness is truly an expert.
Although this portion of an expert's testimony can be overdone, it is essential to bring out every material fact that bears upon the expert's knowledge,
especially when the expert is challenging an opinion by another expert.
Jerome sought to establish Wormley's credentials with a single question:
"Will you just state to the jury your experience in chemistry, what you have
written, what positions you have held, and what you hold now?" In answer
to such a question a typical expert might expound for several minutes on
his or her background, training, and experience. Wormley, however, was a
modest man. He answered with a single sentence: "At the present time I
hold the position of Professor of Chemistry and Toxicology in the Medical
Department of the University of Pennsylvania, in Philadelphia."[26]

Jerome followed up by getting Wormley to admit that he had written a
book on poisons, but he neglected to have Wormley testify that the book
was in its second edition. Jerome should also have gone on to have Wormley tell of his professorships at Capital University and Starling Medical

College; his position as chemist to the Ohio State Geological Survey; his editorship of the *Ohio Medical and Surgical Journal;* his vice presidency of the 1874 Centennial of Chemistry; his lecture on toxicology delivered to the 1876 International Medical Congress held in Philadelphia; and his medical service during the Civil War. These omissions almost certainly caused the jury to give Wormley's testimony far less weight than it deserved.[27]

Dr. Wormley testified in sum that of all the tests Dr. Witthaus conducted to detect the presence of quinine, no single one of them conclusively ruled out the presence of quinine in Helen's body. Jerome neglected, however, to inform Dr. Wormley of one test performed by Witthaus. Wellman was happy to enlighten Wormley of Witthaus's results on that test when he cross-examined the doctor. In fact, that was the first thing Wellman did on cross-examination.

Wellman asked, "If you were informed that Professor Witthaus, in connection with the bromine test, used alongside of him as a blank test one-eight-thousandth of quinine, and that it showed an emerald green under the amount of bromine that he used in this test, would that modify your opinion?" It certainly would. Wellman then asked Wormley what tests he would use to determine if quinine were in Helen's body. Wormley testified he would use the exact same tests that Dr. Witthaus had used. And if he got the same results Witthaus got, would Wormley be willing to testify that there was no quinine in Helen's body? He certainly would.[28]

The sum total of Wormley's testimony, then, was that although the tests Witthaus used couldn't conclusively rule out the presence of quinine, they were the tests that Wormley would have used; and if Wormley had used the tests and gotten Witthaus's results, he would have been willing to testify that there was no quinine in Helen's body. The defense really needed to produce some better witnesses.

Dr. Charles L. Dana took the witness stand as the first witness after the lunch break, and at first sight he looked to be a very positive witness—he regularly served as a witness on behalf of the prosecution in New York City. Jerome began by asking, "based upon your researches, reading and personal experience, can you make an absolutely sure diagnosis of opium or morphine poisoning from the symptoms alone?" Dana allowed as how it was sometimes possible to do so, but not in this case.[29] Dana went on to explain how he had, in his own personal experience, had a patient who went into a coma with symmetrically contracted pupils and died. He said that upon autopsy, it was discovered that she had trouble with her kidneys.[30] At this point Wellman interjected and asked if there was a chemical analysis done. Dana said, "No, sir." Jerome continued on the case of the woman with the symmetrically contracted pupils and the bad kidneys. If someone took a small dose of morphine and then died of uremic poisoning, would there necessarily be any visible changes to the kidney? Dana said he couldn't give a definitive expert opinion on that point, but he would expect very little change visible to the naked eye.[31]

Jerome then gave Dr. Dana the facts from Wellman's hypothetical question and asked, "Can it be positively said in your opinion as a scientific man that, assuming the fact in this question to be true, that the death was caused from morphine poisoning and that alone?"

"It cannot," Dana replied.

Wellman again showed himself to be a good listener. When he began his cross-examination he went directly to the Achilles' heel of the testimony on direct: "Did you write out these questions for Mr. Jerome to ask you?"

Dana temporized: "I suggested the line of inquiry, but I did not write out the questions except two or three of them."

"You wrote out some of them?" Wellman wanted to hammer home this point.

"I wrote out some of them," admitted Dana.

Wellman followed up on the admission: "I notice there has been some care from somebody to say in them: 'Can you positively say;' 'must it necessarily be;' 'can it absolutely be said;' those are important factors in your answers, are they not; those phrases and adjectives?"

Dana dodged the question: "I do not think I used them very often."

Wellman pressed the point: "They were used in the form of the question; 'Could it positively be said;' 'must it necessarily happen;' 'can you say with absolute certainty?'"

At this point Jerome objected. Wellman was demonstrating that the questions had been carefully crafted by the expert to get the "right" answer, which was not a fact calculated to enhance Dana's credibility. Smyth ordered Dana to answer the question.

Dana said, "I am perfectly willing to say that they are important factors in that question," but he was willing to make that admission only after trying to dodge the issue and after being ordered by Smyth to give a direct answer.

Wellman ended this line of questioning by saying, "I thought that would be your answer."[32]

Wellman then established that Dana had high regard for the competence and professionalism of Dr. Fowler, and further that Dana had limited experience with cases of opium poisoning. Wellman concluded his cross by getting Dana to admit that the district attorney's office used him only in cases of insanity. In fact, Dana had to admit that he specialized in "diseases of the mind."[33] Today he would be called a psychiatrist, but that term had not yet come into general use.

When Jerome read Wellman's hypothetical question to his next witness, Dr. James West Roosevelt, the doctor replied that the question was so poorly worded he would have to qualify his answer by saying that "it is not possible to say that it occurred from morphine poisoning or from poisoning; I am at a loss to know what some of the phrases mean."[34] Roosevelt went on to say that the autopsy conducted on Helen was worthless and that symmetrically contracted pupils could come from sunstroke, acute meningitis, uremia, and in hemorrhage of, not the pons Varolii, but the surface brain.[35] Finally, Jerome had called a witness who could withstand cross-examination from Wellman. Although Wellman could not damage Roosevelt on cross-examination, he missed an opportunity in final argument to undermine the doctor. He could have argued, "Isn't it strange that Dr. Roosevelt was the only doctor you heard from who wasn't smart enough to understand my hypothetical question?"

Mrs. Potts testifies (*New York Herald*, January 22, 1892)

The defense rested, and Wellman had rebuttal witnesses. Mrs. Potts took the stand once again and identified a letter from Harris to Helen written just a few months before her death. Jerome fiercely objected to the introduction of the letter, but Smyth allowed it into evidence. The letter read:

Dear Helen: I can't go down to the Grove today. If you suspect anything wrong, I will let you have something to take before your time. Unless you have reached the period I would not do anything. If you are sick in the morning have an orange by your bed and suck part of it before you rise. There is no possibility of your having to leave school. I can't do any good by seeing you now. Yours, C.

If you have any more of those opiates left take them for a couple of days before. There is no reason to operate now. I promise to bring you out of it, and never to cause you any worry of the same kind. C.[36]

Strictly speaking, this was not rebuttal evidence and should not have been allowed into evidence. The letter seems to suggest that a few months before her death Helen mistakenly thought she was pregnant a fourth time, and Harris was promising to get her through it and never get her pregnant again until their marriage was made public. These facts do not call into question any of the testimony of the defense experts. The letter should have been put on during the prosecution's case in chief. There is only one justifiable reason for the prosecution not having put it on at that time— Mrs. Potts didn't discover the letter until after the prosecution rested.

With the conclusion of Mrs. Potts's testimony, the trial was virtually over. There were two more inconsequential witnesses to hear from, but Mrs. Potts would be the last witness on the last full day of testimony. Recorder Smyth recessed court until the following morning at 11:30.[37]

CHAPTER TEN

Taylor Sums Up

The next morning Mrs. Harris arrived in the courtroom at 11:10 A.M. Her face was drawn and she was painfully nervous. Despite her worries she smiled at the reporters assembled in the courtroom as she placed a package on the defense table. She opened it, took out a handful of books, and began distributing them among the reporters. "This is a gift," she said, "to each of the newspaper men who have been fair to my boy." The book was *Plain Talks with Young Home-Makers,* which she had written under the nom de plume Hope Ledyard.[1] Mrs. Potts was not there this last day of trial. During the summations by the attorneys she sat weeping in a room at the district attorney's office.[2]

Recorder Smyth arrived, gaveled the proceedings to order, and Wellman and Jerome put on two more witnesses. Wellman recalled one of Helen's roommates to testify that Helen never suffered from insomnia. Jerome objected, and Recorder Smyth ruled it inadmissible.[3] The only evidence it rebutted was Harris's statements to Deputy Coroner Weston and Dr. Peabody that he had prescribed the capsules to Helen for insomnia. The testimony would have been proper during the prosecution's case in chief, not as rebuttal evidence. Then Jerome announced he wanted to call a rebuttal witness to testify that Harris gave himself up for arrest. This testimony should have been put on during the defense case in chief and was just as improper in rebuttal as Wellman's attempt to show Helen didn't suffer from insomnia, but Recorder Smyth ruled that he would allow the testimony before Wellman had a chance to voice an objection. Wellman didn't try to talk the judge into reversing his ruling.

With the testimony finally over, Taylor began his summation for the defense. Frederick A. Philbrick described Taylor's speech as "a char-

acteristic specimen of the emotive forensic style used in a bad case."[4]
There is an old saying among lawyers that when the law is against you,
you should pound the facts; when the facts are against you, you should
pound the law; and when both law and facts are against you, you should
pound the table. Taylor's speech consisted mostly of pounding the table,
but he did make some logical arguments relating to the law and the facts.
Taylor began his argument by telling the jury that they held Harris's life,
his mother's peace of mind, and the good reputation of the State of New
York in the palms of their hands. If they found Harris guilty, Harris's life
would be forfeit, his mother would be crushed, and the reputation of the
state would be indelibly stained—"the foundation stones of the temple of
jurisprudence would indeed be shaken."[5]

He continued with similar sonorous statements for another 740 words
before he got down to dealing with the issues in the case. Yet even when
he came to grips with the issues, he could not resist using the most florid
language imaginable. He told the jury that the prosecution had to prove
three things. First, they had to prove that Helen had been poisoned with
morphine. He said that this requirement "stands at the very threshold of
the indictment."[6] He said, "That is the gate of the temple. It is the vesti-
bule of the structure. If it shall not open to your intelligent apprehension
you are forever shut from going in the direction of the crime."[7] Second,
the prosecution had to prove that Harris, and nobody else, gave Helen
enough morphine to kill her. Third, they had to prove that Harris deliberately killed Helen. Taylor conceded the third point by telling the jury
if they were satisfied that Helen was poisoned by morphine, and Harris
gave her enough morphine to kill her, then Harris deliberately killed her.
If Harris gave Helen a fatal dose of morphine, then he "conceived . . . an
unholy design" that became "a virus in his heart" that "damnified" his
giving her the morphine.[8] Taylor's ornamental word choice may well have
tickled the fancy of the audience (the *Herald* said, "Mr. Taylor's summing
up was the work of a swordsman"),[9] but it did little to forcefully make the
points he needed to make.

Having stated the central facts at issue as: Did Helen die of morphine
poisoning? And if so, did Harris give Helen a lethal dose of morphine?
Taylor was almost ready to tell the jury why the answer to the two questions was no, but first he needed to make sure that they understood the
burden of proof in a criminal case. In a civil case, both sides have the same

burden of proof. The plaintiff must prove his case by the greater weight of the evidence, and the defendant must prove his innocence by the greater weight of the evidence. In a criminal case, the defendant theoretically has to prove nothing, and the prosecution must prove the defendant's guilt beyond a reasonable doubt. Taylor wanted to hammer home for the jury how heavy a burden the prosecution bore. He read the jury an instruction on reasonable doubt that Recorder Smyth had given in a recent murder case, and then he expounded on the subject of reasonable doubt at length.

Taylor gave two examples of how difficult it was to prove a fact beyond a reasonable doubt. He spoke of the elder McIntyre's claim that he'd never made a mistake and how the defense had disproved it with the $1,000 claim for damages. Then Taylor called the jury's attention to how the prosecution had failed to come forward with proof of two claims made in the prosecution's opening statement: that Harris had been an actor and a book agent.[10]

Taylor then turned to his attack on the proof that Helen had died from morphine poisoning. He began by asserting that Dr. Fowler didn't say as a matter of fact that Helen died from morphine poisoning, he had only stated his opinion that she had died from morphine poisoning.[11] Since Fowler had stated a mere opinion, his testimony was worthless as proof that Helen died from morphine poisoning. Dr. Baner, who had arrived second, came into the sickroom expecting to find a case of morphine poisoning because Dr. Fowler sent for him and told him to bring equipment to treat morphine poisoning. Baner, therefore, was predisposed to unquestioningly accept Fowler's opinion and merely parroted it from the stand when he testified.[12] Dr. Kerr was the only attending physician who testified as a matter of fact that Helen died from morphine poisoning. What would he know about it? He was the youngest and most inexperienced of the three physicians attending Helen, and besides the prosecution did not offer him as an expert witness anyway.[13] Having rhetorically demolished the attending physicians, Taylor turned to the autopsy.

Taylor proclaimed Dr. Hamilton unworthy of belief because Dr. Peabody and Dr. Thomson disagreed with him on several points. Taylor said he wouldn't bore the jury by enumerating those points of disagreement. He should have. Taylor then made a convoluted argument trying to discount the testimony of all the prosecution witnesses in one fell swoop. Shorn of its redundancies, the argument went something like this:

Despite the fact that Drs. Fowler, Baner, Kerr, Hamilton, Smith, Peabody, and Thomson all say Helen died from morphine poisoning, you may ignore their testimony because, while the field of science is valuable, the genius of our jurisprudence makes men who are taken from the ordinary walks of life the supreme arbiters of fact.[14]

The jurors might wonder how men taken from the ordinary walks of life could decide whether a case was morphine poisoning by ignoring the testimony of experts on morphine poisoning, but Taylor told them that they weren't left in the lurch because the defense had produced even better qualified experts to testify that there was no proof that Helen Potts died of morphine poisoning.[15] In other words, Taylor told the jury, "Pay no attention to the prosecution experts because science is worthless when compared to common sense, but let the science of the defense experts guide you in your application of common sense." With this contradictory argument, Taylor turned to a discussion of the defense experts, postponing his discussion of the testimony of Dr. Witthaus to the end of his argument.

When he spoke of Dr. Dana and Dr. Roosevelt, he spent most of his time talking about how wonderfully well qualified they were, outlining their accomplishments and achievements, and spent little time discussing their findings. The bottom line of his argument concerning these two doctors was simply this: The inability of Dana and Roosevelt to say why Helen died raises a reasonable doubt as to whether she died of morphine poisoning.[16]

Taylor then turned to a discussion of Dr. Wood. He employed two standard rhetorical tricks for defending the indefensible. First, Taylor picked out the weakest argument against Wood—the fact that Wood was from Philadelphia—and made that the centerpiece of his defense. It's silly to discount someone's testimony because of the city he comes from, therefore you shouldn't discount his testimony. Second, Taylor reinterpreted the strongest argument against Wood, that he had almost no experience with morphine poisoning. Because Wellman's cross-examination exposing Wood's lack of experience was too devastating to answer, Taylor characterized Wellman's cross as being a memory test. It's silly to discount someone's expertise merely because he can't remember arcane details of some long-ago cases, therefore you shouldn't discount Wood's testimony. Besides, Taylor argued, didn't the jury hear all the wonderful things the prosecution witnesses said about Wood's textbook? Just to make sure they hadn't forgotten, Taylor read some of the praise for Wood from the transcript of testimony.[17]

Taylor next sought to rescue Dr. Biggs's credibility from Wellman's scathing cross-examination. Despite the fact that Taylor had lambasted Dr. Kerr as being young and inexperienced, he argued that the jury shouldn't discount Biggs's testimony simply because he was young. As a matter of fact, Biggs was old enough to be a US senator; he was older than Napoleon when Napoleon conquered Europe; older than Raphael when Raphael produced his incredible artwork, and older than "the Divine Master" when He completed His earthly ministry.[18]

Taylor concluded this portion of his argument by saying that Dr. Hamilton and Dr. Smith were wrong when they ruled out kidney trouble because Dr. Peabody said it wasn't possible to detect kidney trouble after a body had been buried for fifty-three days. Add in the testimony of defense witnesses Dana, Briggs, Roosevelt, and Wood, and you've got reasonable doubt.[19] Having finished his argument that Helen wasn't poisoned, Taylor then turned to the argument that even if she had been poisoned, it wasn't Harris who did it.

Taylor began this next portion of his argument by giving a history of the romance, secret marriage, and abortion, working hard to spin the facts in such a way as to shine the best light possible on Harris's actions. He described the letter that Harris wrote Mrs. Potts upon her discovery of the abortion as "breath[ing] absolute respect for the feelings of a family [and] announc[ing] a clear intention to [deal honorably] with the situation."[20] Taylor told the jury that defense attorneys were usually the ones who made up fantastic scenarios in an effort to free their clients, but in this case it was the prosecution who was making up a fantastic scenario trying to convict his client. The prosecution had presented not one single scrap of evidence that Harris had secretly obtained morphine; not one iota of evidence of any secret acts; and not a particle of proof that Harris reloaded one of those capsules with a lethal dose of morphine.[21]

If the jury accepted the proposition that Helen had died from morphine poisoning, Taylor was working against a strong inference that Harris actually had put morphine in the capsule: Given the facts that the druggist put a safe dose of morphine in the capsule; Harris gave Helen the morphine capsule; there is no evidence anybody else gave Helen morphine; and Helen died from morphine poisoning, then somebody put a lethal dose of morphine in the capsule. Since Harris was the only person who had the capsule between the time the druggist filled it and Helen got it, Harris must have put the lethal dose of morphine in the capsule.

This inference becomes even stronger in light of the evidence that Harris told Mae Schofield he wanted to kill Helen. Taylor had to do something to counteract Schofield's testimony. His first attack was to split hairs. If it had been a real threat, Harris would have said, "I will kill my wife and kill myself before this shall come out" instead of saying, "I would rather kill my wife and kill myself before this shall come out."[22] Besides, Taylor argued, it was just idle talk:

> Gentlemen, go back in your own experience to things that have been said in the midst of your own family. Have you never used expressions like that yourselves? Have you never said, when confronted with some difficulty, "I wish I were dead rather than this should happen," "I would kill you rather than you should do so?" And, gentlemen, when some future complication assails you, would you like to have twelve men bring that up in visitation against you, and connect you with a matter with which no other event connected you at all.[23]

Of course, the flaw in this argument was that many events connected Harris to Helen's death, not just the threat to kill her. Taylor needed more distance between the threat and Helen's death, and he tried to get it by showing that Harris's stated reason for killing Helen was no longer a good reason to kill her when she died. Too many people already knew he was married to her. It was inevitable that the fact of the marriage was going to enter the public domain. Why would Harris poison Helen to keep a secret that was impossible to keep in the first place?[24] Furthermore, the fact that Helen lived for seven months after the threat shows that Harris didn't mean it. If he'd meant it, he would have killed her seven months earlier.[25]

Just as Harris's statements to Mae Schofield were meaningless, so also were the statements to his fellow students about how easy it was to get away with poisoning someone. Students gather together discussing a class they had just heard about poisons and one of them makes an idle comment about how easy it would be to poison someone and get away with it. This was simple innocent banter unworthy of notice except for the unfortunate coincidence of Helen's death.[26]

Taylor belittled the evidence about Harris's access to morphine in Dr. Peabody's lectures. That fact was meaningless because "you know it has been a conceded point in this case that morphine can be obtained at any wholesale druggist in this city upon an order without a prescription; in other words, it must be conceded that any person desiring morphine could obtain it."[27] Apparently Taylor had forgotten that Jerome objected to this testimony and Recorder Smyth ruled it inadmissible. Proof that it was easy to reload capsules was also meaningless. "All those things are possible; they are within the common knowledge of people in the ordinary walks of life."[28]

Taylor argued that the prosecution had failed to prove any motive whatsoever for Harris to kill Helen, therefore Harris was innocent. Harris had agreed to go ahead and publicly marry Helen. She was such a good catch, it was unthinkable that he would want to kill her. Mrs. Potts was going to send them to Europe on their honeymoon. Harris wanted to go to Europe. Why kill Helen and cancel his free ticket to Europe?[29] Warming to his subject, Taylor sought to drive the point home: "Then we find Carlyle W. Harris taking his wife over to Brooklyn to his mother's house. Was it not in pursuance of the plan outlined—this taking his wife over to acknowledge her before his mother?" Taylor paused for dramatic effect, and a voice broke the silence, "That is a mistake!" The *Evening World* described what happened next: "The pleader was disconcerted. He turned hurriedly and found that these words, destructive of the structure he had so carefully reared, had been uttered by Mrs. Harris, the mother of the boy for whose life he was pleading."[30]

Taylor limped along for a few more minutes and then asked the judge to take an early recess. Smyth mercifully granted it. When court reconvened at 2:00 P.M. Taylor had regained his composure and was ready to resume his argument. It is quite likely that over the noon recess either he or Jerome advised Mrs. Harris that they needed no further assistance from her in pleading her son's case to the jury.

Taylor argued that the only thing the prosecution seemed to have going for it was all the evidence of Harris's bad moral character, and evidence of bad moral character is not evidence of guilt for the crime of murder. "Manly men" like those on the jury couldn't possibly be swayed by Harris's moral turpitude and find him guilty of murder.[31]

Besides, the jury had to take all that evidence of Harris's sinfulness with a grain of salt because the three men who testified and "hissed their

Frederick Smyth, recorder of
New York City, 1879–95; justice
of New York City Supreme Court,
1895–1900 (Wellman and Simms,
The Trial of Carlyle W. Harris)

venom" at Harris didn't really know him.[32] Dr. Treverton's testimony was
especially unworthy of belief because his letter to Harris proved him to be
a wretch. Treverton was not only a wretch, he was not even a manly man
like the jurors. He was a money-grubber without a trace of affection for
his niece. Treverton was a blackmailer, and blackmailers are unworthy of
belief. "And yet, gentlemen, you are to murder this young man on the evidence of such a beast?"[33] Taylor ended his assault on Treverton by weak-
ening it. He admitted there was some truth to the things Treverton had
said. "Now, gentlemen, let me be fair with you. I don't offer that situation
as a complete refutation of the facts which Dr. Treverton recited."[34] Taylor
pointed out that even Mrs. Potts, for whom he had the highest regard, had
fibbed a little bit; and if she fibbed a little, Treverton could fib a lot.[35]

Taylor next attacked Dr. Hand, calling him a Bardolph to Treverton's
Falstaff.[36] In Shakespeare, Bardolph was the disreputable henchman of the
comic villain Sir John Falstaff. Such an allusion would be lost on a modern
jury and was quite likely lost on many of the jurors sitting on Harris's
case. In addition to making an arcane reference to a minor Shakespearean

character, Taylor gave no backup facts or reasoning in support of the allegation that Hand was a Bardolph. Taylor's argument seems to be Treverton is a villain, and Hand is his follower, therefore Hand is a villain too. Any jurors familiar with Bardolph would probably be puzzled by the comparison. Falstaff was Bardolph's "mentor," but Hand was Treverton's mentor. Taylor next attacked the Lathams, ridiculing Mr. Latham's pomposity and intimating that if Mrs. Latham was friends with the disreputable Queen Drew, then Mrs. Latham must be disreputable too. Then, after he had thoroughly defamed all and sundry of the witnesses to Harris's misdeeds, Taylor undid it all by saying, "I am not here to suggest to you that you are not to believe these people. I do say that the solemnities of this issue require that you shall make a large abatement on them, and that you shall not accept the statements made by them with an unqualified assurance; that is all."[37]

The thing that Taylor most wanted the jury to disregard about the testimony of Treverton and Oliver was Harris's boasting about the secret marriages. If Harris had multiple secret marriages, then that would be a strong incentive to kill a secret wife who wanted to go public. Harris could end up being prosecuted for bigamy if multiple secret wives found out about each other. Taylor specifically called upon the jury to disregard those boasts. If Harris said such things, he was probably lying. The prosecution searched high and low, and they could find no secret wife. If there were one, they would have found her and she would have testified at trial.[38]

Taylor closed this section of the argument by pointing out that Harris could still love Helen deeply and feel lust for other women. All the evidence showed was that "a man in love with a charming woman was willing to gratify his lust with other women." To show a motive for murder, Taylor argued, the prosecution would have to show that Harris loved Queen Drew more than he loved Helen. It is impossible that he could have loved that woman of ill repute more than his saintly wife. If the jury couldn't believe he loved Queen Drew more than Helen, then they couldn't believe he murdered Helen.[39]

Taylor's next argument is a favorite among defense attorneys even to this day. For Harris to be guilty, that means he carried out the crime in the stupidest way imaginable. If Harris was as cunning and clearheaded as the prosecution contended, he would have gotten rid of the two extra capsules, not kept them.[40] Only an idiot would commit such a crime the way Harris supposedly did it. What idiot poisons someone with morphine by writing the victim a prescription for morphine and signing his name to it? How could a murderer spend such a nice afternoon with Helen knowing he was going to kill her? Would a real murderer be so stupid as to admit giving the capsules to Helen? Would a real murderer hand over the unused capsule? Would a real murderer be so foolish as to propose an autopsy? Harris is no idiot, therefore Harris isn't guilty.[41] The standard reply to this argument is to say that the defendant isn't charged with being a criminal mastermind, he's charged with committing a crime; and crimes don't get solved because the police are so smart, they're solved because criminals make so many mistakes.

Taylor then returned to the first issue, whether Helen was poisoned by morphine, and attacked Dr. Witthaus's testimony. Witthaus's findings meant nothing because all he found was a trace of morphine. Taylor asked the jury if they were going to send Harris to the gallows on a trace. "If there was any mistake about that trace, gentlemen, the whole fabric of this ingenious theory of murder falls."[42] Witthaus's findings were meaningless. He ran fourteen tests for morphine, and he admitted that nine of them were meaningless. His tests for quinine were discredited by Dr. Wormley. The bottom line on Dr. Witthaus was that his testimony was worthless.[43]

Taylor closed his argument by saying that Harris was innocent because he was eager to meet the charges; he went to the district attorney to answer the charges; he turned himself in when he learned of the warrant; he acted like a totally innocent man. Taylor's last words to the jury were, "Gentlemen, if you accept the interpretation which I have presented to you, I beg of you that you shall give back this boy to his mother's arms, and that you shall do it tonight."[44]

Taylor had mapped out three issues: Was Helen poisoned? Did Harris poison her? Did Harris mean to kill her? He began by admitting that if the prosecution could answer yes to the first two questions, then it was certain that the answer to the last question was yes, and he would therefore confine his argument to answering the first two questions in the negative. Francis Wellman would later write that the defense team was so confident that the prosecution could not prove a poisoning, they put all their eggs in the one basket of getting a no to the first question.[45] According to another observer, "Aside from staging ludicrous conflict between scientific men and generally attacking all the witnesses for the prosecution,

Jerome and Taylor contented themselves with an attempt to demonstrate the good character of their client and a general plea that motive was lacking."[46] This was a colossal blunder. From the evidence at trial and Taylor's argument, if the jury answered the first question (Was Helen poisoned?) with a yes, then the answer to the second question (Did Harris poison her?) had to be yes too.

It was incumbent upon the defense to suggest an answer to that second question, which deflected suspicion away from Harris and onto someone else. Harris had robbed the defense of the most promising scapegoat (the pharmacist) by retaining the two capsules and turning one of them over to the coroner. Despite this handicap, they had to find someone else to blame, and they were assisted in the search by the prosecution's burden of proof. The second-best scapegoat after the druggist would be a mysterious disappearing poisoner that the shoddy coroner's investigation failed to uncover. Taylor mentioned the shoddy investigation as good grounds for finding reasonable doubt,[47] but he didn't elaborate on it. A creative mind could devise endless questions to highlight all the people the coroner didn't interview, all the leads the coroner didn't run down, and all the possibilities the coroner's investigation didn't rule out. Anybody could buy morphine? Anybody knew how to switch the contents of a capsule? Then anybody could have poisoned Helen. Had anyone among the students and staff had difficulties with Helen? Were any students suspected of being drug users? Were the capsules kept under lock and key until Helen needed to take one and then doled out to her by a nurse? Or were they just lying around, available for any resident to pick up and tamper with? Did delivery people and other service people have access to the dormitory rooms for business purposes? Were there any suspicious characters employed by any of the service providers who had access to the house? All Jerome and Taylor had to do was ask the questions and raise the doubt. These were questions that should have been asked and answered by a competent investigation. Demonstrating that they weren't may very well have conjured up in the minds of the jurors the specter of the mysterious disappearing poisoner.

Taylor and Jerome share the responsibility for failing to raise the mysterious disappearing poisoner defense. Jerome did not lay the groundwork for the defense on cross-examination of the occurrence witnesses and investigators; no evidence suggesting a mysterious disappearing poisoner was introduced during the defense case; and Taylor did not argue it to the jury. Despite the importance of the omission, none of their contemporaries seem to have criticized them for it. The postverdict faultfinders chose to critique another perceived shortcoming in the defense's presentation.

The critics almost universally agreed that the defense team overemphasized the expert testimony and should have put Harris on the witness stand to deny killing Helen. The most vocal of these critics were the flamboyant criminal defense attorney William F. Howe, who had tried hundreds of murder cases, and his disreputable law partner Abraham H. Hummel. They were dismissive of the way the defense team handled the expert testimony and adamant that Harris should have testified. Howe asked the press, "Why was not Harris put on the witness stand? Surely the prosecution had blackened his character all they could. Then what had he to fear? Harris was the only witness who could swear positively that Harris did not commit the crime." Hummel echoed the opinion: "It was a grave mistake not to let Harris, who was the only person who could do so, go on the stand and swear that he did not give Helen Potts poison."[48] Howe and Hummel may have had motives other than critiquing Harris's defense team when they leveled their indictments. They had originally been retained to represent Harris but had been discharged in favor of Taylor and Jerome.[49] Their vocal criticism may have been part of a campaign to wrest the case away from Taylor and Jerome and defend Harris on appeal.

Regardless of their motives for criticizing the defense team, Mrs. Harris agreed heartily with them. She maintained, "I kept telling Mr. Jerome that all that expert testimony was a fatal mistake, but neither he nor Mr. Taylor would listen to me. Nothing had been proved, they said, and they were right, but oh! My boy had been blackened, and he was not allowed to testify for himself. He begged to get on the stand and he should have been allowed to do so."[50]

Taylor and Jerome did not remain silent in the face of this criticism. When confronted by the press with the chorus of criticism, Jerome responded, "Harris was perfectly willing and anxious to accept our opinion in the matter. When the case of the People had been presented, the matter of putting Harris on the stand was carefully considered. We consulted with some of the greatest leaders at the criminal bar, and it was their general opinion that in this case the defendant should not be called on to testify. At all times Harris was perfectly satisfied with what we thought best to be done."[51]

Wellman agreed with Jerome that the defense should not have put Harris on the stand. In an interview given while the jury was deliberating, he said,

> Lawyers for the defense were wise in not putting Harris on the witness stand. Had they done so I should surely have brought out the story of that other—that prior secret marriage of his to some other girl, who, of course knew nothing of his marriage to Miss Potts. There was such a marriage, there can be no doubt of that, but naturally the girl victim did not reveal herself. Then I should have been able, too, to draw out the story of all his libertinism, and it is a disgusting story ranging over several years.[52]

Wellman later wrote, "The experienced counsel who defended Harris were not guilty of the error of allowing Harris to testify in his own behalf. Had they done so, I was so primed for his cross-examination that the outcome of the trial would never have been in doubt." This was no empty boast. While Harris's case was pending on appeal, Wellman prosecuted another young doctor for poisoning his wife. The prosecution of Dr. Robert Buchanan could have been a carbon copy of the prosecution of Harris except for two things: Firstly, the scientific evidence against Buchanan was so much weaker than that against Harris that when the prosecution rested, courtroom pundits were predicting an acquittal. Secondly, despite his lawyers' pleas that he stay off the stand, Buchanan testified.[53] As Colin Evans put it, "Wellman trapped [Buchanan] in so many lies and contradictions that any doubt created by the scientific dispute was entirely canceled out. Buchanan limped from the stand in tatters."[54] Given Wellman's workmanlike destruction of Harris's defense experts, and given Harris's many vulnerabilities, there is every reason to think that after Wellman finished with him, Harris would also have limped from the stand in tatters.

The postmortem analysis of the defense team's performance was not all negative. In fact, the criticism of Taylor and Jerome was almost drowned out by the praise heaped on them from all quarters. The *Brooklyn Daily Eagle* noted that many newspapers had showered praise on both the prosecution and defense and said that the praise was well deserved.[55] The *Tribune* lauded "the conscientious and painstaking manner" in which Jerome conducted the defense[56] and said that "physicians marveled at the knowledge of chemistry displayed by Mr. Jerome in his examination of the experts for both sides."[57] The *Herald* echoed those sentiments, praising Jerome's "wonderful skill" at cross-examining the experts.[58] Recorder Smyth, speaking from the bench in open court, complimented both the prosecution and defense teams for their ability, industry, and eloquence.[59] It was not lack of skill on the part of the defense team that got Harris convicted.

In the final analysis, Taylor and Jerome put together an intelligent defense that may very well have worked if they had gotten some support from their expert witnesses. Frederick A. Philbrick diagnosed the "cause of death" for Harris's defense as the collapse of Dr. Wood and Dr. Wormley. He called it a disaster and the turning point of the case.[60] Had these two gentlemen weathered the storm of Wellman's cross-examinations, the jury might well have granted Taylor's final plea and "give[n] back this boy to his mother's arms."

CHAPTER ELEVEN

Wellman Sums Up, the Jury Speaks

The *Herald* said Taylor's argument was the work of a swordsman, but it compared Wellman's argument to an attack with a battle-ax. Wellman had obviously done his homework. The three thick typewritten volumes of testimony lay before him, annotated, indexed, and bookmarked so that he could find any reference at a moment's notice. Although he laced his speech with oratorical flourishes, his language was not nearly as ornate as Taylor's. He spent a lot of time reading portions of the testimony to back up his arguments.[1]

Wellman began his speech by complimenting the defense team on their skill, telling the jury that the defense attorney can use "every sophistry that zeal or genius or sagacity can suggest," but the prosecutor must "convince the jury, if he can, by fair, legitimate, and logical arguments, of the guilt of the defendant." Wellman then sought to establish his credibility by telling the jury that he would be as impartial as humanly possible. He intended to strike hard blows, but they would be fair ones. All he wanted to do was enforce the law, and he earnestly asked that the jury not return a verdict that would give "indulgence to the infraction of that divine command, 'Thou shalt do no murder.'"[2] Wellman then got down to arguing the case.

Wellman first observed that when Taylor pointed out the prosecution's failure to prove that Harris had worked as an actor, he tacitly admitted that the prosecution had proved everything else that Wellman had said in his opening statement. He next mentioned that Taylor had promised ten days of defense testimony and delivered only two, and the defense that was presented was like the defense of an octopus. When attacked by a predator, the octopus sprays a cloud of black ink to befuddle its attacker and slips away in the confusion. The defense was nothing more than a cloud of black ink, and the jury should not allow the defendant to escape into that cloud.[3]

Up to this point in his argument Wellman had basically told the jury three things: The defense is allowed to use trickery. The prosecution is the fount of truth. The defense has not put on a legitimate case but has tried to escape behind a smokescreen. Prosecutors today still use Wellman's octopus analogy, but it is a strategy that is fraught with peril. Appellate courts will sometimes approve the octopus analogy as fair comment on the defense,[4] but not always. This is especially true when the prosecutor uses the octopus analogy in tandem with an argument that the prosecutor is the guardian of the truth.[5] Taylor made no objection.

Wellman then stated the questions to be resolved somewhat differently than Taylor: Did Helen die of natural causes or was she poisoned? Did Harris poison her? Wellman attacked the first question by saying that all the evidence pointed to morphine poisoning. All the prosecution experts said it was morphine poisoning, and none of the defense experts said it wasn't morphine poisoning. The best the defense experts would do was say it wasn't "certain" that Helen died from morphine poisoning.

Wellman sarcastically said, "At the time [of Dr. Fowler's cross-examination] Helen Potts apparently had all the diseases known to medicine. It was epilepsy, it was most likely heart disease, it was a brain tumor, it was apoplexy, it was kidney disease." As the trial wore on, though, Wellman said, the possibilities dropped out one by one until the only possibilities were either microscopic hemorrhage of the pons Varolii or an ultra-latent kidney disease aggravated by a one-sixth grain dose of morphine.[6]

Wellman argued that the defense didn't try to prove Helen died of hemorrhage of the pons, they just argued that the prosecution had failed to prove that she didn't die from hemorrhage of the pons. Dr. Hamilton, though, found no disease of the pons after doing a painstakingly thorough examination. He didn't do a microscopic exam because so much time had elapsed it would have been useless, but it made no difference because Dr. Peabody said that small hemorrhages of the pons don't cause death. He also said you could distinguish hemorrhage of the pons from morphine poisoning because hemorrhage of the pons was almost always accompanied by convulsions and some sort of paralysis. Furthermore, Dr. Peabody said that hemorrhage of the pons doesn't produce pleasurable sensations like those Helen reported and doesn't cause numbness like Helen reported. Finally, Dr. Peabody said small hemorrhages of the pons don't happen while people are asleep; they result from trauma.[7]

Wellman next weighed the qualifications of the prosecution experts against those of the defense experts and found the defense experts to be lightweights in comparison. He was especially critical of the wording of Dr. Dana's questions—"absolutely certain," "with positiveness," and so forth. This was an impossibly high standard. Nothing in this world is known with absolute certainty; that's why the prosecution's burden is proof beyond a reasonable doubt, not proof beyond all doubt. Why would the defense engage in such hairsplitting with their questions? They do it "in hopes of befogging the minds of conscientious jurors. This is justifiable [when defending a capital case]; but, while we applaud their zeal and sagacity, let us not be led into error nor deceived by it."[8]

Now what of the issue of death caused by latent kidney infection aggravated by a small dose of morphine? Dr. Thomson disposed of that theory because he said it would appear with the first capsule Helen took, and it didn't appear until her last capsule. Furthermore, Dr. Thomson said profuse perspiration and cold skin are rarely seen in cases of uremia. All the evidence points to Helen being healthy.[9] Dr. Peabody agreed that the first capsule Helen took would have uncovered any latent kidney problem. Furthermore, Dr. Peabody said if Helen had kidney disease, it would have been apparent to the naked eye on autopsy.[10] Dr. Hamilton, who was respected worldwide as a medical man, testified that Helen didn't have uremic coma because there was no report of twitching muscles, no frothing at the mouth, and none of the odor symptomatic of uremia. According to Dr. Hamilton, Helen's kidneys were normal.[11] Even the defense's book authority, Da Costa, whom they were so fond of quoting on cross-examination, negated uremia. Da Costa said uremic coma is preceded by convulsions—Helen had no convulsions. Da Costa said uremic coma is not profound—Helen's coma was profound. Da Costa said in uremic coma the pupils are dilated—Helen's pupils were contracted to pinpoints.[12]

Helen didn't die of natural causes. Did she die of suicide? The defense didn't claim suicide. She was happy the day of her death. That very day she had been told Carl was going to publicly marry her. There was no medicine in her room other than the empty pillbox bearing the initials

C. W. H. Helen showed her mother the capsule that very afternoon, said Carl gave it to her, and said she didn't want to take it. Her mother talked her into taking the capsule. Helen died that night. Unquestionably the capsule killed her.[13]

It was neither natural causes nor suicide. Was it an accident? Taylor said nothing about the druggist making a mistake in his summation. Two druggist clerks testified that the capsules had been properly prepared. Two reputable chemists examined the remaining capsule and found that it had been properly prepared. It wasn't natural causes. It wasn't suicide. It wasn't an accident. It had to be murder. Harris gave Helen the capsule and it had at least three or four grains of morphine in it. How did it get there? Harris put it there. That was no accident.[14]

Testimony from Helen's grave showed that the capsule was filled with morphine and had no quinine in it. Dr. Witthaus's examination proved it. Taylor practically admitted in summation that Dr. Witthaus's examination was correct. When they had Dr. Wormley on the stand, the one question they didn't ask him was whether Dr. Witthaus's examination was correct. That meant nobody contradicted Dr. Witthaus's testimony that he found morphine. Why didn't they find an expert to contradict Dr. Witthaus? They had the eminent chemist Professor Doremus sitting at counsel table with them. Why didn't they put him on the stand? Because he knew Witthaus was right. Wormley himself admitted on cross-examination that if he were going to look for the absence of quinine, he would run the exact same tests run by Dr. Witthaus.[15] In closing his argument on this first question, Wellman demonstrated that he knew his Shakespeare as well as Taylor. "Murder," he said, "though it hath no tongue, yet shall it speak a miraculous language."[16]

Wellman, satisfied that he had proven that Helen was murdered, next moved on to establish that Harris was the murderer. Although proof that she was murdered, standing alone, gives rise to a strong inference that Harris murdered her, Wellman was not satisfied to pin his hopes of conviction on a mere logical inference. He wanted to hammer home Harris's guilt.

Wellman first argued that Harris's actions at Helen's deathbed proclaimed his guilt. When Dr. Fowler sent him to the druggist to check the prescription, Harris said he went and it checked out as being properly compounded. An innocent husband would have rushed to the druggist to find out what was in the capsule, but Harris lied when he said he went. Why didn't he go? He already knew what was in the capsule. Later that morning, when he finally did go down to the druggist to check out the prescription, he was "perfectly cool and self-possessed," he simply asked what was in the prescription, said "Thank you," and left. Wellman at that point reminded the jury what an innocent fiancé did when a botched prescription killed his future wife not long before the Harris case arose. The distraught man went to the drugstore and blew the druggist's brains out with a pistol.[17]

This is the second time that Wellman referred to facts that had not been introduced into evidence. It is a rule of long standing that "The District Attorney representing the majesty of the people, and having no responsibility except fairly to discharge his duty, should put himself under proper restraint, and should not, in his remarks in the hearing of the jury, go beyond the evidence."[18] This is especially true when the matters outside the evidence could be considered inflammatory. Taylor should have objected, but he remained silent.

Harris's concern at the deathbed was not the concern of an innocent husband, but concern whether he might be held responsible for her death. Wellman asked, "Why, had you taken your own wife's life by accident . . . would the uppermost thought in your mind be whether you could be held liable for her death or not?"[19] Wellman again made an improper argument, sometimes called a "Golden Rule" argument, by calling on the jurors to put themselves in the place of one of the parties to the case.[20] Taylor did not object, but he had made the same sort of improper argument himself when he asked the jurors if they hadn't at some time in their lives made an idle threat.

When allowed time with Helen's dead body, Harris showed no interest whatsoever. Harris lied to the coroner when he said he gave Helen the capsules for insomnia. She had sick headaches, not insomnia. Harris's retaining two capsules was not the act of an innocent man. He thought they would protect him. Harris told Dr. Hayden that the capsules would insure that no jury would convict him. Wellman reminded the jury of an old French proverb, "He who excuses himself, accuses himself."[21]

Wellman then recounted Harris's conflicting statements about how Helen died: He told Mrs. Potts it was the druggist's mistake; he told Dr. Rogers it was Mrs. Potts's fault for not telling him about Helen's latent heart defect; he told Dr. Mapes she had a brain tumor; he told Dr. Peabody it was the druggist's mistake; he told Hearn Powers Helen died of heart trouble.

Are these the words of a guiltless man?[22] Wellman misspoke in one place: Harris told Dr. White, not Dr. Mapes, that Helen died of a brain tumor.

Wellman then turned to motive. Taylor wanted evidence of motive, Wellman said, but evidence of motive is only of secondary importance when there is no evidence that anyone else wanted to kill the victim. Besides, although sometimes it is difficult to prove motive, that is not the case with Harris. Wellman told the jury that a motive that would be insufficient for good men like them could easily be a motive for a scoundrel like Harris. Wellman then recounted Harris's boasts to Oliver about his many conquests of women—"not a companion of fallen women, but a seducer of virtuous women"—even going so far as to secretly marry them if he could conquer them no other way. Wellman told the jury that based on what Harris told Oliver, "we are justified in this case in believing and asserting that Harris never intended to recognize Helen Potts as his wife." Other evidence that he never intended to recognize Helen comes from the secret marriage under assumed names and the burning of the marriage certificate.[23]

Wellman said Harris was a libertine, and then he told the jurors if they wanted to see the "evil, misery, and woe existing in the world" caused by libertines such as Harris, they should "go to your asylums, go to your gilded palaces of ill-fame, behold their fallen inmates and learn the cause of their ruin. . . . Go to the lower dens of degradation and behold their miserable inmates, once pure, . . . now lost . . . living in filth. . . . Go to our asylums for the insane. . . . Ah, gentlemen, no man can describe the misery that exists in this city alone, today, following on the track of the libertine!"[24]

Wellman was now ready to answer some of Taylor's specific arguments. Taylor argued that when Harris told Mae Schofield about the secret marriage, it meant he was ready to make the marriage public. Nonsense, Wellman said, it merely meant that telling Mae Schofield about the marriage was the only way he could get Helen to agree to another abortion. Taylor's attack on Treverton was ill founded. Treverton could have worded his letter to Harris more diplomatically, but it was appropriate under the circumstances. Harris had started an abortion on Helen, and Treverton couldn't finish it without becoming liable for the manslaughter of an unborn child.[25] As to Taylor's argument that if Harris had really had another secret wife, the prosecution would have produced her, how was that to be done? They were married under false names at a time and place completely unknown.[26]

What Wellman was saying about the first wife was completely consistent with the evidence at trial, but it was not quite true. Despite the argument being not quite true, it might not have been a lie. This apparent paradox will take some explaining. Toward the end of the first week of Harris's trial, a Connecticut man sent a letter to the district attorney's office saying that he knew a lady named Lulu Van Zandt who had married Carlyle Harris in New York.[27] Harris had put the name Charles on the marriage certificate. The letter went on to say: "After the marriage the groom, who was only sixteen years old, took his fourteen-year-old bride to live in Brooklyn. At the end of two weeks she found that his real name was Carlyle and that he had an uncle who was a famous physician. Charles (or Carlyle) Harris's wife lived a while in Connecticut with him. Then she caught him flirting with a girl. She left him, returned to New York, went to a hospital and had an operation performed and never had anything more to do with Harris."[28] The Connecticut man's statement that Van Zandt had "an operation" was a delicate way of saying she had an abortion.

Wellman had a search made of the Bureau of Vital Statistics. Researchers found a record of an 1880 marriage of Lulu Van Zandt to Charles Harris. The name of the groom's father was given as Charles Harris.[29] Coincidentally, the Helen Potts marriage certificate listed the groom's name as Charles Harris and the groom's father as Charles Harris.[30] In 1880, however, Harris would have been ten years old according to his generally accepted birth date. Wellman theorized he was actually twenty-six or twenty-seven, which would have made him fourteen or fifteen when the marriage occurred.[31] Wellman asked that a thorough search be made for anyone answering to the name of Lulu Van Zandt.

Investigators found Miss Van Zandt in South Amboy, New Jersey. She was in chronic ill health, a condition that she attributed to the abortion.[32] She was also frightened. The *Harrisburg Patriot* blamed her fright on threats she had received from Harris.[33] The investigators determined that she was the Lulu Van Zandt who had married Charles Harris aka Carlyle Harris years ago. Was the Carlyle W. Harris on trial in New York the Charles Harris whom she had married? She didn't know. Would she go to New York and take a look at Harris to see if she could identify him? She replied, "Will I go to court and see if I can identify Carlyle W. Harris as my former husband? No, I will not. Why not? Oh, because a rich uncle of mine who helps mama and me has written saying he will disown both of us if I have anything to do with this Harris case." She was told that $1,000 would be deposited as a guarantee that she would not be detained if she would only go to New York and look at Harris. "Millions couldn't tempt me to go near him."[34] And that ended the prosecution's attempt to produce Harris's first wife as a witness.

Of course, Wellman could say nothing about any of this to the jury because lawyers are forbidden to argue facts that are not in evidence. He couldn't lawfully argue what he believed to be the truth—that they had found Harris's first wife but just couldn't get her to come to New York to testify—so he made the argument that it would be impossible to find Harris's first wife. Which begs the question, was Wellman lying? Is an attorney lying to the jury when he gives a plausible but untrue explanation because the rules governing the conduct of trial won't allow him to give the true explanation?

Taylor wanted to know why, if Harris wanted the marriage kept private, didn't he just point-blank refuse to acknowledge her? Because Helen "had it in her power to destroy him [by reporting him for performing an unlawful abortion]."[35] That threat alone was enough motive for murder. Then Harris attends Peabody's lecture, and like manna from heaven a jar of morphine falls into his hands. He takes some, and the very day he writes agreeing to the February 8 marriage, he goes to McIntyre's and fills the prescription for quinine and morphine.[36] Wellman pointed out how anxious Harris was to have the prescription filled immediately when he wasn't going to give the capsules to Helen for at least a day. Why couldn't he wait? He needed to take the capsules home and load one of them with morphine.[37]

Although Taylor had made much of the fact that Harris suggested an autopsy to Mrs. Potts, it meant nothing. He knew full well that she did not want an autopsy, which might reveal that Helen had been pregnant and undergone an abortion. If Harris had really been innocent, he would not have allowed his wife to be buried without an autopsy. Under the circumstances of Helen's death, a cloud of suspicion would hang over him forever. If he were innocent, he would have demanded an autopsy.[38]

Wellman then answered Taylor's argument that Harris wouldn't have killed his wife because it would have deprived him of an all-expense paid trip to Europe. "Don't you remember," he asked, "at Davison's office he used these words: 'I wouldn't take half a million dollars and acknowledge the marriage'? What does this mean? They are his own unexplained words. Surely, there was some terrible reason why he could not acknowledge Helen as his wife."[39]

Wellman was winding to a close, but he had a few more points to make. He called the jury's attention to the mighty effort of the defense to keep Mae Schofield's deposition out of evidence. He recalled for the jury how hard they fought to keep it out. He reminded the jury that they hadn't asked a single question at the deposition. What conclusion can be drawn from this? "[Can you] come to any other conclusion than the one dreadful one of guilt? I protest I can suggest none."[40]

Wellman argued that "Circumstantial evidence, gentlemen, is not like a chain, where one weak link can weaken the entire chain. It is like a rope or cable; each fact is a strand of that rope; and as we pile one circumstance on another, one fact on another, so we add strands and strength to the rope until we get a cable strong enough to bind the prisoner to justice."[41]

Wellman ended his argument by inviting the jurors to go with him in their imagination to the grave of Helen Potts to stand over that grave and "say a few words in praise of her innocent young life," which had been taken and "hurled into eternity. Let us write an epitaph on her tomb. 'Murdered innocence.' Would to God, gentlemen, we could call her back. . . . But it is too late. She has gone. Her lovely spirit has left the earth. The die is cast. A terrible doom has settled over this defendant. And we can now only listen to the command of the great Jehovah, 'Whosoever sheddeth man's blood, by man shall his blood be shed!'"[42] When Wellman boomed, "Would to God, gentlemen," pointing his finger directly at Harris, Harris blinked and his facial muscles twitched. He looked as though he was about to leap from his chair and flee the courtroom.[43] Not a few eyes were full of tears as Wellman ended. Sobs could be heard.

Wellman's ending, a blatant appeal to emotion conjuring up imaginary facts not in evidence, would be grounds for a mistrial today, but it made for a thunderously good conclusion to his summation. Interestingly enough, it wasn't original. It had been suggested to him by William F. Howe, Harris's first lawyer, who so criticized Taylor and Jerome for not calling Harris as a witness. Howe wrote a letter to Wellman in which he said, "Will you pardon me for suggesting that in the Harris case, in the course of your speech, you should say to the jury, 'Accompany me to the grave of this poor girl.'"[44] Howe went on to sketch out a closing even more florid than the one Wellman actually delivered. Howe correctly predicted that if Wellman pulled off the closing while looking Harris directly in the eye, Harris would flinch.[45] Despite being constant adversaries in murder cases, Howe and

Wellman were fast friends. Whenever Wellman tried a case against another defense lawyer, Howe advised Wellman on courtroom tactics, lent him books on similar cases, and otherwise tried to help in any way he could. In his memoirs, Wellman explained Howe's conduct by writing, "He did not seem to want anybody else to win any case against me— that privilege he reserved for himself!"[46] Howe might have had another motive in this case—to punish Harris for firing him.

William F. Howe, appellate and postconviction counsel for Harris (King, *Notable New Yorkers*)

As Wellman closed his speech, Mrs. Potts sat praying in the corner of the courtroom on the sofa that had been provided for her. A keen-eared reporter for the *Evening World* was able to copy down her words: "O God, O God above, hear me, and say that Carl is guiltless. Give the jury the strength and the light to know the truth. O God, say that he is innocent."[47] Why would Mrs. Potts want Harris to be innocent? If Harris was guilty of murdering Helen, Mrs. Potts had helped him kill her daughter. Helen was going to throw away the poisonous capsule until Mrs. Potts persuaded her to take it and thereby sealed her fate. A not-guilty verdict against Harris could go a long way toward absolving Mrs. Potts of the guilt she felt for encouraging Helen to take the fatal capsule.

Wellman finished his speech at 6:00 P.M. Recorder Smyth announced that he had intended to give the jury instructions immediately following the summations, but given the hour, he would wait until after supper to instruct them.[48] As the jury filed out, Mrs. Harris walked up to Recorder Smyth, who still sat on the bench. She began, "I want to ask your honor . . ." but Smyth cut her off, saying, "Pray, madam, do not approach me."[49]

When court reconvened after supper, it was Smyth's turn to speak, and he talked for approximately one hour and forty minutes.[50] He first defined the different degrees of murder and manslaughter and then described the factual issues in much the same fashion that Taylor had. The first item in question was "whether Helen Potts's death was caused by morphine poison." The second question was: "Who administered the poison to the deceased?" Smyth's final question was: "If you find that the deceased died of morphine poisoning and that it was administered by Harris, then the next thing is to determine the intent. Was it felonious, or was it honest to relieve headache and insomnia?"[51] Smyth also gave a lengthy explanation of circumstantial evidence and how it should be weighed in a criminal case, emphasizing that "If the facts and circumstances taken together are susceptible of two constructions, one pointing towards guilt and the other towards innocence, in criminal cases the accused is bound to receive the benefit of the most favorable construction."[52] Smyth concluded his instructions at 9:23 P.M., and the jury retired to deliberate upon its verdict.[53] Harris would later say that he was confident of an acquittal when the jury recessed for supper, but after Recorder Smyth instructed the jury, he could plainly see that a change had come over their features. When they came back to the courtroom to publish their verdict, he knew before it was published that they had convicted him.[54] Mrs. Harris may have had a similar premonition. After the jury filed out to deliberate, she collapsed onto the floor of the courtroom in tears.

At 10:47 P.M. the jury had their verdict. They filed into the courtroom with bowed heads and took their places in the jury box. Recorder Smyth returned to the courtroom and took his place on the bench. As Smyth sat, the jurors, who had been standing, took their seats as well. The clerk rose from his seat and asked, "Gentlemen of the jury, have you agreed upon a verdict?"

Samuel B. W. McKee, the foreman, responded, "We have."

"Defendant, rise and look on the jury," said the clerk. "Jurymen, rise and look on the defendant." When all had risen to their feet, the clerk asked, "How say you, gentlemen of the jury, do you find the defendant guilty or not guilty?"

"Guilty," the foreman replied.

"Guilty of what?"

"Guilty of murder in the first degree, as charged in the indictment."

"Guilty! O God! Guilty! Carl!" Mrs. Harris screamed and fell into the arms of her younger son, McCready.

Facing page: The jury; *top row, left to right:* Samuel B. W. McKee, foreman; Benjamin F. Stangland; Albert Field; *second row, left to right:* Harvey J. Brown; Charles H. Hinds, John D. Crane; *third row, left to right:* Francis D. Jackson, Samuel P. Mapes, David H. Hilberg; *bottom row, left to right:* Henry Rudolph; Crawford Mason, Joseph Bell (Wellman and Simms, *The Trial of Carlyle W. Harris*)

"Harken unto your verdict, gentlemen of the jury," said the clerk, "you say you find the defendant guilty of murder in the first degree, whereof he stands indicted, and so say you all?" The jurymen nodded their heads. Jerome asked that the jurors be individually polled, and the clerk performed the ritual of calling each juror by name and asking, "Is the verdict you have just heard published your verdict?" Each juror answered "Yes." This part of the proceedings was carried out against a background of shrieks and wails from Mrs. Harris. She had been lifted from the floor and placed onto two chairs. "The verdict is a lie! I know it is a lie!" she cried.

Ignoring the disruption caused by Mrs. Harris, Recorder Smyth spoke to the jury: "Gentlemen of the jury, you are discharged with the thanks of the court for the intelligent manner in which you have discharged your duties. It is my present impression, after listening to all the evidence in this case, that no other verdict than the one that has been rendered by you could have been rendered upon the evidence."[55]

As the jury filed out Mrs. Harris wailed, "How could they have done it?" Foreman McKee replied, "It was hard,"[56] and that was all the news media got in the way of public pronouncements from the members of the jury, who had agreed among themselves that they would not discuss their deliberations with anyone. A "reliable" source provided the press with the results of the jury's balloting: The first ballot stood at eight guilty of murder in the first degree, three guilty of murder in the second degree, and one abstention. The second ballot was eleven guilty of murder in the first degree, one not guilty. The final ballot was twelve guilty of murder in the first degree.[57] Juror Number 11, Crawford Mason, was the holdout who abstained from the first ballot and voted not guilty on the second. The other eleven jurors spent most of their time in deliberations persuading Mason to change his mind.[58] The "reliable" source received an immediate rebuttal. Upon publication of this account, two jurors broke their oath of silence to a certain extent, saying only that Mason was never in favor of an acquittal.[59]

On February 8, 1892, Recorder Smyth sentenced Harris to death, and the last chapter seemed to have been written in the saga of Carlyle W. Harris. That was not to be the case, however. The Harris case would command the attention of the American press for the next fifteen months.

CHAPTER TWELVE

New Evidence?

To say that Harris's case attracted a lot of media attention would be like saying picnics attract ants. The *Evening World* called the case "one of the most startling and remarkable sensations that has ever been disclosed,"[1] with huge crowds attending the trial. As the case progressed, the number of women in the audience got larger and larger,[2] a fact that seemed to irritate the male reporters. The *Philadelphia Inquirer* decried the "mobs of jewel be-decked girls" and "sensation-feeding unhealthy-looking loafers" attending the trial,[3] and the *New York Times* pronounced the "indecent . . . assemblage . . . of crowds of well-dressed but ill-behaved women, who had no business in court" to be "morally the dregs of New York society."[4] Thirty women were in court on the day that the Lathams testified about Harris's affair with Queen Drew. The *Herald* reported that two women became so em-barrassed they left the courtroom, but the other twenty-eight sat blushing and staring at the floor as the four hundred male spectators watched them instead of the testimony.[5]

The jury verdict did not end the public's morbid curiosity about Harris. In the days following his conviction, headlines all over the United States trumpeted the story of Carlyle Harris's life and crimes. The flood of neg-ative publicity fully aired all the details of the sordid story of Lulu Van Zandt. When asked to comment on the story, Harris predictably denied even knowing Lulu Van Zandt. He told a *Herald* reporter that a check of the records of his home church would show that he was ten years old in 1880. The reporter went to the church to check out Harris's claim. He found that the records for the years in question were incomplete and failed to confirm Harris's denial.[6]

The final chapter of the Lulu Van Zandt story was written when Miss Lulu Van Zandt, daughter of Thaddeus Van Zandt, of Plainfield, New Jersey, a lady of high social standing, came forward with the announcement that she was much embarrassed by the news reports of the marriage of Lulu Van Zandt to Carlyle W. Harris and she wanted to set the record straight: She had never been married to Harris. She had a relative named Lulu Van Zandt, who was the daughter of Egbert Van Zandt. Lulu Van Zandt, daughter of Egbert Van Zandt, was the one who had been married to Harris.[7]

The papers also outlined a number of infidelities perpetrated by Harris while he was secretly married to Helen, including a proposal of marriage to another girl living in Asbury Park. When she asked him, "What are you going to do about Helen Potts?" he replied, "Oh, I'm tired of her and I want to shake her."[8] The most serious allegation made against him involved a serving girl by the name of Tillie Benson. In 1888 the fifteen-year-old Tillie went to work for Harris's mother as a serving girl. In short order, Harris had seduced Tillie and impregnated her. When it became impossible to conceal her pregnancy, Harris got her into a maternity hospital, where she gave birth. Upon her discharge she found herself homeless and penniless. Reduced to walking the streets with her child in her arms, she was taken in by a kindly Irish lady. When she appealed to Harris for help, he gave her some money and told her to "get rid of the brat" by leaving it on some doorstep. Eventually Harris arranged to have the baby placed in the Nursery and Child's Hospital at 571 Lexington Avenue. Once Miss Benson was no longer encumbered by a baby, Harris got her a job as a domestic in the hamlet of Orient on Long Island. She had not been at her new job long when she was notified by the hospital that her child had died. Miss Benson told reporters that if Harris received a new trial, she would be happy to testify against him.[9]

The publicity touched off a flood of letters to Harris in the Tombs. They came from all over the country, and although many of the letters were threatening, many were supportive.[10]

Harris occupied Cell 52 in the Tombs for ten months awaiting trial.[11] Cells in the Tombs were twelve feet by six feet with an iron cot, bedding, a tin cup, and a saucepan. A chair and a carpet could be brought in with special permission of the warden.[12] Upon his conviction, the authorities moved him to Cell 10 on Murderer's Row,[13] where he would remain for the duration of his appeal. Harris put up such a good front for the visitors flocking to see him that he became something of a folk hero. The warden of the Tombs told the *Herald,* "I could not have believed any man capable of such nonchalance. He treated his approaching death sentence as a trivial thing in itself. His only concern was about the possible discomfort of moving [from Cell 52 to Murderer's Row]. His indifference made me feel cold. There was not a tremor in his voice. His manner was absolutely the same as it has been ever since he was brought to the Tombs. I cannot understand him. He does not act or speak or look like a criminal."[14]

When the day came for Harris to be sentenced, Taylor presented Recorder Smyth with a motion for new trial alleging that the verdict was contrary to the evidence; there was a variance between the indictment, which charged that Harris administered morphine to Helen, and the proof, which showed that it was sulfate of morphine; Recorder Smyth's charge to jury was unfair; Recorder Smyth erred by refusing to give the jury instructions requested by the defense; Recorder Smyth erred by allowing evidence objected to by the defense; the indictment was improper because it was signed by an assistant district attorney and not the district attorney himself; and the verdict was contrary to law. Smyth summarily denied the motion.

As Harris stood before Recorder Smyth for sentencing, the clerk asked whether he had anything to say prior to the entry of judgment and sentence. Acting on advice of counsel, Harris stood mute.[15] Smyth then pronounced sentence:

> Harris, you were tried in this court by a jury of unusual intelligence; men, I believe, of the strictest integrity, who heard the evidence in this case with great patience and arrived at the result that you were guilty of the crime of murder in the first degree in having deprived your wife of her life by the administration of morphine poison.
>
> I stated at the time that the verdict was rendered, and I believe now, after an examination of the case since the trial, that in my judgment no verdict could have been rendered by the jury in the case other than the one that they did render. The evidence, in my mind was clear and conclusive. You had the benefit, certainly, of a fair trial. You had the benefit of counsel who have left nothing undone that men of intelligence and of great ability could do for the purpose of saving you from the result of your criminal acts. It is rarely that a case, in this or any other country that I know of, has been prepared, tried and presented with such zeal and ability as this case has.

The junior counsel in this case, Mr. Jerome, is certainly entitled to great credit for learning and ability which he displayed in your behalf.

Everything I believe that could possibly be done to avoid this judgment has been done. It is unnecessary for me to and I do not desire to refer to the facts and circumstances of this case. They are within your own recollection and within the recollection of almost every person in this community. It is sufficient for me to say that the crime of which you were convicted, and justly convicted, in my judgment, was one of the most atrocious character. The law permits only one judgment to be pronounced, leaving in the hands of the court no discretion whatever.

I will now proceed to pronounce that judgment upon you. Upon the verdict rendered in this case, Carlyle W. Harris, the sentence is that you suffer the punishment of death upon a day to be determined within the week commencing on the 21st day of March, 1892, and until that sentence is carried out that you be imprisoned in the manner and in the place provided by law. The punishment shall be inflicted upon you in the mode and in the manner provided for by the law of this state.[16]

Harris stood unflinching as Smyth pronounced judgment. The clerk then read the death warrant to him, and he was handcuffed and taken back to the Tombs.

In the wake of the sentencing, reporters tracked down Helen's father and were able to get him to make a comment. He said, "I hope I may be allowed to touch the button of the electrical machine that kills the man that murdered my daughter. I shall make application to the authorities for the privilege."[17]

On Murderer's Row, Harris was treated more like a distinguished guest than a man under sentence of death.[18] The keepers allowed Harris to read the paper, receive callers, and write; and sometimes they allowed him to sit outside his cell and smoke.[19] During the pendency of his appeal he earned money by writing essays and poems for the newspapers, which his mother later collected and had published in a book.[20] Harris wrote on such subjects as conditions in the Tombs[21] and the necessity of prison reform,[22] and the *St. Louis Republic*[23] and the *Herald*[24] published his poetry.

Harris had not been on Murderer's Row for long before a bombshell exploded. A young man calling himself Carl Peterson came forward with the claim that Helen Potts was a morphine addict. According to Peterson, six weeks before Helen's death, he had been with her and Harris in Asbury Park and had seen her with morphine. Peterson said he was a morphine addict, and he had a bottle of morphine on the mantelpiece in his room at Asbury Park. One morning while he was sitting in his room reading the paper, Helen came in, took the bottle from the mantelpiece, and poured a quantity of morphine out onto a sheet of paper.

"My God, Helen!" exclaimed Peterson, "What are you going to do with that? Why, you have enough poison there to kill a dozen men!"

"Don't be a goose," she replied, "I only want to use it to improve my complexion." Helen then wrapped the morphine up, put it in her pocket, and left the room.

The reporter to whom Peterson told this tale naturally wanted to know why Peterson was so tardy in coming forward with it. "I had absolutely forgotten it," he said, "and it was not until I read of my friend Carlyle's conviction that the recollection of this circumstance came back to me. Besides this, my business has obliged me to be away from New York a great deal lately, and I was not aware of the nature of the evidence which resulted in my friend's conviction. I shall at once place myself in communication with his lawyers and if the revelation of this fact will avert his dreadful fate I shall do all I can to rectify the fault at this late date." Peterson went on to say how much in love the two were and how absurd it was to believe Harris capable of killing her. Peterson was a well-spoken, educated, handsome man who claimed to have made two trips around the world. As proof of his assertions, he produced letters, which he said were written to him by Helen.[25] Peterson also mentioned that he had been engaged to marry one of Helen's friends, a Miss Mollie Meeker. One might wonder if it was one of his round-the-world trips that caused Peterson to have overlooked his good friend's misfortune for almost a year. One might also wonder why he was telling these things to the news media in Chicago rather than leaving Chicago and returning to New York to tell them to the lawyers involved in the case.

A reporter from the *Trenton Evening Times* rushed to the Tombs to ask Harris about Peterson's story. Harris's reply: "I remember the gentleman perfectly, and to the best of my knowledge all he says is true. He was an intimate friend of my wife's friend, Miss Meeker, so Helen knew him better than I. No one could be in a better position to speak of the affection between Helen and myself. . . . It is to be hoped that the truth of this terrible tragedy will be proved."[26]

The next stop in the reporter's investigation was the home of Miss Meeker, who denied knowing anyone by the name of Carl Peterson. "Not only that," she said, "but I never even heard of him. I was never more surprised than when I read that he said I had been engaged to him. It is a very strange thing it seems to me that this man Peterson, if there is such a person, did not come forward while Carlyle Harris was being tried for his life." Meeker admitted knowing Harris slightly, and she vehemently denied that Helen had ever used morphine for her complexion. "She did not need anything for her complexion."[27] In an attempt to resolve the conflicting statements, the reporter went to Asbury Park, where everyone he spoke to denied that Helen ever used morphine for any purpose. Every druggist in Asbury Park denied ever filling a morphine prescription for Helen, and the doctors who had treated her since childhood said that Peterson's claim was "preposterous and unquestionably false."[28]

A little more questioning of Peterson got him to admit that he had stolen the morphine from a doctor in Philadelphia "because poison fascinated" him, and further got him to admit that he had not returned to New York during Harris's trial for fear of people to whom he owed money.[29] Then it turned out that Carl Peterson was not Carl Peterson. It seemed that he was really Carl Haaman. A re-interview with Miss Meeker produced evasive answers as to whether she knew a Carl Haaman, but reporters were able to locate mutual friends of Haaman and Meeker who attested to the fact that the two were intimate. While all this was going on, Haaman mailed a letter to Jerome containing what he claimed was a sample of the morphine from which Helen had borrowed.[30]

While the controversy swirled around Carl Peterson/Haaman, a Mrs. Anna Kunn presented herself to Warden Fallon at the Tombs asking to see Harris. She told Fallon a story about overhearing a conversation in Central Park. Fallon asked Harris if he wanted to see her, and Harris told Fallon to send her to his lawyer, William Travers Jerome. She said she had already told Jerome the story during the trial, but he ignored her.[31] Within an hour of Mrs. Kunn being turned away, another woman appeared on the doorstep of the Tombs. She was young, pretty, and richly dressed. She got an audience with Warden Fallon. "Oh sir," she said, "pray let me see Mr. Harris. I know he is guilty, but the Lord commanded me to save him and I can do it. I can't tell you my name because my family goes in the very nicest society and it would offend them to tell. But I am only twenty years old and I was a schoolmate of Helen. Pray let me see Mr. Harris and save him, as the Lord commanded me." Fallon didn't bother to consult with Harris. "Better see his counsel, madam." The young lady left disappointed.[32]

As the two ladies unsuccessfully tried to gain an audience with Harris at the Tombs, the curtain rang down on the saga of Carl Peterson/Haaman. Asbury Park residents recognized his description as being that of a fugitive from justice under the name of Frank Prescott. It seems that Haaman ran the poker room on the third floor of the Neptune Club, and when he got arrested, he gave his name as Prescott. He got released on $200 bail pending action by the grand jury and left town when the grand jury returned an indictment against him. This revelation put the last nail in the coffin of Peterson/Haaman/Prescott's credibility.[33]

While the controversy swirled around Harris, Wellman and Simms had not been idle. They had edited a digest of the trial with a summary of all the testimony, condensing some 1,400 pages of transcript down to 334 pages.[34] The book bore the title *The Trial of Carlyle W. Harris for Poisoning His Wife, Helen Potts, at New York,* and contained pictures of all the major participants in the trial, including the jury. This was Wellman's first, but not his last, venture into the realm of publication, and it proved very successful. Five thousand copies were sold almost overnight.[35]

Toward the end of May the papers were reporting that Harris had retained new counsel. Harris told the reporters he still had the utmost confidence in Taylor, Jerome, and Davison, but he wanted to secure the additional services of William F. Howe,[36] the man who had helped write Wellman's summation and later criticized the defense put up by Jerome and Taylor. Of course, whenever Howe was retained to defend a case, it went without saying that the client also had the services of Howe's partner, Abraham Hummel. Harris may have had the utmost confidence in Jerome, Taylor, and Davison, but they did not have any confidence in Howe and Hummel. They withdrew from the case.

The author of the old joke "Is he a criminal lawyer?" "Yes, very," may not have had Howe and Hummel in mind, but they perfectly exemplified the spirit of the joke. In one of his memoirs Wellman wrote that "The office of Howe and Hummel was a veritable perjury factory. They took in the raw material, perfected it, polished it and turned out the finished article. They seldom ever presented a defense that was not honeycombed with this weapon to thwart justice." Wellman was philosophical about the

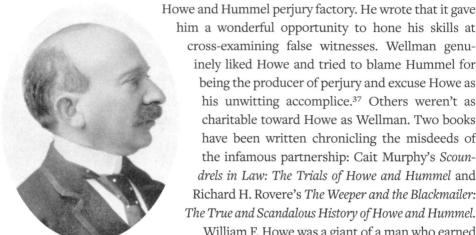

Abraham Hummel, law partner of William F. Howe (King, *Notable New Yorkers*)

Howe and Hummel perjury factory. He wrote that it gave him a wonderful opportunity to hone his skills at cross-examining false witnesses. Wellman genuinely liked Howe and tried to blame Hummel for being the producer of perjury and excuse Howe as his unwitting accomplice.[37] Others weren't as charitable toward Howe as Wellman. Two books have been written chronicling the misdeeds of the infamous partnership: Cait Murphy's *Scoundrels in Law: The Trials of Howe and Hummel* and Richard H. Rovere's *The Weeper and the Blackmailer: The True and Scandalous History of Howe and Hummel*.

William F. Howe was a giant of a man who earned a reputation among the criminal element as being the greatest criminal lawyer of his day by defending over one thousand murder cases.[38] Fat, flashy, and flamboyant, he had an uncanny ability to befuddle a jury. In one sensational murder case prosecuted by Wellman, Howe succeeded in getting the jury to accept his client's preposterous story that she had killed her lover by accidentally pulling the trigger of a gun four times.[39] It was widely agreed that any sort of evidence Howe and his partner Hummel might produce on Harris's behalf would be perjured. Howe was never called to account for offering perjured testimony, but after Howe's death, Hummel got prosecuted, convicted, disbarred, and imprisoned for subornation of perjury.[40] In an odd sort of karmic justice, the man who prosecuted Hummel was district attorney William Travers Jerome.

Howe found himself handicapped by the fact that he had entered the litigation at a stage where his greatest assets—his perjury factory and his ability to bamboozle juries—were of no avail. On appeal there were no witnesses to call and no juries to manipulate; there was just the Court of Appeals, which was made up of judges who had heard all about Howe's questionable tactics. Howe did have one thing going for him on the appeal—the towering intellect of Abraham Hummel.[41] The pair filed a 107-page appellate brief alleging 19 points of error,[42] but Howe's pleas before the Court of Appeals fell on deaf ears.

The Court of Appeals handed down a 23-page, 10,000-word opinion affirming Harris's conviction. But judge John C. Gray, writing for a unanimous court, summed it up in a single sentence: "A careful reading of the evidence contained in this very voluminous record, and a conscientious consideration of the facts disclosed, must inevitably lead to the formation of an opinion that the verdict of the jury was not only justified, but that no other conclusion could have been reached by the fairest mind."[43] Because so much had been made of the inadequacies of circumstantial evidence both in Howe's brief and in the press, Gray felt constrained to explain the force and effect of such evidence:

All evidence is, in a strict sense, more or less circumstantial, whether consisting in facts which permit the inference of guilt, or whether given by eyewitnesses of the occurrence; for the testimony of eyewitnesses is,

John C. Gray, Court of Appeals judge, 1888–1913 (King, *Notable New Yorkers*)

of course, based upon circumstances more or less distinctly and directly observed. . . . The mind may be reluctant to conclude upon the issue of guilt in criminal cases upon evidence which is not direct, and yet, if the facts brought out, when taken together, all point in the one direction of guilt, and to the exclusion of any other hypothesis, there is no substantial reason for that reluctance. Purely circumstantial evidence may be often more satisfactory, and a safer form of evidence, for it must rest upon facts which, to prove the truth of the charge made, must collectively tend to establish the guilt of the accused. . . . The necessity of a resort to circumstantial evidence in criminal cases is apparent in the nature of things, for a criminal act is sought to be performed in secrecy, and an intending wrongdoer usually chooses his time, and an occasion when most favorable to concealment, and sedulously schemes to render detection impossible. All that we should require of circumstantial evidence is that there shall be positive proof of the facts from which the inference of guilt is to be drawn, and that that inference is the only one which can reasonably be drawn from those facts.[44]

. . .

Evidence, as I have suggested, is not to be discredited because circumstantial. It [often has] more reliable elements than direct evidence.[45] Where it points irresistibly and exclusively to the commission by the defendant of the crime, a verdict of guilty may rest upon a surer basis than when rendered upon the testimony of eyewitnesses. . . . The evidence seems to overwhelm the accused with his guilt, and leaves the mind unfitted to accept any other belief than that he intended to make away with his wife in order to free the field of his own life, and to escape from the imminent danger of disgrace or punishment, and that with cold deliberation he planned her death by methods which should conceal him as its author. The circumstances preceding and attendant upon the death of the deceased were such as to associate him inevitably with its cause, and to forge the chain which has drawn him to the bar of justice.[46]

Howe dispatched a junior member of his firm to give Harris the bad news. Distraught, Harris sent telegrams to a male cousin and to his mother, saying, "Come to town at once." He wanted her to hear the bad news from his own lips. The cousin arrived first and had a brief private interview with Harris and then hurried away to meet Mrs. Harris and escort her to the Tombs. Mrs. Harris arrived at the Tombs in deep mourning. "Take me to my poor boy!" she cried. "Let me see him at once!" Leaving her handbag at the gate, she was escorted to her son's cell on Murderer's Row.

No reporters were allowed to be present for the talk between mother and son, but one of the keepers described their meeting: "Harris seemed to be pretty well shook up when his mother came up to his cell. He tried to cheer her up, and showed more nerve than most men would in the same box."

After a half hour, Mrs. Harris emerged weeping from the Tombs. Seeing a group of reporters, Mrs. Harris said, "Oh, gentlemen, for God's sake be kind to my poor boy. As God is my judge he is innocent and I know it, but I cannot give you the proof now of his innocence."[47] Mrs. Harris began to expound on the innocence of her son, the wickedness of Recorder Smyth and the jurors, and the suffering that they had visited upon her children. A reporter interrupted her, "But I am credibly informed that there is every chance that the Governor will commute your son's sentence."

"Thank you, sir," she replied indignantly, "but we wish for no pardon or commutation. What we want is justice."[48] Mrs. Harris broke down and was allowed into the warden's office to compose herself. When she regained her faculties enough to leave the Tombs, she went to the offices of Howe and Hummel.

As she left, one of the keepers remarked, "Well, it's tough to see a woman suffer like that. It is the woman that's always getting the worst of it in a case like this. I suppose that the mother of the poor girl that was killed has had her crying times the same as Harris's mother. Men are devils for making trouble."[49]

Howe was in trial when the news of the court's opinion came down, but he took time to speak to the press: "Harris shall not be executed. On Monday next we shall move for a new trial. Evidence has been discovered which will establish his innocence. We shall show that the young woman for whose death Harris is suffering was a morphine eater. A young man who knew that she was a morphine eater and a druggist who used to sell her the drug have been discovered. I tell you that we shall free Harris."[50] He said he was prepared to take the case all the way to the Supreme Court of the United States if he had to. When reached for comment, De Lancy Nicoll said he could think of no grounds for the case to be brought before the Supreme Court. He went on to say that the motion for new trial was unimportant; the theory that Helen Potts was a morphine eater had been exploded long ago.[51] He did not elaborate on how the theory had been exploded. It is likely that Taylor and Jerome explored the possibility of raising the defense and discarded it as unprovable.

Howe found himself somewhat out of his element in presenting Harris's case to a judge rather than a jury. His flamboyant, bombastic style worked well with lay jurors, but it would have little effect on the "remorselessly just"[52] Recorder Smyth. Although his witnesses would be taken at face value by a jury composed of people who were unaware of Howe's reputation for suborning perjury, Recorder Smyth would automatically look on every witness with a jaundiced eye. Howe worked against a disadvantage of another sort, or possibly it was an advantage. Under then existing New York law, live testimony could not be given on a motion for new trial—all the evidence would have to come in the form of affidavits. On the one hand, reading a paper statement could never be as persuasive as live testimony, but on the other hand the defense witnesses would be spared the ordeal of cross-examination by Francis L. Wellman.

Viewing the case as a realist, Howe probably concluded that the motion for new trial before Smyth was a lost cause. It would, however, serve as one skirmish in the battle to save Harris's life. Howe proposed to wage his battle on several fronts—in the courtroom, in the newsroom, from the pulpit, on the streets of New York, in Madison Square Garden, and finally in the governor's office. Howe intended to arouse such a groundswell of public opinion in favor of Harris that Gov. Roswell P. Flower would risk political suicide by refusing to pardon the man.

Howe's projected battle plan would follow this path: As he recruited witnesses to testify about Helen's supposed drug use, he would leak the details of their statements to the papers. The papers would print lurid stories recounting the uncross-examined details of the statements, and doubts about Harris's guilt would grow. Mrs. Harris would publicly appeal through the media for a letter-writing campaign in support of her son,[53] and favorable letters would fill the op-ed pages of New York papers.[54] Critics would write letters and articles finding fault with expert testimony,[55] circumstantial evidence,[56] the tactics of the prosecution,[57] and the institution of capital punishment.[58] Preachers would expound from the pulpit on Sundays decrying Harris's conviction and impending execution. When Harris was resentenced, he would deliver a stirring speech decrying his mistreatment at the hands of a vindictive prosecutor. A mass meeting in Harris's favor would be held at Madison Square Garden, where a petition drive would be inaugurated pleading for Harris's pardon.[59] Canvassers would take to the streets collecting signatures on the petition. Governor Flower would be presented with a petition containing the signatures of tens of thousands of registered voters. Governor Flower would succumb to the political pressure and pardon Harris or at least commute his sentence.

Articles began regularly appearing in the papers painting Mrs. Harris in the most pathetic hues, Harris in the most sympathetic tones, and the case against him in the darkest colors. The *Tribune* and *Herald* published articles describing Mrs. Harris's fruitless journey to Asbury Park, seeking exculpatory evidence for her son, and her collapse into hysterics when her every effort was stymied.[60] John MacMullen, a former teacher of Harris's, wrote the *Tribune* praising Harris's character, supporting his mother's call for a new trial, and castigating Harris's lawyers. According to MacMullen, they "proved themselves wretchedly inefficient, and in fact made hardly any defense at all."[61] Howe had a report from a phrenologist published in the paper. Dr. Edgar C. Bell had rubbed the bumps on Harris's head and pronounced him neither cruel nor cunning, and certainly not the murderous type.[62] Howe announced that he had a letter from an expert witness, Dr. Walter Scheele, who said that it was impossible to tell if Helen had morphine in her body.[63] Howe did not explain how Scheele's testimony would support a plea that Helen died because she was a morphine eater.

Rev. Thomas Dixon Jr., pastor of New York's 223rd Street Baptist Church, preached a sermon against the verdict, saying he was amazed that Harris could be found guilty when so much reasonable doubt existed.[64] In a later sermon Dixon said that "if Harris is executed, it will be a crime against civilization."[65] Dixon was a man who never left his audience in suspense as to how he felt on any subject. He would later express his views on race relations in such books as *The Leopard's Spots: A Romance of the White Man's Burden—1865–1900* and *The Clansman: An Historical Romance of the Ku Klux Klan,* which he dedicated "To the memory of a Scotch-Irish leader of the South, my uncle, Colonel Leroy McAfee, Grand Titan of the Invisible Empire of the Ku Klux Klan.[66] *The Clansman* served as the basis for D. W.

Rev. Thomas Dixon Jr., pastor of 223rd Street Baptist Church, New York City, 1889–95; pastor of the People's Church, New York City, 1895–99 (King, *Notable New Yorkers*)

Griffith's screenplay of *The Birth of a Nation,* to which Dixon wrote a sequel, *The Fall of a Nation.*

Dixon was not the only clergyman who castigated the verdict. Rev. John L. Scudder of the Jersey City Tabernacle had no doubt about Harris's guilt, but called capital punishment a "useless relic of savagery." He wanted Harris imprisoned for life.[67] Dr. David Mitchell of the Scotch Presbyterian Church in Jersey City said in a sermon that if Harris were tried in Scotland, the verdict would be "Not Proven."[68] The nationally famous evangelist Dwight L. Moody[69] organized a petition drive in Harris's favor.[70]

The most prominent clergyman in New York, Rev. Charles H. Parkhurst of the Madison Square Presbyterian Church, did not add his voice to the chorus of ministerial calls for clemency. Parkhurst had risen to fame in New York through his efforts to root out gambling and prostitution in the city and his accusations of corruption at Tammany Hall and in the New York Police Department.[71] Parkhurst's silence on the issue of Harris's impending execution should not be construed as approval. He was too busy with other matters to speak out on the conviction. During the pendency of Harris's case, Parkhurst had become dissatisfied with official apathy toward vice and had launched a lengthy campaign against it. Parkhurst had castigated the police department and retained his own investigators to expose New York City's underbelly of corruption. The police had responded by bringing criminal charges of extortion against Parkhurst's chief investigator, Charles Gardner. During Harris's posttrial proceedings, Parkhurst was locked in a war of words with Insp. Thomas Byrnes of the police department,[72] and he was preoccupied by the case against Gardner. Coincidentally Gardner had William Travers Jerome as his defense attorney and Francis L. Wellman as his prosecutor.[73] Wellman got the conviction, but Gardner eventually won the case on appeal.[74]

Howe's campaign to get a new trial for Harris began with his announcement that he had changed his mind about going to the Supreme Court of the United States and would instead move for a new trial on grounds of newly discovered evidence. He told the press that Harris had given him "the name of the druggist who used to sell Helen Potts morphine, and also the names of several of the girl's schoolmates who knew that she was a morphine eater."[75] The announcement sent reporters scampering to Asbury Park to find the druggist who sold Helen morphine, but all of the established druggists in Asbury Park vehemently denied doing any such thing.[76] When Harris was brought before Recorder Smyth for resentencing, Howe obtained a two-week delay in order to get his proofs in order. Howe intimated that he had affidavits from a mother and daughter that Helen had once overdosed the daughter on morphine and that he was trying to get affidavits from a doctor and druggist who had provided Helen with morphine. Recorder Smyth granted the delay.[77]

Howe apparently was able to enlist the aid of some fellow members of the bar. The papers made a great fanfare over A. H. Van Buren, a lawyer from Kingston, New York, who claimed to have newly discovered evidence that Helen was addicted to opium and morphine and frequently threatened to kill herself. Van Buren telegraphed Recorder Smyth, saying, "Don't resentence Harris until I see you." He rushed to New York City and had a note delivered to Smyth as Smyth sat on the bench hearing other matters. Smyth said he was capable of handling the case by himself and refused to see the man.[78] The witness Van Buren had turned up was Susan F. R. Jackson, a former principal of the Jackson Seminary, a school that Helen had attended.[79] Howe obtained an affidavit from Jackson, and it was eventually presented at the hearing on his motion for new trial.

Howe next placed ads asking Carl Haaman and Morpheus to communicate at once with him. When questioned about the ads, Howe let the press know that Haaman and Morpheus were people who could provide affidavits about Helen's drug use. It wasn't necessary to disclose Haaman's proposed testimony, but Howe said that he had received a letter from Morpheus, whose handwriting appeared to be a woman's, stating that at the appropriate time she would come forward and tell what she knew about Helen's use of morphine, including hearing Helen threaten to commit suicide by using morphine.[80] Howe also managed to alert the papers to the fact that attorney Frank Fitzsimmons had collected a mass of evidence showing Helen to be a morphine eater and proving Dr. Treverton guilty of insurance fraud.[81]

George Potts, Helen's father, tried to counter Howe's media campaign with some publicity of his own. He announced to the press that Nicoll's office had been to Asbury Park and had collected enough affidavits to conclusively refute the claim that Helen used morphine. He ridiculed the claim by pointing out that "at the trial [the defense] spent $10,000 in securing expert evidence that she never used the drug." Potts went on to say that "If Harris succeeds in getting clear in New York he will suffer for an offense in New Jersey, the penalty for which is death."[82] Mr. Potts was referring to the fact that Harris had been indicted in New Jersey for infanticide in connection with Helen's abortion, and the indictment was being held in abeyance pending the outcome of the New York prosecution.[83]

Meanwhile, Howe had not neglected other stratagems. He made an application to Governor Flower for executive clemency, and Flower requested Nicoll to forward him "a concise statement of the facts of the case, together with your opinion of the merits of the application."[84] In a blatant attempt to garner public sympathy, Harris wrote, and the *Sunday World* published, an essay titled "Carlyle Harris's Hopes," which the paper advertised as "an opportunity to study the mind of an intelligent man condemned to death."[85] Harris continued to hold forth in the Tombs for any reporter who wanted an interview, and there were many. Safe from a searching cross-examination by Wellman, he discounted and explained away any negative publicity about counter-affidavits collected by the prosecution.[86]

Finally, the day of the hearing came. At 11:00 A.M. Recorder Smyth took his seat on the bench and called court to order. Harris, looking pallid and weak, sat at counsel table between his lawyer Howe and his mother.[87] De

Lancy Nicoll himself appeared for the prosecution. The opening skirmish dealt with the admissibility of the papers Howe proffered into evidence. Howe tried to introduce a paper that he said was a copy of an affidavit from Carl Haaman. Haaman had apparently slipped into New York, given Howe an affidavit, and slipped back out without the authorities becoming aware of his presence. Then both Haaman and the original affidavit disappeared. Howe tried to authenticate a copy with the testimony of the notary public, who placed Haaman under oath, but it was not allowed into evidence. Then Nicoll made a formal objection to the legal sufficiency of all the affidavits that the defense had gathered from out of state. Howe apologized for the irregularity of the affidavits: "These affidavits were procured by the mother of the defendant, you know."

"I do not care who they were obtained by," replied Smyth, "read them and they will be considered, but you know they must be authenticated."

Howe, who had a reputation for being able to weep on demand, began to speak, his eyes filling with tears:

> To quench the spark of human life is indeed an awful responsibility. Such is the responsibility now placed on you, Recorder. So surely as anybody takes a part in taking this young man's life, so surely will he have to answer for it. The statute says that if new evidence shall be discovered subsequent to the trial a new trial shall be granted. That is simple justice.
>
> It is claimed that Helen Potts died of morphine poison. That poison was not given to her by Carlyle W. Harris. It was self-administered. Our new evidence will prove that this poor girl was in the habit of taking morphine in secret generally, but sometimes to the knowledge of others. The testimony of these others we shall read to your Honor today. If we can show you that for two or three years prior to her death she was in the habit of taking morphine, who on this earth will dare to say that the morphine which caused her death was not administered by her own hand?
>
> I learn that the District Attorney has several affidavits from the parents, relatives, and friends of Mary Helen Potts, declaring that they never knew that she took morphine or had any in her possession. They amount to nothing. If they call 999 witnesses to swear that they never saw her take morphine, and if we call one who was reliable, to testify that to his or her certain knowledge she had taken morphine, as he or she had seen her do so, the evidence of the 999, being purely negative, would be of no account. We intend

to bring forward witnesses, discovered by Mrs. Harris, who have not only seen Mary Helen Potts taken morphine herself but administer it to others.

With this opening completed, Howe began to read the affidavits one by one. The first affidavit came from Mary M. Frenette, who deposed that she was the mother of Ethel M. Harris (no relation to the defendant), that Ethel was a friend of Helen's, and that one morning after a visit from Helen, she had trouble waking Ethel. After heroic effort, she woke Ethel, who refused to say what was wrong. Later that evening Ethel confessed that the evening before she had taken a pill Helen gave her.

The next affidavit came from Ethel M. Harris, who recounted the incident described by her mother and went on to say that she later went to Ocean Grove to visit Helen. While they were out driving, Ethel complained of a headache and Helen offered her another pill. Ethel at first declined, but Helen insisted. Helen said the second pill would work better than the first and assured Ethel that she, Helen, had taken as many as three pills at a time. Helen then took the pill in Ethel's presence.

The affidavit of Susan F. R. Jackson, the former principal of a young lady's seminary, said that Jackson had Helen as a student. Helen told Jackson that she suffered from headaches and took morphine to combat them. Helen further said that the morphine was prescribed for her by an uncle who was a doctor. Helen was an unruly, quick-tempered student, and once when threatened with being sent home, she told Jackson, "I will not go home; my home is a perfect hell upon earth. I will kill myself first. I will take a dose of opium before I will go home to such a home." Helen frequently asked to go out to a pharmacist's office to get morphine for her headaches, and she once gave a pill to a fellow student who complained of a headache. The fellow student said that the pill cured her headache and made her sleep.

The affidavit of Mary Lewis alleged that she was a domestic in the home of Dr. Treverton while Treverton was treating Helen and that Helen seemed perfectly healthy except for the fact that she slept most of the time and twitched her fingers. Helen once asked if Mary used opium. Mary denied using opium and Helen told her there was no harm in it. Mary frequently saw Helen take pills from a pillbox she carried.

John J. Pratt, a carriage painter from Scranton, gave an affidavit that while he was working for Dr. Treverton, he frequently saw Helen. Helen acted drowsy and appeared to be under the influence of something. On one occasion, when she came in from horseback riding, she left a pillbox in the stable. Pratt looked in the pillbox, and it contained a white powder.

Howe next read the affidavits of a number of Scranton residents who tended to discredit Dr. Treverton's testimony about Helen's botched abortion by swearing that they had seen her riding horses and playing tennis. This was supplemented by an affidavit from a Dr. George B. Reynouls to the effect that Helen couldn't have ridden horses or played tennis if she was recovering from a botched abortion.

Miss Frankie Wallace's affidavit claimed that she overheard Helen telling another girl at the Comstock School that she, Helen, took morphine for insomnia. Wallace swore that she was an invalid and had studied up on medicine and was familiar with the symptoms of opium poisoning, and that she frequently saw Helen exhibiting the signs of opium poisoning.

Howe then read affidavits from jurors Crawford Mason and Joseph Bell that if they had heard Howe's testimony about Helen's morphine use, they would have acquitted Harris, and affidavits from jurors Charles Hines and S. B. W. McKee said that the testimony might have affected their verdicts.

Howe next presented an affidavit from Joseph R. Lefferts, who swore he worked as a druggist's clerk in Asbury Park in 1890, and he said Helen was a steady customer of his. He sold her a dozen lots of one-quarter grain morphine pills and on three occasions he had sold her as much as a dram. He hadn't come forward with this information during the trial because he didn't want to get involved.

The last affidavit came from Harris himself, and it was a study in self-serving rhetoric. He said he did not fault Jerome and Taylor for keeping him off the stand, but he should have been allowed to testify: "As an innocent man, wrongfully, and cruelly, and unjustly convicted, I do boldly say to you, Recorder Smyth, as my earthly judge, that if I had been permitted to take the stand and give my testimony, and consequent explanation of the facts arraigned against me, I would have been acquitted."

When it was Nicoll's turn to speak, he characterized the evidence presented by Howe as falling into two categories—hearsay and perjury. He then read into the record counter-affidavits that fairly impeached the evidence of all the affidavits. Frenette and Harris were proven to be disreputable, and to be totally unknown to Helen's parents or any of her friends. Jackson retracted most of her more salacious statements in an interview given to Dilworth Choate. Lewis was a Salvation Army reject, and Pratt had a reputation in Scranton for being a liar. Wallace was totally unknown to any of Helen's friends, and Lefferts had just been arrested for keeping a disorderly house. Further, the Potts family was out of the state of New Jersey when Lefferts was working in the drugstore. Nicoll backed up his assertions with an avalanche of affidavits. Nicoll made one telling point on the issue of Harris's being allowed to testify: If Harris's testimony could have cleared him, he should have put that testimony into his affidavit for a new trial.

Then Harris spoke. If none of Helen's family knew Frenette and her daughter, neither did Harris, and he certainly couldn't have bought their testimony. He was broke, and Howe had taken him on as a charity case. He didn't know that he was allowed to put his exculpatory testimony in his affidavit. When he finished speaking, he collapsed back into his chair and Howe made a concluding argument to the court. When Howe finished speaking, Mrs. Harris jumped to her feet.

"Recorder," she cried, "can I speak?"

"You cannot." With that rebuke, she broke down and had to be taken to another room, where she cried and raved for a full fifteen minutes before regaining her composure. She returned to the courtroom just in time to hear Smyth adjourn the court.

The hearing was held on February 29, 1893, and Smyth did not release his order on the motion for two weeks. In the interim, both sides continued to press newly obtained affidavits upon Smyth.[88] On March 15, the day Smyth had set for the announcement of his ruling on the motion, six hundred people crowded the General Sessions Building to hear his announcement. They went away disappointed when he announced that he was going to withhold the decision until the following morning.[89] The next morning he released his order, weighing and evaluating the evidence of each affidavit presented. In the order he "pulled to pieces every affidavit made in behalf of [Harris]"[90] and denied the motion for new trial. Smyth summed up his 15,000-word decision in the following language: "A careful examination of all the facts and circumstances established upon the trial of this case as well as of the additional facts which have been presented upon this motion by way of newly-discovered evidence, or so much of such evidence as could have been legally admitted upon the trial, it would not have changed the verdict which was then rendered against him."[91]

Ironically, Smyth found Harris's affidavit to provide one of the strongest pieces of evidence that Helen was not addicted to morphine. Harris was a trained medical man, intimately familiar with Helen, in a position to closely observe her, and unable to discover any sign whatsoever that she was addicted to morphine or any other drug. "To my mind," Smyth wrote, "this is a strong and most convincing circumstance, that it was impossible that the deceased should have been addicted to the use of morphine and the defendant not observe it."[92]

CHAPTER THIRTEEN

The Raines Commission

Harris had lost in the Court of Appeals, and he had lost the motion for new trial. Neither defeat should have been surprising. As for the appeal, the trial had been "clean"—that is to say it was tried by able, intelligent lawyers before a competent, well-respected judge who had committed no serious errors. As for the newly discovered evidence, if it had been of any real value, two such skilled attorneys as Jerome and Taylor would have discovered it and presented it at the trial. For Howe, the hearing on the motion for new trial was aimed as much at public opinion as at Recorder Smyth. Howe felt his best chance of saving Harris lay in Gov. Roswell P. Flower's office with a petition for pardon, and almost everything he had done after taking the case was calculated to recruit as much public opinion as he could in favor of his client. He had two more stages on which to play out a melodramatic plea for sympathy—Harris's resentencing hearing and the mass meeting he planned for Madison Square Garden.

The plan for the mass meeting hit a snag when Howe couldn't book Madison Square Garden. Undeterred, he booked the Cooper Union,[1] the site of the famous antislavery speech that served as Abraham Lincoln's launching pad for his presidential campaign. "I do not know who will preside," Howe told the press, "but you may depend upon it that the chairman will be a lawyer of national fame. Joseph H. Choate, John E. Parsons, James C. Carter and other prominent men have been suggested to me, but the project is still nebulous."[2] In tandem with Howe's announcement of a mass meeting, Mrs. Harris sent a long, rambling letter to the *New York Times* criticizing Recorder Smyth's denial of a new trial and begging the public to do three things: attend the mass meeting, write letters to the papers and to her supporting a pardon for her son, and sign petitions for Harris's pardon.[3]

Joseph Choate, the premier trial lawyer of the age,[4] threw a pail of cold water on the mass meeting project when he told the press that he would not preside. Choate said he supposed that Harris was guilty and he left the whole matter of Harris's pardon up to Governor Flower.[5] A further dose of cold water came from the press. A *New York Times* editorial called the proposed mass meeting "a violation of public decency" and said, "The attempt to bully the Governor, by a false showing of public opinion, is an outrage upon civilization."[6] The *Brooklyn Daily Eagle* characterized the mass meeting as mob rule. Saying that a mass meeting could do nothing but appeal to sentiment, the *Eagle* concluded that "The unanimous decision of disinterested and expert judges of evidence that the prisoner is a murderer, should be enough to satisfy everyone except his mother."[7] Almost too late, Howe realized that he needed to find a graceful way to abandon his plan for a mass meeting.

Harris himself busily assisted the public relations campaign. He saw an estimated twenty reporters per day, holding forth on his innocence, the unfairness of his trial, and the speech he planned to make when he was brought before the court for resentencing. He and Howe even staged a conference for the benefit of the press.

"They don't dare to give me a new trial," he told Howe. "They seem to be afraid. They know that I would be acquitted. But when I am taken to court on Monday I'll make Rome howl. I'll lash them. When I was last in court the Recorder kindly allowed me to speak on sufferance. This time I shall stand on my statutory right. They dare not stop me. I will not die with my mouth shut. I shall vindicate myself. Some people will hear things they won't like."[8]

Harris's threat to "make Rome howl" was an allusion to the popular antebellum play, *The Gladiator,* by Robert Montgomery Bird, a tragic tale of Spartacus's slave rebellion against Rome. Just before his final battle with the Roman general Crassus, Spartacus is told of the crucifixion of thousands of his captured slave-soldiers. In response, Spartacus vows to make Rome howl because of the vengeance he takes. He then leads the remnant of his army into battle. Knowing that all is lost, Spartacus believes he can win a Pyrrhic victory by personally killing Crassus. Spartacus cuts his way to a face-to-face confrontation with Crassus before being overwhelmed and killed by superior numbers. Crassus, in deference to the gladiator-general's courage, orders that he be buried as a nobleman.[9] Harris seemed to be saying that he realized his case was lost, but like Spartacus, he would vindicate himself with his attack on the New York authorities. This allusion would be lost on Gilded Age readers, who would more readily associate Harris's statement with the vow of Gen. William Tecumseh Sherman, who wrote that he would "make Georgia howl" when he embarked upon his March to the Sea.[10]

"Harris," Howe replied, "I want you to act according to your own judgment. I place no restrictions on your words or actions in court. I shall not take responsibility."[11]

Harris continued to accuse Helen of drug use. He told one reporter,

Only day before yesterday a woman called on me and told a startling story. Her niece, she said, was an intimate friend of my poor wife in Asbury Park in the summer of 1889. She used morphine habitually, and one day my informant surprised her dividing with Helen the contents of a bottle that was marked with a skull and crossbones. The niece is now in an asylum, a mental and physical wreck from the use of morphine. But what is the use of dragging the lady's name into the matter now? I should only bring unpleasant notoriety upon her and her unfortunate niece. Dilworth Choate or some other person from the District Attorney's Office would call on my informant and then make an affidavit that she completely retracted all she had said. This case has been a triumph of Choate over justice. But wait until Monday. If my strength does not desert me he shall hear something from my lips.[12]

Harris produced a letter signed by Susan F. R. Jackson that purportedly refuted Dilworth Choate's affidavit about his interview with her. In the letter she said she refused to talk to Choate and then went on to say that she told Choate pretty much exactly what Choate said in his affidavit but gave explanations for why she said it. For example, Choate had sworn that Jackson told him she never said anything to Helen's parents about Helen's drug use. Her letter admitted she never spoke to Helen's parents but gave as an excuse that she only needed to report the drug use "if I had visual evidence and could prove it by one who was present at the time."[13]

Finally, the day of resentencing came, and the man who had appeared so strong and confident in the Tombs came to court beleaguered and weak. When asked, as the law requires, if he had any cause to show why sentence should not be imposed upon him, he gave a lengthy speech in which he excoriated everyone associated with the prosecution, especially Dilworth Choate and Francis L. Wellman. He castigated Wellman so vociferously that Wellman got up and left the courtroom during that part of the speech. He claimed that assistant district attorney Vernon M. Davis had coerced Mae Schofield into giving a false deposition. He complained that he had not been allowed to cross-examine the affidavits the prosecution had offered in opposition to his motion for new trial. In his concern over this point, he forgot to mention the prosecution could not cross-examine his affidavits either. He claimed that the jury had been "sandbagged" by technical terms. Howe wept at appropriate points in the oration.[14] According to the *New York Times*, "[Harris] stood at the bar trembling like an aspen, saving himself from collapse by frequent drinks of brandy and water, and talked as though he were a lawyer arguing the case of another." The *Times* characterized his speech as "a sarcastic, unimpassioned, critical analysis of the case against him."[15]

The speech was not all dry logic. As he neared the end of his speech, Harris spoke of the jurors who gave affidavits saying they might have changed their verdicts had they heard the testimony about Helen's drug use.[16] He turned to Howe and asked that the affidavit of one of those jurors, Crawford Mason, be placed in his coffin with him. Harris thanked Howe for taking up his case without hope of compensation and gave the lawyer a set of his cufflinks as the only thing of value he had. Howe wept appropriately.[17] Then came an odd parallel between Wellman's summation and Harris's speech. He ended his speech with an account of his visit to Helen's grave, saying that he secretly went there shortly after the funeral. He said:

> I little thought that I should never visit it again; and yet today, standing by the brink of another grave, of my own, I thank God that in the light of this new testimony he who will may read inscribed upon that grave, your Honor, not "Suicide," but "At Rest." Perhaps when my poor body and brain are laid at rest someone may mark that spot with a little slab of stone. I ask that there be engraved there in justice to those men who sat there a year ago "we would not if we had known," and signed "The Jury." I will leave the rest of my epitaph to Your Honor.[18]

Of course, at the time Harris spoke, only Wellman and Howe knew of Howe's connection to the two conclusions. There is reason to believe that Howe wrote the script for Harris's account of his visit. One can only speculate whether Harris would have closed his speech with a graveside visit if he had known that Howe had urged Wellman to use the same conclusion. Smyth asked Howe if he had anything to say, and Howe declined to speak. He had already spoken through the carefully stage-managed speech of his client. It was now Smyth's turn to speak.

> My duty is made doubly painful in your case because you are undoubtedly a man of extraordinary intelligence, and I regret to see you standing in the position in which you do today. No one regrets it more sincerely than I do, and no one regrets more sincerely than I do that my sworn duty impels me to say that after listening to you with patience through all you have had to urge in your own behalf, I still adhere to what I stated upon your motion, that the evidence of your guilt was overwhelming in my view.[19]

Smyth then sentenced Harris to death by electrocution and set his execution date for the week beginning May 8, 1893. As Harris sat back at counsel table, Smyth left the courtroom. Nicoll, Wellman, and the rest of the district attorney's staff were close on Smyth's heels as spectators mobbed Harris to shake his hand. Harris's custodians separated him from the well-wishers, manacled him, and escorted him out of the courtroom.[20]

A crowd had formed outside the courthouse waiting to catch a glimpse of the condemned man as he was escorted back to the Tombs. Someone yelled "Lynch him!" as Harris and his guards emerged from the courthouse. Someone else shouted "Harris! Three cheers for Harris!" and the cheer was taken up by hundreds of voices. Harris took off his hat and bowed to the crowd.[21] As Harris and his guards walked down Centre Street toward the Tombs, mobs of cheering people surrounded them. The cheering kept up all the way down the street to the Tombs and continued even after Harris had been taken inside.

"If those people think I am guilty why don't they lynch me instead of cheering me?" Harris wanted to know. After being locked in his cell, he gave an interview to a *New York Times* reporter. "I am happier today," he said, "than I have been for two years, because I have been able to free my

Roswell P. Flower, thirtieth
governor of New York, 1892–94
(King, *Notable New Yorkers*)

mind and establish my innocence before the public. You heard them cheering me. It was sweet music to my ears." When the reporter caught up with Howe, the lawyer said that the mass meeting idea had been abandoned because Harris did not want it. Howe declared that he would go to Governor Flower with a monster petition for pardon within the next two weeks.[22]

As Harris made his way under guard from the Tombs to Sing Sing, Howe's public relations campaign got into full swing. Howe announced to the *Herald* that he had received hundreds of letters supporting Harris and that one of them came from a retired justice of the Supreme Court, Frothingham Fish. Justice Fish had written saying that although there was considerable evidence against Harris, it was not sufficient to remove all reasonable doubt, and for that reason "I therefore join in asking His Excellency the Governor of the State to interfere with the execution of the sentence."[23] Five hundred petition distributors were recruited and sent onto the streets of New York to collect signatures on petitions asking the governor to "grant the said Carlyle W. Harris such clemency as may be deemed just."[24] By March 26, less than a week after the resentencing, Howe was reporting that they had already collected nearly thirty thousand signatures.[25] Letters to the editor flooded the New York papers, most of them supportive of Harris. One of them threatened to kill Dilworth Choate and Francis Wellman. Instead of affixing a signature, the writer drew a picture of a heart impaled by a knife.[26]

Upon his arrival at Sing Sing, Harris was taken to the Death House, which was on the prison grounds just south of the main building. It was separated from the other housing units but was connected by an archway to the office of Principle Keeper Connaughton. The one-story building had a hallway with a row of eight cells divided into two cellblocks consisting of four cells. In the middle of the hallway between the two cellblocks a corridor led off at a right angle to a smaller building, which housed the electric chair. The cells were not built into the wall, but they were huge cages eight feet wide and ten feet high. The front wall of each cage was hinged and served as a door. The ceiling loomed fifteen feet overhead.

The first cell one came to upon entering the hallway was designated Cell No. 1, and the cells were numbered sequentially, with the farther cell being Cell No. 8. Cells No. 1, 6, 7, and 8 had no tenants when Harris arrived.[27] The keepers locked him in Cell No. 8, which had recently been vacated by the execution of a notorious killer known as Murderer Mellvaine.[28]

His mother announced that if Harris should be executed, she would insist on being allowed to witness it. Warden Brown insisted that she would do no such thing.[29] For the rest of Harris's stay in the Death House, the *Herald* would print every detail that could be gleaned about Harris's living conditions, deportment, and state of mind; and the details usually cast Harris in a favorable light.[30] Among other things, the *Herald* reported on his sleeping habits, his appetite, the books he was reading, and the favorable attitude of the keepers toward him.[31]

On another front, Sen. Henry J. Coggeshall introduced a bill in the New York Senate "providing that a defendant convicted of a capital offense may take an appeal from the decision of a judge refusing to grant a new trial on the production of new evidence." Coggeshall initially denied that he introduced the bill to provide relief for Carlyle Harris, saying he thought on general principles that a person convicted of a capital offense should be entitled to the relief the bill provided.[32] Eventually he admitted that Howe had prevailed upon him to introduce the bill.[33] On general principles, such a bill was a good idea, but passing it to benefit a single defendant was not. In any event, it provided no relief for Harris. It languished in the legislature until it was finally defeated almost two months after Harris's execution.[34]

As Harris bided his time in the Death House, Howe's public relations campaign began to snowball. Anne E. Inman wrote a letter to the *Herald* saying that she had attended a séance in St. Louis, Missouri, and gotten a message from beyond the grave. Helen Potts's spirit had come to her and told her that Harris was innocent. Helen purportedly told her, "I want to let you all know that my husband is innocent. He did not poison me. I took the deadly drug myself. It is true we did live unhappily together. I am in darkness and very miserable, but my husband is not guilty."[35] Mrs. Harris pled her case with Richard Croker, who had begun his career as a prizefighter and Tammany Hall muscleman, gotten himself elected coroner, and eventually became Boss Tweed's successor as head of Tammany Hall.[36] There was much speculation that Mrs. Harris had convinced Croker to prevail upon Flower to commute Harris's sentence,[37] but he squelched the speculation by announcing, "I have made no request in re-lation to the case, and it is not my purpose to interfere in any way con-cerning it."[38]

Howe next wrote Flower asking for a full clemency hearing on April 17. Flower wrote back saying Howe could have his hearing on April 10 at 3:30 P.M.[39] Flower grew up on a farm in Jefferson County, New York, where he earned a name for himself as an accomplished hunter and a crack shot. He married money, moved to New York, formed a brokerage firm on the New York Stock Exchange, and became a mover and shaker in Democratic pol-itics. Although derided by his opponents as a "flamboyant millionaire," he won his first public office by defeating William Waldorf Astor for a seat in Congress from the Eleventh District of New York. In 1891 he won the election for governor on the Tammany Hall ticket. Although he served a single term as governor, he remained active in Democratic politics until his untimely death in 1899.[40]

Howe saw to it that the clemency hearing got lavish publicity, and a huge crowd of spectators was expected to attend the hearing.[41] Howe did not show up for the hearing. Around noon on the morning of the scheduled hearing, he wired Flower saying he could not attend due to engagements in court. He asked that the hearing be postponed. Flower notified him that the hearing was canceled,[42] and he didn't intend to reset it.[43] When Howe heard the news, he managed to get the murder case he was set to try postponed and caught a train for the capital,[44] arriving that evening. He pleaded with Flower for five minutes of his time on Tuesday, and Flower granted him a brief interview on that day.[45] Howe presented Flower with 110 letters, many from scientists and members of the bench and bar, urging clemency for Harris.[46] Howe also tried to ramp up the pressure of public opinion upon Flower with petitions containing thirty-five thousand signatures, but the mounting pressure seemed to be having a negative effect. Flower let it be known that he disapproved of Howe's "buttonholing people on street corners to secure their names on petitions." Pundits were predicting that Flower would not interfere with Harris's sentence.[47]

District Attorney Nicoll and Recorder Smyth swam against the tide of public opinion by writing letters to Flower urging him to deny clemency. Nicoll wrote a lengthy letter describing the course of the prosecution from indictment to Smyth's denial of the motion for new trial and concluded by saying that every court that had reviewed the case had found "no facts or circumstances . . . to justify any interference with the execution of the judgment pronounced against the prisoner." Smyth's letter was shorter, but it arrived at the same conclusion: "I am forced to the conviction that no legal or sufficient reason exists against the enforcement of the judgment pronounced against the defendant."[48]

One newspaper reporter for the *Herald* swam against the tide of favorable press Harris was getting. The reporter had discovered Matilda Bergston, a twenty-four-year-old Swedish immigrant who had worked for Frances McCready Harris as a serving girl in 1889 immediately after Tilly Benson left to have her baby. Though Bergston had been in America for several years, she was not fluent in English and consequently was very shy. Harris took an instant liking to her and treated her very well until one night he entered her bedroom by use of a duplicate key and forced himself upon her. When she told him she had become pregnant, he promised to marry her; when her pregnancy could no longer be concealed, he promised to take care of her if she would just go away. A few days before Harris married Helen, Matilda had his child in a charity hospital, gave it into the custody of another woman, and found another job as a domestic servant in Brooklyn. She had been working at that job for five months when she was notified that her baby had died. When Harris was indicted, Matilda told her story to the district attorney, and he had her arrested as a material witness. She sat in jail until the district attorney decided not to call her as a witness at trial.[49]

As Flower procrastinated over making his decision, efforts to lobby him continued. Mrs. Harris went to the governor's office and was allowed to see him. She spent a half hour pleading for her son's life, and he assured her that he would give the matter his careful consideration and have a decision by April 25.[50] Dr. Hugh S. Kinmouth, who had given Howe an affidavit saying he sold Helen morphine, got an audience with Flower and repeated his allegations against Helen. He also declared that the affidavits of the district attorney impeaching his testimony were "utterly false."[51]

The very night that Kinmouth met with Flower, something happened that changed the situation and gave Harris new hope that he might escape the electric chair—two inmates, Frank W. Roehl and Thomas Pallister, escaped from the Death House at Sing Sing. After overpowering the keepers, they escaped through a trapdoor in the roof of the Death House, and Harris loudly proclaimed that he had declined an invitation to go with them.[52] Harris wrote a letter describing the escape attempt, but the soon-to-be

Aerial view of Sing Sing, early 1900s (Courtesy of the Library of Congress)

ex-Warden Brown refused to let it be published. The contents of Harris's letter remain a mystery, but speculation at the time centered around the possibility that Harris contradicted the official version of what had happened.[53] There can be little doubt that it contained a melodramatic description of how Harris valiantly refused to join in the escape.

Howe began to proclaim loudly that Harris's refusal to escape made it almost certain that Flower's decision would be favorable.[54] Flower certainly felt some heat as a result of Harris's purported refusal to escape. He decided to do what many executives do when faced with a difficult decision—delegate. Howe had been lobbying for a commission to take testimony on the issue of the newly discovered evidence,[55] so why not delegate the decision to a commissioner? Of course, the final decision would be Flower's, but he would have the excuse that he was merely following the recommendation of the commissioner. Flower announced that he was appointing Sen. George Raines to take testimony on the application for clemency.[56] Raines was an accomplished criminal trial lawyer who had served two terms as district attorney of Monroe County, New York. Resigning his post as district attorney to run for the state senate, he won election on the Democratic ticket.[57] Given his background, talent, and experience, Raines was an excellent choice to serve as commissioner. Whether Flower made an excellent choice in deciding to appoint a commission is open to question.

Shortly after the announcement, some information came to light that, had it been known sooner, might have led Flower to deny clemency without referring the case to a commissioner. J. L. Osmond, who had been sentenced to death for the murder of his wife, was returned to New York for resentencing after the Court of Appeals upheld his conviction and death sentence. While Osmond was in the Tombs awaiting resentencing, a *New York Times* reporter interviewed him about the escape. According to Osmond, when Keeper Hulse opened Roehl's cell door to give him his supper, Roehl threw some sort of powder into Hulse's face, grabbed him by the throat, and pushed him against Pallister's cell. Pallister grabbed Hulse's arm and took the keeper's revolver. They got the keys and locked Hulse in a cell, and then they ambushed Keeper Murphy when he entered the Death House. After securing Murphy, they made some tea to fortify themselves for their run. They invited Osmond and another inmate to join them. Both men declined. Osmond explained his refusal: "I knew that they were desperate men and if anybody interfered with them they would surely kill him. I thought to myself, I must go to the chair for the crimes with which I have been charged, and I did not want to go before my Maker with any more blood on my hands." The two then demanded Osmond's coat and vest, which he willingly handed over. Rather than inviting Harris to join them, they threatened to kill him and robbed him of his cigarettes. Then the two worked for some three hours trying to get out through the bathroom window before they thought to climb the ladder to the roof, where they found a trapdoor, which they used to gain their freedom.[58]

The two escapees were considered dangerous in the extreme. Roehl was an ax murderer and Pallister had shot and killed a police officer.[59] The authorities began a massive manhunt that continued for several weeks until they found the two escapees' bullet-riddled bodies lying on the bank of the Hudson River five miles from Sing Sing. Investigators never determined who killed the two men.[60]

On April 24 Commissioner Raines met with District Attorney Nicoll and William F. Howe to outline the procedure for his inquiry into the matter of clemency for Carlyle Harris. Raines directed Howe to begin the hearing by producing the witnesses upon whose affidavits he had relied for the new trial. They would be examined by Howe and cross-examined by the district attorney, and Howe would be allowed to present any further testimony he desired. After Howe finished presenting his evidence, the district attorney would present the testimony and evidence of rebuttal witnesses, but he would not rehash testimony that had been given at the trial.[61]

The very next day Commissioner Raines began taking testimony in a courtroom in City Hall.[62] Howe appeared for Harris, who remained at Sing Sing, and Francis Wellman appeared for the prosecution with the assistance of deputy district attorney George Gordon Battle.[63] The timing of the hearing seriously hampered both Raines's inquiry and another murder case that Wellman was supposed to try. The Raines Commission hearing began on April 25 and ended on April 30. Wellman's other trial, *People v. Robert W. Buchanan*, began on March 21 and ended on April 27.

Buchanan was another doctor who had purportedly murdered his secret wife with morphine. The case was very similar to Harris's case, except that where Helen was young and beautiful, Dr. Buchanan's wife was old and the only thing attractive about her was her wealth. Helen was the picture of innocence, while Mrs. Buchanan made her fortune as the madam of a bordello. Harris claimed Helen was just a friend; Dr. Buchanan passed his wife off as his housekeeper. Harris's case was hard enough to obtain a conviction, but Buchanan's was even harder. Mrs. Buchanan did not have the telltale symmetrically contracted pupils. This was explained at trial by a witness who testified that Buchanan had told him "Harris was a [expletive deleted] fool. He didn't know how to mix his drugs. If he had put a little atropine with his morphine, it would have dilated the pupil of at least one of his victim's eyes, and no doctor could have deposed to death by morphine."[64] As luck would have it, De Lancy Nicoll had decided to serve as Buchanan's lead prosecutor,[65] and Wellman could shuttle back and forth between the two trials.[66]

Mrs. Anna B. Carman took the stand as Harris's first witness, and Wellman immediately began objecting to Howe's questions. Commissioner Raines advised the lawyers that he was not going to follow the strict rules of evidence and allowed the testimony. Mrs. Carman testified that in 1889 she lived in Ocean Grove across the street from the Pottses, and she also knew Carl Haaman. She said that in April 1892 Mrs. Potts came to her and told her that she hoped Harris would not be executed because she had a doubt in her mind about his guilt. If Harris were executed, it would drive her crazy because she always suspected that Helen had taken her own life. Mrs. Carman also attested to the good character of Dr. Kinmouth, who had given an affidavit in favor of Harris.

Mrs. Carman's daughter, Grace, testified next. She said that she heard Mrs. Potts make the same statements that her mother had described about the possibility of Helen committing suicide. Miss Carman was a very good friend of Helen's, but she never saw Helen take morphine and never heard anything said about Helen taking morphine. When the prosecution's turn came to put on witnesses, Mrs. Potts vehemently denied having any such conversions with either of the Carman ladies. The testimony of the two Carmans took up the entire morning, and that afternoon, Anna Waddell testified that Helen had given her a morphine pill.

Francis Lange, an Asbury Park druggist, testified that in 1890 he twice sold a half-dozen quarter-grain morphine pills to a young lady in Asbury Park. He didn't know the girl, but he had seen her in the company of Carlyle Harris, and she had asked him not to tell "Carl" about her purchases. He had gone to Howe's office and been shown a picture of Helen, and he testified that the picture resembled the girl who bought the morphine from him, but he added that pictures can be deceiving. Wellman pounced on that statement in cross-examination.

"But you said that photographs were deceiving?" Wellman asked, sarcasm dripping from his tone of voice.

"Yes," Lange replied, "but I didn't mean this one," indicating a photograph Howe had produced in evidence.

"Which ones did you mean?" Wellman insisted.

"Oh, others in general," Lange evaded.

"What particular one?"

"Oh, my own," was the best Lange could do for a reply, provoking a horse laugh from the audience. Wellman continued his cross-examination to the point that, according to the *Tribune*, he "got the young man so mixed up that he didn't seem to know where he was 'at.'"[67]

The last witness of the day was Mrs. Ida Bayha, who had worked as a domestic servant for Helen's aunt from December 1886 to March 1887. She testified that she bought arsenic wafers for Helen. Mrs. Bayha said that when she warned Helen against taking the wafers, Helen replied that she took them to get a handsome complexion. Wellman asked two questions on cross-examination.

"That was six years ago?"

"Yes, sir."

"When Helen Potts was fifteen years old?"

"Yes, sir."[68]

Dr. Hugh Kinmouth testified as the first witness on April 26. He said that in the summer of 1890 Helen came into his drugstore with two other women and asked for morphine pills for her mother. Kinmouth wrote a prescription for the pills and had his clerk, Henry M. Woolman, fill the prescription and give the pills to Helen. On cross-examination Kinmouth admitted to having been arrested for the illegal sale of liquor in his store. He blamed his arrest on one of his clerks. After Wellman wrung this embarrassing admission from Kinmouth, he challenged the doctor to produce corroboration for his claims.

"When did you see the Potts prescription last?" Wellman wanted to know.

"Only yesterday. It is in my book at Asbury Park," which Kinmouth had thoughtfully neglected to bring with him to court.

"In what part of the book?"

Despite his claim that he had seen the prescription "only yesterday," the best Kinmouth could do for an answer was: "Between the covers."[69] Kinmouth followed up this evasive answer by being unable to give Wellman the date of the prescription. Wellman then forced Kinmouth to admit that he may have told several people that he never sold Helen morphine. Kinmouth explained his prior inconsistent statements by saying that he believed the morphine was for Helen's mother. Wellman hectored Kinmouth into admitting that he lied to one person when he told a Mr. King that he never sold Helen morphine. Wellman pursued this admission by violating one of the Ten Commandments of Cross-Examination, which states that the examiner should never ask "Why?"[70]

"Why did you tell that lie?"

"Because it is the duty of a physician to refuse to disclose the weaknesses and failings of his patients."[71] On the surface, Kinmouth gave a plausible explanation, but it had problems. First, assuming he was telling the truth about selling morphine to Helen, she wasn't his patient, she was his customer. Second, there is a marked difference between saying "It's none of your business" and lying.

Commissioner Raines asked whether Kinmouth could identify the prescription he wrote for Mrs. Potts. Kinmouth said he couldn't, but he promised to search his records and bring the prescription in on the following Friday.

Susan F. R. Jackson testified next. She said that once when she threatened to send Helen home, the girl exclaimed, "I am going to drown myself or cut my throat or take opium or something of the kind. My home is a hell on earth!"[72] Jackson admitted on cross-examination that she did not know that Helen ever took morphine.

Howe then called Henry M. Woolman, who corroborated Kinmouth's testimony. On cross-examination Wellman surprised Woolman by producing a copy of a letter that Woolman had written Kinmouth. The facts recited in Woolman's letter were in hopeless conflict with the facts Woolman had testified to on direct examination,[73] and Wellman fully exploited those contradictions. The press reported that Wellman got Woolman "completely tangled up in his testimony and he contradicted himself several times."[74]

Ethel Harris, who was not related to Carlyle Harris, was the next witness, and she testified that Helen had given her morphine pills. On cross-examination Wellman asked her whether she had registered under assumed names in numerous hotels with different men. Harris refused to answer questions, citing her Fifth Amendment privilege against self-incrimination. Harris's mother was present in the courtroom but did not testify.

The final witness of the day was Alexandrine Le Brun, who testified that she was a governess at the Comstock School while Helen was there, and Helen was not the bright, popular girl everyone else said she was. Le Brun characterized Helen as a dull, listless pupil. Le Brun said that Helen was often irritable and complained of headaches and that she took pills and powders for her headaches. Le Brun did not know what was in the powders and pills, and she certainly could not say that they contained morphine.

And so the testimony continued. One witness who was prominent in his absence was Joseph H. Lefferts, the pharmacy clerk who had given an affidavit that he had sold large lots of morphine to Helen a half-dozen times. At the beginning of the hearing the district attorney's office had produced affidavits refuting his testimony and had announced that should he show up in New York City to testify, he would be arrested for perjury. When Howe rested, the prosecution put on a spirited rebuttal. Miss Day, the principal of the Comstock School, took the stand to testify about Helen's cheerful, bright personality and to say that there was nothing about her to even hint that she might be a morphine user.

"After she was dead," Miss Day said, "we found no medicines of any kind in her room except the box of pills which bore the initials of Carlyle W. Harris."

Howe had little success cross-examining Miss Day: "Isn't it possible that Miss Potts might have obtained medicine outside without your knowledge?" Starting a question with the phrase "Isn't it possible" is a standard defense tactic that is sometimes successful when trying to get the jury to agree that a reasonable doubt exists, but such a tactic would probably have little effect on Commissioner Raines.

Miss Day rose to the challenge: "Yes, sir, but it is not probable. It was against the rule for any scholar to go out unattended, and from what I know of Miss Potts she was not a girl to break the rules of the school."[75]

Assistant Principal Reed also testified to Helen's good character and the complete absence of any signs that she might be addicted to morphine. Then she spoke of the night Helen died. "I met the girl on the stairs a few hours before she died. She then told me that she had been given some medicine by the doctor which required that she should not be disturbed after retiring. 'He gave me the same kind of medicine once before,' she said to me, 'but he told me afterward that it did not have the desired effect because I was aroused too soon.'" Upon hearing this, Howe jumped to his feet in surprise. Everyone in the courtroom knew that when Helen spoke of "the doctor," she meant Harris. He interrupted Reed's direct examination:

"Miss Reed, you didn't testify to these facts at the trial of Harris?" Howe interjected.

"No, sir," she replied.

"Did you tell the District Attorney of the occurrence?"

"I did, sir."[76] Wellman had failed to find any lawful way to get this hearsay before the jury at Harris's trial, but he happily put it before Commissioner Raines, who had suspended the rules of evidence.

True to his promise, Dr. Kinmouth returned to the courtroom with a prescription book containing seven thousand prescriptions written in his store during 1889 and 1890. He assured Commissioner Raines that Helen's prescription was in there somewhere, but he couldn't quite pinpoint it. He pointed out three different prescriptions as possibly being Helen's prescription. Wellman put on a number of witnesses who testified that they would not believe Kinmouth under oath. When James Watson, the Asbury Park assessor, testified that he had heard a number of people say Kinmouth's testimony was bought and paid for, Mrs. Harris erupted, "Oh! How can you?"

Commissioner Raines was severe. "If you speak another time, Mrs. Harris, I shall have you put out of the room."

Against all expectation, Joseph H. Lefferts walked into the courtroom ready to testify. He outlined the circumstances of his purported drug sales to Helen, totaling 150 to 200 grains of the drug. He remained cool and unruffled through most of his cross-examination, denying that he had told anyone that he had been paid $500 for his testimony and swearing that his employer knew full well he sold morphine without a prescription. This was rebutted by the affidavit of an Asbury Park lawyer's clerk named Cook, who swore that Lefferts had bragged about earning $500 to lie under oath, and the affidavit of the Asbury Park druggist for whom Lefferts had worked. Druggist Van Mater swore that no morphine was ever sold in his store without a prescription and, further, that Lefferts was a part-time employee who worked only one hour per day during his employment.

Lefferts's testimony was further refuted by evidence that Helen was out of town with her family during most of the time he worked in the drugstore. Lefferts's window of opportunity for selling morphine to Helen was a mere twenty-one days. This gave Wellman a powerful closing for his cross-examination.

"Now, you say that you sold Miss Potts . . . about 150 to 200 grains altogether?"

"Yes, sir," Lefferts replied.

Wellman shot back, "It is acknowledged that Miss Potts did not return from Scranton until September 23, so that between that time and October 15 she must have consumed nearly 10 grains of morphine a day. Now you probably know that two grains are enough to kill a person, so that you would have us believe that she bought enough to kill her 100 times over?"

Lefferts became defiant: "I know that two grains are enough to kill an ordinary person, but it would probably surprise you to know that in my own family I have seen a person take twelve grains at a dose without injury."

Wellman replied, "Oh, nothing in your family would surprise me."[77] He asked the embarrassed young man two or three more questions and let him go without having him arrested for perjury.

On the final day of the hearing the prosecution called only two witnesses and read a few affidavits into evidence, but the fireworks were essentially over. Wellman had become so ill during the hearing that he missed the last day, and Assistant District Attorney Battle came in his place. Howe was so hoarse that he was subject to violent fits of coughing. He was also subject to the constant harassment of Mrs. Harris, who sat directly behind him and repeatedly bothered him with remarks and suggestions. Harassed beyond endurance, he told her that he could not go on unless she left the room or moved to a different seat. She left the room to pace in the corridor, but within a few minutes Howe relented and allowed her back in the courtroom.

When the testimony ended, Commissioner Raines complimented both sides on the professionalism they had shown as they had plowed so quickly through such a mass of evidence. Raines adjourned the hearing, and the waiting game began. How soon would he have his report ready to send to Governor Flower?

CHAPTER FOURTEEN

The Curtain Falls

The *New York Times* was skeptical of the Raines Commission. Voicing the opinion that the hearing "can have no possible bearing on a legitimate exercise of clemency by the Governor,"[1] the *Times* said that the Raines Commission was nothing more than a rehash of the motion for new trial heard by Recorder Smyth. Since the governor could not order a new trial, the entire hearing was an exercise in futility. The *Times* concluded by saying, "There can be no other logical outcome of the Raines inquiry except to let the sentence of the court stand."[2]

Almost a week after the conclusion of the hearing, Commissioner Raines sent his report to Governor Flower.[3] It was not as long as Recorder's Smyth's order denying Harris a new trial, but Raines's conclusion was the same. Raines found that of all the witnesses whom Howe called to testify, only Jackson and Waddell gave any credible testimony suggesting that Helen might have possibly abused morphine. Raines dismissed Jackson's complaint about Helen's deportment while a student at Jackson's school, but he did credit that at one time during the winter of 1888–89 Helen had said her uncle (Dr. Treverton) had given her a pill of morphine or opium for a headache.[4] Raines found that Miss Waddell probably had some interaction with Helen regarding a pill or pills of some sort, but she was such "a strong partisan for the defendant, Harris, as evidenced by her manner and admissions in her testimony [that she] seemed to be making as much of the facts within her knowledge as possible for a deeply interested witness." Due to her obvious bias, "the line could not be drawn by me between the facts and the additions made by the witness in her zeal as a partisan." Regardless, Waddell's testimony related to a time almost two years before Helen's death.

Raines found Ethel Harris "destitute of moral character" and contradicted by Mrs. Potts. He completely disregarded her testimony. Raines found that Dr. Kinmouth's testimony was not inherently improbable, but it was in hopeless conflict with his "corroborating" witness, Henry M. Woolman. Woolman had credibility problems of his own, due to the fact that his testimony at the hearing was in hopeless conflict with the letter he wrote to Dr. Kinmouth. The three-way contradictions of Kinmouth's testimony, Woolman's testimony, and Woolman's letter were not the only factors discrediting Kinmouth's testimony. Raines was not at all impressed with Kinmouth's explanation that he lied about not selling morphine to Helen because he was observing the physician-patient privilege. Raines wrote: "Dr. Kinmouth is a most intelligent physician, and is not, in my opinion, so lacking in tact that he would at any time resort to a plain falsehood in preference to silence or evasion." Raines likewise was not impressed with the character witnesses called by the prosecution to besmirch Kinmouth's reputation for truthfulness. If that had been the only evidence against Kinmouth's credibility, Raines said he would have accepted Kinmouth's testimony, but given the conflicts in testimony, the lies Kinmouth told, and the weak excuses he gave for lying, Raines rejected his testimony completely.

Raines dispatched Lange's testimony in a sentence or two and then turned to the witness whom he characterized as "far the most important to the issue"—Joseph Lefferts. Raines outlined Lefferts's testimony in detail, including his weak excuse for not coming forward during the trial, and then summed it up in a few words: Lefferts testified that in a period of two weeks he had sold "sixty fatal doses of morphine" and that "such sales were made by him without question or caution to a girl nineteen years of age, as if he had given her soda water." Raines could not believe it, especially in light of others' testimony that during the time Lefferts claimed to be poisoning Helen with morphine, she gave no signs of being anything other than a "bright, buoyant, ruddy girl . . . of the purest character and highest intelligence." Raines dismissed Howe's suggestion that Helen was stocking up for the next semester at Comstock School by pointing out that a thorough search of Helen's effects revealed no stash of morphine.

Raines then outlined all the testimony produced by the prosecution that while at Miss Jackson's school Helen never took morphine, while at the Comstock School Helen never took morphine, and at no other time pertinent to his inquiry did anyone see Helen taking morphine. Raines concluded his review of the testimony by mentioning two damning pieces of evidence that the jury never heard—Helen asking Miss Reed to warn her roommates against waking her because Harris told her the pill wouldn't work if she were awakened from sleep and her deathbed statement to her roommates, asking whether Harris might have poisoned her.

Raines did not quote that deathbed statement, but we would do well to review it. When her roommates urged her to go back to sleep, Helen replied, "If I go to sleep, it will be a death sleep."[5] Then, urging her friends to continue to check on her if she went to sleep, she uttered her final words: "Carl said I could take one of these pills every night for twelve nights in succession and he had taken them himself. Carl would not give me anything that would hurt me—would he?"[6] Helen believed she was dying. If she had been dying from a self-administered overdose of morphine, she would not have been wondering if Harris had killed her.

Raines ended his report by saying, "A careful and conscientious discharge of my duty compels my mind to the conclusion upon the evidence before me that the deceased took morphine medicinally prescribed for her and not otherwise." After reading the report, Flower denied clemency and, on the eve of Harris's execution, released the full text of Raines's report to the press.

On the morning of May 4 two telegrams arrived at Sing Sing. Warden Durston, who had replaced Warden Brown in the wake of the escape of Roehl and Pallister, personally took the telegrams to Cell No. 8 in the Death House. When Harris saw the stern look on Durston's face, he became visibly nervous. "Harris," Durston said, "here are two telegrams which were received a short time ago. One is from your counsel and the other from the Governor." Harris reached a trembling hand through the bars and took the telegrams. When he had finished reading the telegrams, Harris said, "Warden, will you kindly telegraph my mother to come and see me. . . . I haven't seen her since I came here." Durston agreed to send the telegram and left Harris to his thoughts in Cell No. 8.[7]

Howe was not through with his efforts. He announced he was going to the capital to plead with the governor for a month's reprieve so he could take Harris's case to the Federal Circuit Court of Appeals. His office also produced a letter from a woman who said she supplied Helen with morphine. They said the letter came in some time ago and was lost in the excitement of preparing Harris's case, and it had only recently come to light.

Death chamber at Sing Sing, early 1900s (Courtesy of the Library of Congress)

They had lost the envelope it came in, and they knew the sender only by her signature—Lillie D.[8]

In the excitement following Flower's announcement, Howe again vowed to take the case to the Supreme Court of the United States "if I can see the faintest hope for Harris." Howe then dug into the law books, looking for any precedent that might support faint hope for an appeal to the Supreme Court. He found none. The next day Howe had to sing a different tune to the press: "To carry the case to the U.S. Court without a ghost of a chance of success would be simply to prolong the suffering of Carlyle. . . . They will electrocute him Monday."[9]

Mrs. Harris arrived at Sing Sing the morning after receiving Durston's telegram, and she was immediately escorted into the Death House to see her son. While she met with Harris, the preparations for his execution got under way. They mailed out invitations to the official witnesses, placed the electric chair in position in the death chamber, and began testing the electrical apparatus to make sure that it worked properly.[10]

Harris played his part to the end. He fought to maintain his composure, treated everyone with courtesy, promised to die bravely, and vehemently maintained his innocence.[11] He behaved so nobly that the majority of the keepers in the Death House came to believe he was innocent.[12] The papers continued to report Harris's every action in the Death House, usually in a light most favorable to him. Even the *New York Times* remarked on his "bravado," describing his eating and sleeping habits, and telling how he joked with the keepers. One thing the papers seemed to obsess on was the state of Harris's salvation, and the *Times* was careful to quote Harris as saying that any reports about him scoffing at religion were untrue.[13] Warden Durston tried to staunch the flood of information about Harris's activities being given to the press. He ordered that he and he alone would speak to the press about Harris, and his standard answer to any questions about Harris's welfare was to say, "Very well indeed" and nothing more. His efforts proved futile.[14]

Mrs. Harris and her youngest son, Allen, took a room at Ambler's Boarding House near the prison. Her elder son, Robert McCready Harris, who had vied with Carlyle for Helen's affection, did not accompany her to Sing Sing. McCready had begun to wash his hands of his infamous brother, and he would eventually change his name to Robert Harris McCready.[15] From their room at Ambler's, Mrs. Harris and her son Allen had a view of the roof of the warden's house and would be able to see the raising of the black flag, which would announce Harris's execution. She made her final visit to the Death House to see her son on Saturday. Her husband Charles L. Harris made his first appearance in the case on Sunday, arriving by train and going with Allen to the Death House to visit his son. After spending a half hour with his son, the husband went to the boardinghouse and saw his wife for the first time in five years. After a brief meeting, he got back on the train and went home to Syracuse.[16]

At 8:20 on Monday morning, Warden Durston sent his wife and child away from the prison and went to the Death House to read the death warrant to Harris. The reading of the warrant completed, the chaplain, Rev. John C. S. Weills, arrived at 9:00 to pray with Harris. After Weills left, Dr. Irving examined Harris, finding him to be showing some signs of nervousness. Morphine was available for Harris had he asked, but he did not. The first witnesses began arriving at 9:20. Ten minutes later a column of smoke curled up from the chimney of the engine room as the state electrician, who went by the pseudonym "Davis," fired up the generator to power the electric chair. Only Warden Durston knew the true identity of State Electrician

"Davis." Outside on the hill overlooking Sing Sing a crowd began to gather, jostling each other and jockeying for a good vantage point from which to see the black flag raised.

At 10:30 a prison barber shaved Harris and cut his hair. Harris then put on a new suit of clothes furnished him by the prison. Principle Keeper Connaughton slit the lower right leg of the pants with a knife to accommodate one of the electrodes that would be attached Harris's body. At 11:40 "Davis" entered the death chamber and made final tests to make sure that the electric chair was in proper working order. At 12:16 Warden Durston, the official witnesses, and members of the press entered the death chamber. "Davis" ran one more test on the chair and announced it was ready.

Principle Keeper Connaughton and two guards escorted Harris into the death chamber. He walked without assistance, with Connaughton in the lead and the two guards following. Upon entering the room Harris looked about uncertainly until Connaughton pointed to the electric chair. Harris walked to the chair and sat down. The guards moved to strap him in. When his arms and legs were strapped down, he began to talk.

"I have a word to say if the warden will permit." Silence. Harris repeated, "I would like to say something if I have the warden's consent."

Durston asked, "What did you wish to say?"

"I have no further motive for any concealment whatever. I desire to state that I die absolutely innocent of the crime of which I have been convicted." He then settled back in the chair and the electrode was attached to his right leg through the slit in his pant leg. The other electrode, consisting of a skullcap, was lowered into place on his head. "Davis" made sure the connections were secure and he and the guards stepped away from the chair. "Davis" walked over to the switchboard and said "All ready."

Dr. C. M. Daniels, who had been placed in charge of the execution, raised his hand, and "Davis" threw the switch, sending a current of 1,760 volts through Harris's body. Harris tensed as the electricity flowed through him and the securing straps creaked. After four seconds Daniels lowered his hand and "Davis" cut the current back to 150 volts. After 51¾ seconds at 150 volts, Daniels raised his hand and then lowered it and "Davis" shut off the current. Harris's body relaxed and the straps creaked again as the tension subsided. Two physicians immediately stepped to the body to examine it. One of them cut open Harris's shirt with a scalpel and placed a stethoscope to his chest. "He is dead," said the doctor, and the other took the stethoscope. After finding no heartbeat, the second doctor concurred that Harris was dead. The two doctors then invited other physicians among the witnesses to examine the body. All the doctors said they were satisfied that death was instantaneous. "Davis" turned to the other witnesses and said, "That is all." As the witnesses filed out of the death chamber, one of the reporters fainted.

Two keepers carried in a long black walnut board and laid it beside the chair. They unbuckled Harris and placed his body on the board. Lifting the board, they carried Harris's body to a dissecting table at the other end of the death chamber. Within ten minutes they had begun the autopsy, and they completed it by 2:00 P.M. Dr. Daniels told the press that the execution was the most successful of the seven he had witnessed. "Harris died without pain, and I do not see how his execution could have been bettered, from a humane standpoint."

Mrs. Harris, watching from the window of her room, saw the black flag raised over the warden's house. She turned to her son Allen and said, "They have murdered him." Allen left the boardinghouse to go to Sing Sing and claim the body. When Allen arrived, Principle Keeper Connaughton escorted him to view the body, and Allen told Warden Durston that an undertaker would call at the prison that afternoon to remove it. At 3:00 the undertaker arrived and placed Harris's body in an oak casket bearing a silver plate. The plate was inscribed:

CARLYLE W. HARRIS
Murdered, May 8, 1893
Aged 23 years, 7 months, 15 days
"We would not if we had known."
THE JURY

The undertaker then placed the casket in a hearse and removed the body from the grounds of the prison to transport it to its final resting place at a private cemetery. Harris's remains were the first to receive such treatment. All previous inmates executed at Sing Sing had been buried at the prison.[17]

Mrs. Harris had said she would make an announcement to the press after her son's execution, and she did so late that afternoon. When she spoke she was dry-eyed, but her complexion was chalky-white and her features worked convulsively. She said, "They have murdered my son because he did not wail and gnash his teeth when he heard of his wife's death. But see how calm I am. Would they say that I murdered my son because I do not carry on? I have not shed a tear. I may not do so. Yet do you not know that I loved my murdered boy dearly?" She carried on in a similar vein for some time, blaming Tammany Hall and the Potts family for her son's death, until she challenged the assembled reporters. "Did he not die innocent?" Silence. "Did he not die innocent?" she repeated.

One man spoke up and said, "He bore himself like an innocent man." More silence.

"Did he not die innocent?" Mrs. Harris shrieked, "Shame on you all! Have the courage to break away from politics and answer with a hearty yes." She didn't get the hearty yes. She said a few more words about false conviction and bade the reporters good day.

Harris had written a valediction, and Durston had promised Mrs. Harris he would give it to her after the execution. When she went to retrieve it, Durston refused to give it to her. He would give her no explanation for his change of heart, but he told her that he had mailed the valediction to the capital, and she might possibly be able to get it there.[18]

It was also revealed after the execution that Harris, who had often said that he would never attempt suicide,[19] had done just that. On the Saturday evening before his execution, Harris chewed up a large quantity of newspaper and stuffed the keyhole to his cell door full of thick paper pulp. After securing himself against interference, he began swallowing newspaper pulp in an attempt to close off his windpipe and suffocate himself. When the keepers discovered what he was up to, they immediately tried to force their way into the cell. For an hour and thirty minutes they worked to gain entry while Harris swallowed newspaper pulp. Gaining entry to the cell, the keepers subdued Harris and ended his suicide attempt. When the prison doctor arrived, he examined Harris and proclaimed him fit to be executed.[20]

Mrs. Harris had her son's remains buried with Episcopal ceremonies at Albany Rural Cemetery in Menands, which was located approximately halfway between Albany and Troy, New York. Originally founded in 1841 and used for the burial of Union soldiers during the Civil War, the cemetery serves as the final resting place for many famous people, including President Chester A. Arthur and Judge Learned Hand.[21] Mrs. Harris piled flower arrangements upon the grave until it was completely covered. The

Albany Rural Cemetery in Menands, New York (Courtesy of the Library of Congress)

centerpiece was a wreath of roses inscribed "At rest, Innocent."[22] After Mrs. Harris and her friends left the cemetery, a swarm of people, mostly women, descended upon the grave and started carrying off the flowers Mrs. Harris had left. The cemetery staff had to place a guard upon the gravesite to prevent the thefts.[23]

One person stood out in the small funeral party with Mrs. Harris. She was a young lady dressed all in black who seemed to be the most grief-stricken person in attendance. When reporters asked her who she was, she gave the name "Carrie Jones," but nobody believed her.[24] Nobody knew at that time that Carrie had met Harris in the Tombs one Sunday in December 1891 when she went with a church group to sing hymns for the inmates. When she saw him, it was love at first sight. She visited him almost daily after that, sometimes spending hours with him. Warden Fallon temporarily put a halt to the visits because they were not engaged, but upon receiving a pleading letter from Harris, he allowed the visits to resume. Fallon later said that he was never told in so many words that they were engaged, but their actions were "of a very tender character." The keepers often saw Carrie and Harris embracing through the bars of his cell, but never tried to stop them. Her last visit with Harris was just before Recorder Smyth denied the motion for new trial. After that only family could visit condemned prisoners. She was almost but not quite family, having broken an engagement with another man to become engaged to Harris. Had he escaped the gallows, he might very well have entered into a public marriage with her—she was independently wealthy. Mrs. Harris heartily approved of the match. She told a friend, "Just as soon as Carl comes out of prison he will marry Miss Jones. She has an income of $2,000 a year, and they can live nicely on that while Carl is making a career for himself." Carrie steadfastly believed him innocent and worked as hard as his mother in trying to find evidence for a new trial. Up until the funeral her existence was known only to Harris and his mother, the keepers, and the staff at Howe and Hummel. Having spied her at the funeral, the newshounds set off on a relentless quest to learn everything they could about her.

The day after Harris's funeral the *Herald* broke Carrie's story. Somehow, a *Herald* reporter connected the "Carrie Jones" at the funeral with a "Carrie Brun" who often visited Harris at the Tombs. He went to the Tombs and interviewed the keepers. There he got a description of "Carrie Brun" and was told that she gave her address as the intersection of Seventy-Fourth Street and Western Boulevard, no number. Going to that intersection, the reporter made inquiry and learned that a young lady matching the description given to him by the keepers lived in an apartment house at 202 W. Seventy-Fourth Street, just east of Western Boulevard. The young lady was named Carrie Bruning. When he arrived at the address, the elevator operator refused to take him up to Miss Bruning's apartment. Instead he called on the speaking tube, and a lady came downstairs and identified herself to the reporter as Carrie Bruning. The young lady, who looked nothing like the description he had been given of Carrie Bruning, denied knowing Carlyle Harris, but she volunteered that she thought he was innocent. The reporter made a second visit to the apartment house, hoping to get an interview with the real Carrie Bruning, but all he got on this second visit was a note that read "I desire to deny most emphatically the publication in the *Herald* of today that I had anything to do with Carlyle Harris. Carrie Bruning."[25] And that ended the matter. The newshounds lost interest and left Carrie to grieve for Harris in anonymity. She was a lucky young lady.

Mrs. Harris, however, stayed in the news. She was apparently trying to suppress her grief by lashing out at others—the Pottses, Tammany Hall, the district attorney, the prison officials, and even her son's lawyers. She claimed that she had hired John A. Taylor to represent her son for an agreed-upon fee of $2,500, but Taylor had taken $12,000 and left her destitute. Had it not been for the self-sacrifice of her heroic son, who stepped into the financial breach by writing poetry and essays for newspapers, she would have been penniless.[26] When he was reached for comment, Taylor said, "I do not want to get into a controversy with the bereaved mother. As a matter of fact she was never my client. I acted for Miss McCready, who is my client now, while I am also counsel for the McCready estate. Mrs. Harris seems to think $5,000 an excessive fee for my services, but I will leave it to any fair-minded lawyer whether $5,000 is too much in pay for six months' service in taking charge of a capital case and assuming all the responsibility."[27]

Then Mrs. Harris set her energies to corkscrewing her son's valediction out of the hands of the officials in Albany. Although Durston had hindered her quest by sending the valediction to the capital, she found no resistance to its release there. The valediction, consisting of six pages of foolscap, was a rehash of the self-serving statements he had made all along during the course of his prosecution.[28] The *Illustrated American* wrote a more even-handed postscript to the Harris case:

> There will always be a question in the minds of many whether Carlyle Harris did or did not kill his young wife. . . . He alone is conscious whether he is an innocent man or the most cowardly, cunning wretch of our own times. . . .
>
> Our sympathy, however, goes with the mother who, without means, has made a valiant fight to save her son. The sin of the child has fallen with a heavy hand on the parent. He has punished her far more than Society has punish him. He escapes shame in Death; she lives to bear the sorrow.[29]

For the next several years controversy raged over every aspect of the trial—Harris's guilt or innocence; circumstantial evidence; scientific evidence; the fairness of allowing so much evidence of Harris's sexual indiscretions; whether a new trial should have been ordered. Rather than letting Harris's valediction be the last word on his guilt or innocence, let us look to "Some Notable Murder Cases," an article that his lawyer William F. Howe wrote for *Cosmopolitan Magazine* in 1900.

"My God, what will become of me?" was what Carlyle Harris said when informed by Doctor Fowler of the death of his unacknowledged wife. I have always considered Carlyle Harris, a doctor in embryo, one of the cleverest of all the murderers I have known. He provided against every possible complication, it would seem, by giving his young wife a box of pills all but one of which contained a harmless sedative dose of morphine. The deadly dose, in a pill that looked just like all the others, was by an almost inconceivable chance not taken by the artless victim till after all the others had been used. What was more damning still, it was not taken until the very night on which Carlyle Harris called upon her, this call (made doubtless with fearful self-questionings, bewildering surprise that all still was well) serving to feed her brain with thoughts of him and of their relations, which found expression from her lips in the temporary reaction from the first stupor which is so characteristic. Her words could not have failed to direct attention to Harris, even had his own (subsequent) exclamation not done so. What then had become of his undoubted mental acuteness, his cold prudence, his patient calculations! He came very nearly escaping—yet he made the fatal slip.[30]

Howe was in a better position than anyone else except Harris himself to know beyond peradventure that Harris was guilty, and we must give his statement great weight. Howe was correct when he said it was a masterfully conceived and executed crime that would have succeeded had it not been for some unfortunate (for Harris) circumstances. Howe was wrong, however, to identify Harris's cry, "What will become of me?" as the fatal misstep that led to the gallows. Standing alone it could do no more than raise suspicion. Four circumstances contributed more than anything else to Harris's conviction: Helen's roommates woke her up when they came in from the concert. Harris outsmarted himself by keeping two capsules for "proof" of his innocence. Harris's ill-advised attempt to talk Nicoll into dropping the investigation caused the district attorney to resurrect it. When Nicoll resurrected the case, he reassigned it to Francis Wellman and Charles Simms.

The Harris Case Today

What course would the Carlyle Harris case take today? Would he be indicted? Could he be proven guilty beyond a reasonable doubt? Would a modern jury convict him? If not, how can we say he was proven guilty beyond a reasonable doubt when he was tried over one hundred years ago? Our study has demonstrated that Wellman did not prove Harris guilty beyond all doubt. Given the limitations of human ability, few things can be proven beyond all doubt, and many things thought to have been proven beyond all doubt have later been shown to be wrong.[1] Helen died of morphine poisoning. Harris gave her morphine. She got morphine from no other known source. The most probable interpretation of the evidence is that Harris must have poisoned her. There is room to doubt, but is the space large enough to accommodate a reasonable doubt? Based on my thirty-two years in the courtroom handling thousands of cases and trying hundreds of jury trials, I believe that the evidence Wellman presented would not satisfy a modern jury, and they would most likely acquit Harris. Modern juries have come to expect better investigations and more compelling scientific evidence than what they had in the Harris case. I do not mean by this statement to argue that Harris was innocent. I merely mean to make a dispassionate evaluation of the persuasive effect that the available evidence would have on a modern jury.

One might argue that the term *reasonable doubt* is an eternal concept that means the same thing yesterday, today, and forever, and that if a twenty-first-century jury would acquit Harris, the nineteenth-century jury should have acquitted Harris. One would be wrong. I had listened to judges read the instruction for reasonable doubt approximately half a hundred times before I noticed a seldom-realized paradox—Florida's "definition" of reasonable doubt did not define what a reasonable doubt is. Instead it told the jury what a reasonable doubt is not—it is not an imaginary, speculative, or forced doubt, nor is it based on bias, prejudice, or sympathy.[2] Checking the jury instructions of other states shows that their "definitions" of reasonable doubt also fail to define the term. In Washington State, judges tell jurors that a reasonable doubt is "such a doubt as would exist in the mind of a reasonable person after fully, fairly, and carefully considering all of the evidence or lack of evidence."[3] Colorado judges tell juries that it is a doubt "based on reason and common sense" that is not "vague, imaginary, or speculative."[4] Reasonable doubt is so hard to define because it is not an objective standard. According to James Q. Whitman, it is not even a legal standard. In his 2008 work *The Origin of Reasonable Doubt: Theological Roots of the Criminal Trial*, Whitman argues that it is a religious standard. To greatly oversimplify Whitman's argument, "beyond a reasonable doubt" originated as the quantum of satisfaction that would save a juror's soul from Hell if he mistakenly condemned an innocent man to the gallows. It has now transformed into something that, to paraphrase Justice Potter Stewart, we could never succeed in intelligibly defining, but we know it when we see it.[5] It is also something that changes over time. As science and technology advance, jurors demand more stringent proof. The march of forensic science has caused reasonable doubt to fit into smaller and smaller spaces. In the final analysis, whether a modern jury would convict is irrelevant to the question of whether the actual jury properly convicted.

Whether the case would be filed today is a harder question. Many prosecutors looking at the state of the evidence would answer with an emphatic "No." Some prosecutors, not realizing the weakness of the case, would soon come to regret filing it. Other prosecutors, probably the smallest percentage, would file the case, fully recognizing its weaknesses. I would be inclined to count myself in this third group. Why? I assess the Harris case as being a peculiar type of case that prosecutors sometimes confront—The Case That Must Be Tried. This type of case is one where the prosecutor is satisfied that: The defendant committed a horrific crime. Marginal evidence is available to prove the defendant is guilty. The evidence is not going to get any better. There is a fair chance of winning, but a bigger chance of losing. The only hope of doing justice is to try the case and attempt to get a conviction.

Over the years, I've tried several homicide cases that fell into this category. I won some, and I lost some. I don't regret trying any of them. One final observation about The Case That Must Be Tried: If there is reasonable doubt about the defendant's guilt, charges should not be filed. If the chances of winning are miniscule, charges should not be filed. Charges should be filed when there is a full, firm, and abiding conviction that the defendant is guilty and there is a chance to convict. So long as probable cause exists, so long as the prosecutor believes the defendant is guilty, so long as the prosecution is conducted ethically, so long as there is a fighting chance of convicting, the prosecutor has done nothing wrong by filing charges.

If by some sort of magic we could move Carlyle Harris and Helen Potts forward in time 125 years, their story would take a far different course than it did. First, were Carlyle Harris to commit his murder today, the prosecutor's office would most likely receive a very different case from law enforcement. The modern medical examiner's office normally has a far better working relationship with the police than the New York coroner did in Harris's time, and the typical medical examiner has received rigorous training in the subspecialty of forensic pathology. Forensic science, technology, and police procedure have all taken giant strides since 1891, and the modern prosecutor would receive more evidence from the police and medical examiner than Francis Wellman could have imagined.

Second, there is very little likelihood that Harris would have ever thought it necessary to kill Helen. This second point requires a lengthier explanation than the first. Sexual mores, the status of women, and medical science are so far removed from what they were when Harris proposed to Helen that it is almost inconceivable that their romance could have traversed the path it did or ended the way it did. We will take up the differences in reverse chronological order. The situation spiraled out of control when Harris nearly killed Helen in a botched attempt to perform an abortion on her. This led to her mother's discovery of the secret marriage and her pressuring Harris to the point that he felt murder was his only option.

Let us assume that a modern-day Mrs. Potts discovers a secret marriage between her daughter and Harris. Today the institution of marriage doesn't have the same status as it did in the Gilded Age. A modern-day Mrs. Potts would be far less likely to become upset about Harris's liaison with Helen. A modern-day Dr. McCready would be far less likely to disinherit Harris for sexual dalliance. And modern society is not going to make a social pariah of Helen or any of the other women whom Harris despoiled.

Today it is possible to get safe abortions in a clinical setting. We don't quite have abortion on demand, but with pluck and determination, a safe abortion can usually be had. Today, Helen has her safe abortion, comes through it with flying colors, Mrs. Potts never learns of the secret marriage, and Harris's life goes on until he gets himself into another jam. If we turn the clock back a few more ticks and put Helen on birth control, she never has the abortion in the first place.

Let us turn the clock back a little further in the romance of Harris and Helen. Would they ever have gotten married in the first place? In many ways nineteenth-century women were considered as property. There was a legal presumption that if a married woman did something in the presence of her husband, she was acting under the compulsion of her husband.[6] In chapter 51 of *Oliver Twist*, when Mr. Brownlow explained the presumption to Mr. Bumble, Mr. Bumble famously replied, "If the law supposes that, the law is a ass—a idiot." Notwithstanding Mr. Bumble's opinion, for most intents and purposes Gilded Age women were the property of their husbands. For example, when a woman married, her husband became the owner of a life estate in her real property,[7] and she was considered incompetent to enter into a contract.[8] Possibly the most important asset that a young woman brought to the marriage was her virginity. Social purity was the clarion call of the 1890s, and we can see from the trail of ruined women that Harris left in his wake that the socially impure young woman was not fit for polite company.

Helen refused Harris's sexual advances because she feared becoming a social pariah. Harris overcame her objections and achieved his conquest by talking her into a secret marriage that would prevent her becoming damaged goods. When her mother discovered the marriage, she was so distraught over the possibility of Helen losing status through the appearance of impropriety that she attempted to coerce Harris into a "respectable" marriage. Today women are not property; today premarital sex does not transform a woman into something unworthy of a respectable man. Gender roles are so different today that there would be escape valves at each stage of the progression of Harris's pathological relationship with Helen.

How would Harris's romance with Helen play out today? There are two possibilities. First, Helen might not be so insistent upon maintaining her virginity; Harris might have gotten what he wanted and moved on to another conquest; Helen would have nursed a broken heart for a while; and then she would have moved on with her life. Second, if Helen withstood Harris's advances to the point of his making her a secret wife, there would most likely be no pregnancies, and the marriage would most likely end in divorce. (Divorces are much easier to obtain today than they were in the 1890s.) Helen would then move on with her life, and Harris would move from one act of villainy to another until he finally wound up in prison. Harris might have been such a psychopath that he would murder Helen to get out of a lesser mess than the one he created in the 1890s, but it is not likely. He would not consider murder to extricate himself from the sort of a scrape he would get into with Helen today. He had already gone through several much worse scrapes with other women and managed to get through them without killing anyone. The foregoing discussion is not meant as an indictment of Victorian moral standards or an endorsement of modern morality. It is simply meant as a dispassionate analysis of how the social consequences of sexual behavior have evolved.

Although Carlyle W. Harris was a thoroughgoing scoundrel, he would not have killed Helen had he not felt compelled to do so by the negative social consequences of exposure. The tragic death of Helen Potts came about because the second-class status imposed upon nineteenth-century women, the unforgiving moral code of the times, and Harris's insatiable sexual appetite all combined to lead him to despoil Helen with a clandestine marriage and later destroy her with a capsule of morphine.

Notes

INTRODUCTION

1. *People of the State of New York . . . against Carlyle W. Harris,* 413 (hereafter cited as Transcript).

2. Transcript, 395.

3. "Harris Denies the Van Zandt Marriage," *New York Herald,* Feb. 5, 1892 (hereafter cited as *Herald*), http://genealogybank.com.

4. Transcript, 414.

5. Boswell and Thompson, *The Carlyle Harris Case,* 28.

6. Transcript, 429.

7. Transcript, 415.

8. Transcript, 415.

9. Transcript, 417.

10. Transcript, 429.

11. "Raines' Report in Harris' Case," *Herald,* May 7, 1893; Wellman, *Luck and Opportunity,* 46.

12. Transcript, 396.

13. Transcript, 430.

14. King, *Notable New Yorkers,* 349; "Dr. Edward P. Fowler Dead," *Times,* Jan. 30, 1914.

15. Transcript, 476.

16. Heidler and Heidler, *Civil War Encyclopedia,* 3:1307.

17. Crothers, *Morphinism and Narcomanias,* 29–32.

18. Crothers, *Morphinism and Narcomanias,* 33.

19. Transcript, 396.

20. Transcript, 404.

21. Transcript, 477.

22. Transcript, 397.

23. "History of CPR," http://cpr.heart.org/AHAECC/CPRAndECC/AboutCPR FirstAid/HistoryofCPR/UCM_475751_History-of-CPR.jsp.

24. Transcript, 477.

25. Boswell and Thompson, *The Carlyle Harris Case,* 10.

26. Wellman and Simms, *The Trial of Carlyle W. Harris*, 122.

27. Transcript, 478.

28. Transcript, 480.

29. Transcript, 480, 481.

30. Sun and Moon Data for One Day, U.S. Naval Observatory, Astronomical Applications Department, http://aa.usno.navy.mil/data/docs/RS_OneDay.php.

31. Wellman and Simms, *The Trial of Carlyle W. Harris*, 126.

32. Wellman and Simms, *The Trial of Carlyle W. Harris*, 22.

33. Transcript, 483, 484.

34. Transcript, 486.

35. Transcript, 484, 485.

36. Wellman and Simms, *The Trial of Carlyle W. Harris*, 128.

37. Transcript, 486.

38. Transcript, 486, 487.

39. Transcript, 489.

40. Transcript, 757–61.

41. *Dictionary of American Biography*, 4:558.

42. A court of first instance is a court that initially takes up a potential criminal case, such as a coroner's inquest or a preliminary hearing before a committing magistrate.

43. Train, *Courts and Criminals*, 33.

44. Train, *Courts and Criminals*, 33.

45. Wellman and Simms, *The Trial of Carlyle W. Harris*, 131.

46. Transcript, 763, 764.

47. Wellman and Simms, *The Trial of Carlyle W. Harris*, 129.

48. Transcript, 767, 768.

49. Transcript, 764.

50. Transcript, 813, 814.

51. Transcript, 610.

52. Philbrick, *Language and the Law*, 192.

53. Transcript, 766, 767.

54. Transcript, 609, 610.

55. Transcript, 779, 780.

56. Transcript, 786.

57. Ledyard, *Articles, Speeches and Poems of Carlyle W. Harris*, 121.

58. Boswell and Thompson, *The Carlyle Harris Case*, 16.

59. Transcript, 788.

60. Transcript, 785.

61. Boswell and Thompson, *The Carlyle Harris Case*, 16.

62. Transcript, 785–87.

63. "To Confound Young Harris," *Herald*, Mar. 23, 1891.

64. "Are Such Inquests Common in New York?," *Herald*, May 15, 1891.

65. "Tried for Murder," *Rocky Mountain (CO) News*, Jan. 14, 1892, http://

genealogybank.com. Ironically, Harris's grandfather, Dr. Benjamin W. McCready, testified as an expert witness for the prosecution in that previous trial. "The Harris Murder Trial," *New York Tribune*, Jan. 31, 1892 (hereafter cited as *Tribune*), http://genealogybank.com.

66. "The Harris Case," *Irish American Weekly*, Apr. 1, 1893, http://genealogybank .com.

67. "On Trial for His Life," *Tribune*, Jan. 24, 1892.

68. "Another Victim for the Electric Chair," *Harrisburg (PA) Patriot*, Feb. 3, 1892, http://genealogybank.com.

69. "Last Act in the Harris Drama," *Watertown Daily Times*, May 8, 1893, http:// genealogybank.com; "Now to the Jury," *New York Evening World*, Feb. 2, 1892 (hereafter cited as *Evening World*), http://genealogybank.com.

1. THE SECRET MARRIAGE

1. "Inauguration of the Bellevue Hospital Medical College," *New York Times*, Oct. 17, 1861 (hereafter cited as *Times*), http://www.nytimes.com/ref/member center/nytarchive.html.

2. "Bellevue Hospital Medical College, New York: Announcement for 1861–62," 442.

3. "Twenty-Sixth Annual Statement of the Washington Life Insurance Company," *Washington (DC) Evening Star*, Feb. 10, 1886, http://www.genealogybank.com.

4. "Dr. McCready's Funeral Sermon," *Evening World*, Aug. 11, 1892.

5. "Carlyle Harris Disinherited," *Herald*, Jan. 14, 1892.

6. For example, Ledyard, *Bible Stories and Scenes for Young People*.

7. "Nelly Ryder's Tea Triumph," *Bossier (LA) Banner*, Dec. 5, 1878, http://news papers.com.

8. "Sunday School Convention," *Watertown (NY) Re-Union*, Sept. 17, 1884, http://nyshistoricnewspapers.org.

9. Wellman, *Luck and Opportunity*, 32.

10. "Social Purity," *The Churchman*, Apr. 12, 1890, 483.

11. "Teach Children to Speak Correctly," *Pacific Commercial Advertiser (Honolulu)*, Feb. 16, 1889, https://chroniclingamerica.loc.gov.

12. Ledyard, "Nellie Ryder's Tea Triumph."

13. Ledyard, "False Pride as to Work," *Vancouver (WA) Independent*, May 31, 1877, https://chroniclingamerica.loc.gov.

14. Frances "Fanny" McCready Harris (1846–1919), Find a Grave Memorial, http://www.findagrave.com/cgi-bin/fg.cgi?page=gr&GRid=113250950.

15. "Story of Harris' Life," *Herald*, May 9, 1893.

16. "His Record of the Worst," *Kansas City Times*, Feb. 4, 1892, http://news papers.com.

17. Ledyard, *Articles, Speeches and Poems of Carlyle W. Harris*, 10.

18. "Story of Harris' Life."
19. "Story of Harris' Life."
20. "Story of Harris' Life."
21. "Story of Harris' Life."
22. "Story of Harris' Life."
23. Daniels, *Story of Ocean Grove*, 25–28.
24. Wellman, *Luck and Opportunity*, 32.
25. Wellman and Simms, *The Trial of Carlyle W. Harris*, 11.
26. Transcript, 444.
27. Boswell and Thompson, *The Carlyle Harris Case*, 9.
28. Wellman and Simms, *The Trial of Carlyle W. Harris*, 67.
29. Transcript, 446.
30. Transcript, 447.
31. Transcript, 624, 625.
32. Transcript, 448, 449.
33. "He May Be at Bar," *Evening World*, Mar. 23, 1891.
34. Transcript, 449, 450.
35. Transcript, 451, 470a, 470b.
36. Transcript, 467.
37. "He May Be at Bar."
38. "Story of Harris' Life."
39. Ledyard, *Articles, Speeches and Poems of Carlyle W. Harris*, 12.
40. "More of Young Harris," *Tribune*, Feb. 3, 1891.
41. "The Harris Conviction," *Tribune*, Feb. 4, 1892.
42. Transcript, 1300–1304.
43. Transcript, 455, 456.
44. Transcript, 664–66.
45. "To Confound Young Harris," *Herald*, Mar. 23, 1891.
46. Transcript, 688.
47. Transcript, 673, 674.
48. Transcript, 653.
49. Transcript, 683–99.
50. Transcript, 387, 388. Given what happened between Oliver and Harris over the next two days, it is highly unlikely that either Treverton or Harris told Oliver of Helen's predicament.
51. Transcript, 652–83.
52. Transcript, 838–40.
53. Transcript, 686.
54. Transcript, 657–59.
55. Transcript, 659.
56. Transcript, 660.
57. Transcript, 661.
58. "More of Young Harris."

2. THE SACRED MARRIAGE

1. "The Railroads," *Fort Worth* (TX) *Daily Gazette*, Feb. 2, 1887, http://news papers.com.

2. See, for example, Transcript, 467, 584, 588, 593, 596, 599, 612, 613, 655, 662, 1434.

3. Transcript, 629.

4. Transcript, 632.

5. Transcript, 649.

6. Voorhees, *The Holland Society*, chap. 1.

7. The Holland Society, http://www.hollandsociety.org/?.

8. Transcript, 461–64.

9. Transcript, 464.

10. Transcript, 465. What Davison was talking about was that it was a crime to try to extort money from someone by threatening to report his criminal activity to the authorities. Patterson v. State, 33 Vroom 82, 62 N.J.L. 82 (1898).

11. Transcript, 464–68.

12. Transcript, 577.

13. Transcript, 1436.

14. Transcript, 578.

15. Transcript, 679.

16. Transcript, 579.

17. Transcript, 579.

18. Transcript, 594.

19. Transcript, 595.

20. Transcript, 596.

21. Transcript, 598, 599.

22. Transcript, 598, 599.

23. Transcript, 639, 640.

24. Transcript, 600.

25. Transcript, 711.

26. Transcript, 712.

27. Wellman and Simms, *The Trial of Carlyle W. Harris*, 97, 98.

28. Transcript, 432.

29. Transcript, 603.

30. Transcript, 604.

31. Transcript, 605.

32. Ledyard, *Articles, Speeches and Poems of Carlyle W. Harris*, 13.

33. Transcript, 606, 607.

3. A WORLD OF CONCERN FOR HARRIS

1. Transcript, 1211–12.

2. "Thought to Be Alive, Although in Her Coffin," *Herald*, Feb. 7, 1891; "Her Mother's Fault, Said Carlyle Harris," *Herald*, Jan. 26, 1892; Wellman and Simms, *The Trial of Carlyle W. Harris*, 136.

3. "Phrenological Tests of Carlyle W. Harris," *Herald*, Jan. 29, 1893.

4. Transcript, 614, 615.

5. Mrs. Potts maintained that she gave the money to Mrs. Harris. Transcript, 616. Mrs. Harris contended that she declined the offer of the money. Ledyard, *Articles, Speeches and Poems of Carlyle W. Harris*, 14.

6. Ledyard, *Articles, Speeches and Poems of Carlyle W. Harris*, 14.

7. "He May Be at Bar," *Evening World*, Mar. 23, 1891.

8. Wellman, *Luck and Opportunity*, 31.

9. *National District Attorneys Association National Prosecution Standards*, 4–1.3m.

10. *ABA Standards for Criminal Justice Prosecution Function*, Prosecution Standard 3–3.1(a).

11. "Harris Indicted," *Evening World*, May 13, 1891.

12. *World 1908 Almanac and Encyclopedia*, 34.

13. "A Crime Newspapers Brought to Light," *Brooklyn Daily Eagle*, Feb. 3, 1892, (hereafter cited as *Daily Eagle*), http://newyorkshistoricnewspapers.org.

14. "He May Be at Bar," *Evening World*, Mar. 23, 1891.

15. "To Confound Young Harris," *Herald*, Mar. 23, 1891.

16. Transcript, 682.

17. Boswell and Thompson, *The Carlyle Harris Case*, 18.

18. "To Confound Young Harris."

19. Matter of Choate, 8 N.Y. Crim.Rep. 1 (Court of Oyer and Terminer, New York County, 1890); People ex rel. Dilworth v. Barrett, 30 N.Y. State Rep. 728 (Sup.Ct., 1st Dept., 1890); "Sentenced!" *Evening World*, Mar. 31, 1890; "Their Case Goes Over," *Tribune*, Mar. 29, 1890.

20. "Dilworth Choate Free," *Evening World*, May 16, 1890.

21. "Ready with Bail," *Evening World*, Mar. 22, 1891.

22. A diligent search of all available online newspaper sources has failed to find any article on the Carlyle Harris case dated either Mar. 20, 1891, or Mar. 21, 1891, other than the article written by Dilworth Choate for the *Evening World*.

23. As Unger recalled the meeting, he sent for the morning paper and read the article. "Opinions on Harris' Case," *Herald*, May 9, 1893. This appears to be impossible for the reason stated in the previous note. If he sent for anything, it was the closed-out file.

24. "Ready with Bail."

25. *Dictionary of American Biography*, 13:512.

26. "De Lancy Nicoll, Noted Lawyer, Dies," *Times*, Apr. 1, 1931.

27. "Odds and Ends of Politics," *Tribune*, Sept. 17, 1893; "The News This Morning," *Tribune*, Oct. 17, 1893.

28. Wellman, *Gentlemen of the Jury*, 232.

29. Wellman, *Luck and Opportunity*, 39.

30. "Clearing House for All Crimes," *Herald*, May 7, 1893.

31. Wellman, *The Art of Cross-Examination*.

32. "First in Ten Years," *Evening World*, Mar. 20, 1891.

33. "For Killing Young Ronan," *Herald*, Feb. 10, 1891; "Stroud's Trial for Murder," *Herald*, Feb. 18, 1891; "Guilty of Murder in the Second Degree," *Tribune*, Feb. 21, 1891.

34. "Stephani on Trial for Murder," *New York Evening Post*, Mar. 25, 1891, http://nyshistoricnewspapers.com.

35. "Got His Symptoms Mixed," *Sun*, Apr. 3, 1891; "Gledhill Takes the Stand," *Evening World*, Apr. 7, 1891; "Curious Effect of Cross-Examination," *Rochester (NY) Democrat and Chronicle*, May 21, 1891; "Fanning's Trial for Murder," *Evening World*, June 5, 1891; "To Try Mrs. Nelson for Murder," *Sun*, June 12, 1891; "Yarns That Frenchy Told," *Sun*, July 1, 1891; "Michael Carroll Convicted," *Tribune*, Oct. 21, 1891; "Gallivan on the Stand," *Herald*, Dec. 3, 1891; "Why 'Billy' M'Glory Owns the Place," *Tribune*, Dec. 29, 1891.

36. "On Trial for His Life," *Tribune*, Jan. 24, 1892.

37. "Clearing House for All Crimes," *Herald*, May 7, 1893.

38. King, *Notable New Yorkers*, 80.

4. WORKING UP A CASE ON HARRIS

1. Hall v. Sudyam, 6 Barb. 83, 1849 WL 5119 (Supreme Court, New York County, New York, 1849).

2. Hall v. Sudyam, 6 Barb. 83, 87, 1849 WL 5119.

3. *ABA Standards for Criminal Justice Prosecution Function*, Standard 3-3.9(b).

4. "Carlyle Harris Must Die," *Times*, Mar. 21, 1893.

5. "Lawyer Choate Brings Suit," *Chicago Daily Inter Ocean*, July 10, 1893, http://genealogybank.com.

6. Conway, *The Big Policeman*, 52–65.

7. *Dictionary of American Biography*, 3:386; "Ex-Chief Byrnes Dies of Cancer," *Times*, May 8, 1910.

8. "The Third Degree," *Watertown Daily Times*, Oct. 12, 1901.

9. "He May Be at Bar," *Evening World*, Mar. 23, 1891.

10. "Mr. Nicoll Sends for Mrs. Potts," *Tribune*, Mar. 23, 1891; "To Confound Young Harris," *Herald*, Mar. 23, 1891.

11. "The Inquiry into Mrs. Helen Harris's Death," *New York Sun*, Mar. 26, 1891 (hereafter cited as *Sun*), http://chroniclingamerica.loc.gov.

12. "Her Mother's Fault, Said Carlyle Harris," *Herald*, Jan. 26, 1892.

13. "Carlyle W. Harris in Custody," *Daily Eagle*, Apr. 1, 1891.

14. "Dr. A. M'L. Hamilton, Alienist, Dies at 71," *Times*, Nov. 24, 1919.

15. Hamilton, *Recollections of an Alienist*.

16. People v. Harris, 136 N.Y. 423, 33 N.E. 65, 68 (1893).

17. Wellman, *Luck and Opportunity*, 42.

18. Hamilton, *Recollections of an Alienist*, 276.

19. Wellman and Simms, *The Trial of Carlyle W. Harris*, 147

20. "Her Mother's Fault, Said Carlyle Harris."

21. Wellman and Simms, *The Trial of Carlyle W. Harris*, 141–42.

22. "Her Mother's Fault, Said Carlyle Harris." The pons Varolii is a portion of the brain near the brain stem.

23. "Extensive Brain Lesion with Slight Symptoms," 187.

24. Transcript, 974.

25. "Her Mother's Fault, Said Carlyle Harris."

26. Wellman and Simms, *The Trial of Carlyle W. Harris*, 149.

27. Transcript, 1051.

28. "The Inquiry into Mrs. Helen Harris's Death."

29. Wellman, *Luck and Opportunity*, 42.

30. Wellman, *Luck and Opportunity*, 42.

31. Wellman, *Luck and Opportunity*, 42, 43.

32. Dr. Peabody lectured on poisoning on Dec. 18, 23, and 24, 1890, and Jan. 6, 7, and 8, 1891. Transcript, 1438.

33. Wellman, *Luck and Opportunity*, 42.

34. Transcript, 1158.

35. The account of Harris's arrest comes from the following sources: "Harris Charged with Murder," *Herald*, Apr. 1, 1891; "Carlyle Harris Arrested," *Sun*, Apr. 1, 1891; "Carlyle W. Harris in Custody," *Tribune*, Apr. 1, 1891.

36. The original article reads "tell him," suggesting that the young man wanted Davis to tell the judge where to commit him. Since the judge knew full well where he was going to be committed, this is obviously a typesetting error, and he was asking "tell me" where he was going to be committed. "Carlyle Harris Arrested."

37. "Harris' Examination Postponed," *Herald*, Apr. 2, 1891; "Carlyle Harris's Case Adjourned," *Tribune*, Apr. 21, 1891; "Home News," *Tribune*, Apr. 28, 1891.

38. "Harris Indicted," *Evening World*, May 13, 1891.

39. Joyce, *Treatise on Indictments*, 738.

40. "There is no general constitutional right to discovery in a criminal case." Weatherford v. Bursey, 429 U.S. 545, 559, 97 S.Ct. 837, 846, 51 L.Ed.2d 30 (1977); Gray v. Netherland, 518 U.S. 152, 116 S. Ct. 2074, 135 L. Ed. 2d 457 (1996).

41. "City and Suburban News," *Times*, May 15, 1891.

42. People v. Molineaux, 14 N.Y.Crim.R. 1, 27 Misc. 60, 57 N.Y.S. 936 (General Sessions, New York County, NY, 1899).

43. "Harris Not Ready to Plead," *Herald*, May 15, 1891.

44. "Harris Indicted."

45. "Harris's Trial Delayed," *Times*, Dec. 16, 1891.

46. "Carlyle Harris's Trial Transferred," *Tribune*, Dec. 16, 1891.

47. "Lawyers in the Harris Case in a Wrangle," *Times*, Jan. 26, 1892.

5. WELLMAN STATES HIS CASE AGAINST HARRIS

1. "Harris Murder Trial," *Daily Eagle*, Jan. 14, 1892. Smyth was called a "recorder" because judges in his position used to be required to keep certain official records. Rovere, *The Weeper and the Blackmailer*, 18.

2. "On Trial for His Life," *Tribune*, Jan. 24, 1892.

3. Wellman, *Gentlemen of the Jury*, 229.

4. As recorder, Smyth had certain record-keeping duties, but his primary function was to serve as the chief judge of the Court of General Sessions.

5. "Justice Smyth Is Dead," *Times*, Aug. 19, 1900.

6. Wellman et al., *Success in Court*, 204, 205.

7. "On Trial for His Life."

8. "People vs. Harris," *Daily Eagle*, Jan. 31, 1892.

9. "Summing Up," *Herald*, Feb. 3, 1892.

10. Wellman, *Gentlemen of the Jury*, 237.

11. Czitrom, *New York Exposed*, 145.

12. Boswell and Thompson, *The Carlyle Harris Case*, 21, 22.

13. "Jerome Dies at 74; Long Tammany Foe," *Times*, Feb. 14, 1934.

14. "The Harris Jury Now Complete," *Tribune*, Jan. 19, 1892.

15. "The Trial of Carlyle Harris," *Daily Eagle*, Jan. 19, 1892.

16. "On Trial for His Life."

17. "'I Would Kill Her and Kill Myself,'" *Herald*, Jan. 20, 1892.

18. "The Trial of Carlyle Harris."

19. "'I Would Kill Her and Kill Myself.'"

20. Wellman and Simms, *The Trial of Carlyle W. Harris*, 9, 10.

21. Wellman and Simms, *The Trial of Carlyle W. Harris*, 14.

22. Philbrick, *Language and Law*, 194.

23. Wellman and Simms, *The Trial of Carlyle W. Harris*, 15, 16.

24. Wellman and Simms, *The Trial of Carlyle W. Harris*, 24.

25. Wellman and Simms, *The Trial of Carlyle W. Harris*, 24, 25.

26. People v. Kerr, 6 N.Y.Crim.R. 406, 6 N.Y.S. 674, 675 (Court of Oyer and Terminer, New York County, 1889).

27. Wellman and Simms, *The Trial of Carlyle W. Harris*, 25.

28. Wellman and Simms, *The Trial of Carlyle W. Harris*, 26.

29. Wellman and Simms, *The Trial of Carlyle W. Harris*, 25, 26.

30. Wellman and Simms, *The Trial of Carlyle W. Harris*, 26; emphasis added.

31. Wellman and Simms, *The Trial of Carlyle W. Harris*, 27, 28.

32. Wellman and Simms, *The Trial of Carlyle W. Harris*, 28, 29.

33. Wellman and Simms, *The Trial of Carlyle W. Harris,* 31.

34. Wellman and Simms, *The Trial of Carlyle W. Harris,* 33, 34.

35. "'I Would Kill Her and Kill Myself.'"

36. "On Trial for His Life."

37. In 1926 the New York legislature changed the law to require the defense to give their opening before the prosecution presented their evidence. People v. Seiler, 246 N.Y. 262, 269, 158 N.E. 615, 618 (1927).

6. THE PROSECUTION CASE—WEEK ONE

1. "Harris Denies the Van Zandt Marriage," *Herald,* Feb. 5, 1892.

2. See, for example, People v. Rose, 41 A.D.3d 742 840 N.Y.S.2d 363 (Sup.Ct., App.Div., 2d Dept., 2007); People v. Kimes, 37 A.D.3d 1 831 N.Y.S.2d 1 (Sup.Ct., App.Div., 1st Dept., 2006); People v. Martinez, 257 A.D.2d 410 683 N.Y.S.2d 81 (Sup.Ct., App.Div., 1st Dept., 1999).

3. The following exchange comes from Transcript, 441, 442.

4. Transcript, 441, 442.

5. Pierson v. People, 34 Sickels 424, 79 N.Y. 424 (1880).

6. Transcript, 472, 473.

7. Transcript, 475.

8. Transcript, 475.

9. This description is paraphrased from "Harris on Trial," *Evening World,* Jan. 20, 1892.

10. Transcript, 484–85.

11. "Morphine, He Swears, Killed Miss Potts," *Herald,* Jan. 21, 1892.

12. Transcript, 487.

13. Transcript, 487–88.

14. Transcript, 489–90.

15. "Morphine, He Swears, Killed Miss Potts."

16. Boswell and Thompson, *The Carlyle Harris Case,* 36

17. Transcript, 491.

18. Transcript, 554–55.

19. Transcript, 557.

20. Transcript, 525.

21. Transcript, 528–30.

22. Transcript, 501.

23. "Harris on Trial."

24. Transcript, 501.

25. Transcript, 539.

26. Transcript, 532, 533.

27. Transcript, 534–36.

28. "Morphine, He Swears, Killed Miss Potts."

29. "Morphine, He Swears, Killed Miss Potts."

30. "'I Would Kill Her and Kill Myself,'" *Herald,* Jan. 20, 1892.

31. "Did Harris Twice Try to Kill Helen?" *Herald,* Jan. 23, 1892.

32. "Mrs. Potts's Story," *Evening World,* Jan. 21, 1892.

33. "Dark for Harris," *Evening World,* Jan. 22, 1892.

34. "Combination Capsules—Their Manipulation May Hang Harris," *St. Louis (MO) Republic,* Jan. 22, 1892, http://www.genealogybank.com.

35. "Did Harris Twice Try to Kill Helen?"

36. Boswell and Thompson, *The Carlyle Harris Case,* 43.

37. Transcript, 604.

38. Transcript, 604–5.

39. "Morphine, He Swears, Killed Helen Potts."

40. Transcript, 580.

41. Transcript, 592.

42. Transcript, 617.

43. Boswell and Thompson, *The Carlyle Harris Case,* 45.

44. "Did Harris Twice Try to Kill Helen?"

45. "Did Harris Twice Try to Kill Helen?"

46. Transcript, 670–71.

47. Transcript, 672.

48. The transcript reads "your mother" (Transcript, 673), but the newspaper reports quote Jerome as saying "her mother." "Did Harris Twice Try to Kill Helen?" "Her mother" makes more sense in the context of the question.

49. Transcript, 694.

50. Transcript, 698–99.

51. Transcript, 703–8.

52. Transcript, 706.

53. Transcript, 707, 708.

54. Transcript, 711.

55. Transcript, 723.

56. Transcript, 724.

57. "Did Harris Twice Try to Kill Helen?"

58. Transcript, 715–17.

59. Transcript, 722.

60. Transcript, 726–50.

61. Transcript, 740.

62. Transcript, 748.

63. Transcript, 739, 740.

64. Transcript, 751–57.

65. Transcript, 756–57.

66. Lawrence v. State, 294 So.2d 371, 373 (1st D.C.A., Fla., 1974).

67. Transcript, 775–76.

68. Transcript, 778.

69. Transcript, 779–87.

70. Transcript, 786.

71. Transcript, 789.

72. Transcript, 790, 793.

73. Transcript, 794.

74. Boswell and Thompson, *The Carlyle Harris Case*, 51. The official transcript reads "I am not acquainted with the gentleman." Transcript, 799.

75. Transcript, 805.

76. Transcript, 807.

77. Transcript, 807.

78. Transcript, 809–12.

79. Transcript, 813.

80. "'Give Him a Pill—I Can Fix That,'" *Herald*, Jan. 25, 1892.

81. John Robortella, "That Time Canandaigua Had a Spy in Its Midst," *Rochester (NY) Democrat and Chronicle*, May 29, 2015, http://democratandchronicle.news papers.com.

82. Robortella, "That Time Canandaigua Had a Spy in Its Midst."

83. Transcript, 827.

84. Transcript, 833.

85. Transcript, 835, 836.

86. "Gotham Gossip," *New Orleans (LA) Times-Picayune*, Jan. 28, 1892, http://www.newspapers.com.

87. Transcript, 827–33, 837.

88. Transcript, 844.

89. Transcript, 844–47.

90. Transcript, 848.

91. Transcript, 848, 849.

92. Transcript, 850.

93. "Harris Has a Bad Record," *Times*, Jan. 26, 1892.

7. THE PROSECUTION CASE—WEEK TWO

1. Transcript, 854, 855.

2. Transcript, 856.

3. Transcript, 857.

4. Transcript, 858–75.

5. Transcript, 879.

6. Transcript, 879.

7. Transcript, 880–88.

8. Transcript, 888–91.

9. Transcript, 891–922.

10. Transcript, 922–42.

11. Transcript, 942–60.

12. Transcript, 927.

13. Transcript, 957.

14. "Her Mother's Fault, Said Carlyle Harris," *Herald,* Jan. 26, 1892. The court reporter did not see fit to include this exchange in the official transcript of testimony.

15. Transcript, 963–65.

16. Transcript, 965–68.

17. "For Harris's Life," *Evening World,* Jan. 26, 1892.

18. Transcript, 969–76.

19. Transcript, 1000.

20. Transcript, 1022.

21. Transcript, 1024.

22. Wellman and Simms, *The Trial of Carlyle W. Harris,* 147.

23. Transcript, 1048, 1049.

24. Transcript, 1050.

25. ABA Model Rule of Professional Conduct 3.4(e), https://www.american bar.org/groups/professional_responsibility/publications/model_rules_of_profes sional_conduct/rule_3_4_fairness_to_opposing_party_counsel/.

26. Wellman, *The Art of Cross-Examination,* 390, 391.

27. Transcript, 1083, 1084.

28. Transcript, 1084, 1085.

29. Transcript, 1092, 1093.

30. Transcript, 1156.

31. Transcript, 1157.

32. Transcript, 1163.

33. Transcript, 1163.

34. Transcript, 1164, 1165.

35. Transcript, 1166–68.

36. Transcript, 1168.

37. Transcript, 1169, 1170.

38. Transcript, 1170.

39. Transcript, 1172, 1173.

40. Transcript, 1212.

41. Transcript, 1212.

42. Transcript, 1215, 1216.

43. Transcript, 1216–26.

44. "Lawyers in the Harris Case in a Wrangle," *Times,* Jan. 29, 1892.

45. Transcript, 1249.

46. Transcript, 1277–1300.

47. "Lawyers in the Harris Case in a Wrangle."

48. Transcript, 1306.

49. Transcript, 1312, 1313.

50. "Lawyers in the Harris Case in a Wrangle."

51. "'I Would Kill Her and Kill Myself,'" *Herald*, Jan. 29, 1892.

8. THE DEFENSE CASE—DAY ONE

1. "In Harris's Defense," *Evening World*, Jan. 29, 1892.

2. "In Harris's Defense."

3. Wellman and Simms, *The Trial of Carlyle W. Harris*, 200.

4. Wellman and Simms, *The Trial of Carlyle W. Harris*, 200.

5. Wellman and Simms, *The Trial of Carlyle W. Harris*, 200.

6. Wellman and Simms, *The Trial of Carlyle W. Harris*, 200, 203.

7. Wellman and Simms, *The Trial of Carlyle W. Harris*, 203, 204.

8. "Mr. Jerome Ill in Court," *Tribune*, Jan. 30, 1892.

9. Wellman and Simms, *The Trial of Carlyle W. Harris*, 204. The Upas tree has a poisonous sap that is used on arrowheads and blowpipe darts. Robinson and Ling, "Blowpipe Dart Poison from Borneo," 82.

10. Wellman and Simms, *The Trial of Carlyle W. Harris*, 204.

11. Wellman and Simms, *The Trial of Carlyle W. Harris*, 205.

12. Wellman and Simms, *The Trial of Carlyle W. Harris*, 205.

13. Quintilian, *Institutes of Oratory*, IV.ii.31. See also Cicero, *Rhetorica ad Herennium*, I.ix.14.

14. Wellman and Simms, *The Trial of Carlyle W. Harris*, 207.

15. Wellman and Simms, *The Trial of Carlyle W. Harris*, 208.

16. "People vs. Harris," *Daily Eagle*, Jan. 31, 1892.

17. Philbrick, *Language and the Law*, 201.

18. Philbrick, *Language and the Law*, 202.

19. Philbrick, *Language and the Law*, 202.

20. Colton, *Lacon*, 36.

21. Stryker, *For the Defense*, 549.

22. Transcript, 532, 533, 566, 870, 871, 961, 962, 1007, 1267, 1268.

23. *Dictionary of American Biography*, 20:459.

24. "The Harris Murder Trial," *Tribune*, Jan. 31, 1892.

25. Transcript, 1319.

26. Transcript, 1320.

27. Transcript, 1321.

28. Transcript, 1322, 1323.

29. Transcript, 1322, 1323.

30. Transcript, 1325.

31. "Striving to Save Carlyle Harris," *Philadelphia (PA) Inquirer*, Jan. 30, 1892, http://genealogybank.com.

32. Transcript, 1327.

33. Transcript, 1328.

34. Transcript, 1329.
. 35. Transcript, 1329.
36. West, "Report on the Microscope," *Transactions of the State Medical Society of Indiana,* 34–38, 38.
37. See Harsha, "The Diagnostic Value of the Medical Laboratory," 1:86–91.
38. Transcript, 1330.
39. Transcript, 1330, 1331.
40. Transcript, 1332.
41. "Striving to Save Carlyle Harris."
42. Transcript, 1333; Wellman and Simms, *The Trial of Carlyle W. Harris,* 215.
43. Wellman, *The Art of Cross-Examination,* 326.
44. Transcript, 998.
45. Transcript, 1332, 1333.
46. Wellman and Simms, *The Trial of Carlyle W. Harris,* 215. Once again, the court reporter seems to have omitted an indelicate remark by one of the lawyers.
47. "Young Lawyer Jerome Breaks Down in Court," *Herald,* Jan. 30, 1892.
48. Wellman, *The Art of Cross-Examination,* 386.
49. "Young Lawyer Jerome Breaks Down in Court."
50. "The Harris Murder Trial."
51. Wellman et al., *Success in Court,* 33, 34.
52. Wellman et al., *Success in Court,* 41, 42; Wellman, *Luck and Opportunity,* 44; Wellman, *The Art of Cross-Examination,* 392–96.
53. Wellman, *The Art of Cross-Examination,* 396.
54. Wellman et al., *Success in Court,* 41 (five thousand); Wellman, *Luck and Opportunity,* 44 (six thousand).
55. Wellman et al., *Success in Court,* 40.
56. "I have thought that inequality of the pupils is proof that a case is not one of narcotism; but Professor Taylor has recorded an instance of opium-poisoning in which it occurred" (Hamilton, *Medical Jurisprudence,* 7th Am. ed. 1873, p. 205). Wood, *Therapeutics,* 166.
57. Taylor, *A Manual of Medical Jurisprudence,* 205.
58. Transcript, 998; Wellman et al., *Success in Court,* 41, 42.
59. Transcript, 998.
60. Transcript, 1249.
61. Taylor, *The Principles and Practice of Medical Jurisprudence,* 1:362.
62. "Symptoms Like Those of Poisoning by Opium—Pupils Contracted—Autopsy: Apoplexy of the Pons Varolii—Bright's Disease," *Medical Times and Gazette,* 1:214.
63. "Symptoms Like Those Produced by Large Doses of Opium—Death—Fracture of the Base of the Skull," *Medical Times and Gazette,* 1:214.
64. Wellman et al., *Success in Court,* 42.
65. Transcript, 1347.
66. "Young Lawyer Jerome Breaks Down in Court."

67. Transcript, 1335.

68. Transcript, 1336.

69. *Dictionary of American Biography,* 2:264.

70. "Opening of the Defense," *Times,* Jan. 30, 1892.

9. THE DEFENSE CASE—DAY TWO

1. "Lawyer Jerome Out Again," *Herald,* Jan. 31, 1892.

2. "The Harris Murder Trial," *Tribune,* Jan. 31, 1892.

3. "Lawyer Jerome Out Again."

4. "The Harris Murder Trial."

5. "Opening of the Defense," *Times,* Jan. 30, 1892.

6. "Lawyer Jerome Is Resting," *Evening World,* Jan. 30, 1892.

7. "Lawyer Jerome Out Again."

8. "Lawyer Jerome Out Again."

9. "Mr. Jerome Ill in Court," *Tribune,* Jan. 30, 1892.

10. "Lawyer Jerome Is Resting."

11. "Harris's Defense," *Evening World,* Feb. 1, 1892.

12. "Harris's Defense."

13. Transcript 1353, 1354.

14. "Harris' Trial Closing," *St. Louis (MO) Republic,* Feb. 2, 1892, http://genealogy bank.com.

15. Transcript, 1351; emphasis added.

16. Transcript, 1354, 1355.

17. Transcript, 1358.

18. "Harris's Defense."

19. Transcript, 1355.

20. Transcript, 1365, 1366.

21. Transcript, 1367.

22. Transcript, 1370–73.

23. Transcript, 1379.

24. Transcript, 1382.

25. *Dictionary of American Biography,* 20:535, 536.

26. Transcript, 1383.

27. Transcript, 1383; *Dictionary of American Biography,* 20:535.

28. Transcript, 1392, 1393.

29. Transcript, 1402.

30. Transcript, 1405.

31. Transcript, 1407.

32. Transcript, 1411, 1412.

33. Transcript, 1419.

34. Transcript, 1421, 1422.

35. Transcript, 1423.

36. Transcript 1435, 1436.

37. Transcript, 1440–41.

10. TAYLOR SUMS UP

1. "Now to the Jury," *Evening World*, Feb. 2, 1892.

2. "Summing Up," *Herald*, Feb. 3, 1892.

3. Transcript, 1439–40.

4. Philbrick, *Language and the Law*, 212.

5. Wellman and Simms, *The Trial of Carlyle W. Harris*, 241.

6. Wellman and Simms, *The Trial of Carlyle W. Harris*, 243.

7. Wellman and Simms, *The Trial of Carlyle W. Harris*, 243.

8. Wellman and Simms, *The Trial of Carlyle W. Harris*, 243.

9. "Summing Up," *Herald*, Feb. 3, 1892.

10. Wellman and Simms, *The Trial of Carlyle W. Harris*, 245, 246.

11. Wellman and Simms, *The Trial of Carlyle W. Harris*, 247, 248.

12. Wellman and Simms, *The Trial of Carlyle W. Harris*, 248, 249.

13. Wellman and Simms, *The Trial of Carlyle W. Harris*, 249.

14. Wellman and Simms, *The Trial of Carlyle W. Harris*, 250.

15. Wellman and Simms, *The Trial of Carlyle W. Harris*, 250.

16. Wellman and Simms, *The Trial of Carlyle W. Harris*, 251, 252.

17. Wellman and Simms, *The Trial of Carlyle W. Harris*, 252, 253.

18. Wellman and Simms, *The Trial of Carlyle W. Harris*, 255.

19. Wellman and Simms, *The Trial of Carlyle W. Harris*, 254, 255.

20. Wellman and Simms, *The Trial of Carlyle W. Harris*, 257.

21. Wellman and Simms, *The Trial of Carlyle W. Harris*, 257–57.

22. Wellman and Simms, *The Trial of Carlyle W. Harris*, 268, 269.

23. Wellman and Simms, *The Trial of Carlyle W. Harris*, 269.

24. Wellman and Simms, *The Trial of Carlyle W. Harris*, 270.

25. Wellman and Simms, *The Trial of Carlyle W. Harris*, 268.

26. Wellman and Simms, *The Trial of Carlyle W. Harris*, 260.

27. Wellman and Simms, *The Trial of Carlyle W. Harris*, 260.

28. Wellman and Simms, *The Trial of Carlyle W. Harris*, 260.

29. Wellman and Simms, *The Trial of Carlyle W. Harris*, 261, 262.

30. "Now to the Jury."

31. Wellman and Simms, *The Trial of Carlyle W. Harris*, 262.

32. Wellman and Simms, *The Trial of Carlyle W. Harris*, 263.

33. Wellman and Simms, *The Trial of Carlyle W. Harris*, 264.

34. Wellman and Simms, *The Trial of Carlyle W. Harris*, 264.

35. Wellman and Simms, *The Trial of Carlyle W. Harris*, 265.

36. Wellman and Simms, *The Trial of Carlyle W. Harris*, 265.

37. Wellman and Simms, *The Trial of Carlyle W. Harris*, 265.

38. Wellman and Simms, *The Trial of Carlyle W. Harris*, 267.

39. Wellman and Simms, *The Trial of Carlyle W. Harris*, 266.

40. Wellman and Simms, *The Trial of Carlyle W. Harris*, 261.

41. Wellman and Simms, *The Trial of Carlyle W. Harris*, 270–72.

42. Wellman and Simms, *The Trial of Carlyle W. Harris*, 273.

43. Wellman and Simms, *The Trial of Carlyle W. Harris*, 274.

44. Wellman and Simms, *The Trial of Carlyle W. Harris*, 275.

45. Wellman et al., *Success in Court*, 39.

46. Smith, *Famous American Poison Mysteries*, 43.

47. Smith, *Famous American Poison Mysteries*, 272.

48. "Harris Feels Sure of a New Trial," *Herald*, Feb. 4, 1892.

49. "Harris Not Ready to Plead," *Herald*, May 15, 1891.

50. Ledyard, *Articles, Speeches and Poems of Carlyle W. Harris*, 16.

51. Boswell and Thompson, *The Carlyle Harris Case*, 109.

52. "Harris Must Die," *Evening World*, Feb. 3, 1892.

53. Wellman, *Luck and Opportunity*, 59, 60.

54. Colin Evans, "Robert Buchanan Trial: 1893."

55. "A Crime Newspapers Brought to Light," *Daily Eagle*, Feb. 3, 1892.

56. "The Harris Murder Trial," *Tribune*, Jan. 31, 1892.

57. "Carlyle W. Harris to Die," *Tribune*, Jan. 18, 1893.

58. "'I Would Kill Her and Kill Myself,'" *Herald*, Jan. 29, 1892.

59. "A Crime Newspapers Brought to Light."

60. Philbrick, *Language and the Law*, 204.

11. WELLMAN SUMS UP, THE JURY SPEAKS

1. "Summing Up," *Herald*, Feb. 3, 1892.

2. Wellman and Simms, *The Trial of Carlyle W. Harris*, 276.

3. Wellman and Simms, *The Trial of Carlyle W. Harris*, 277.

4. Crump v. State, 622 So.2d 963 (Fla. 1993); People v. Flores, 191 A.D.2d 306, 595 N.Y.S.2d 173 (Sup.Ct.App.Div., 1st Dept., New York County, 1993).

5. People v. Jackson, 143 A.D.2d 363, 532 N.Y.S.2d 303 (Sup.Ct.App.Div., 2nd Dept., New York County, 1988).

6. Wellman and Simms, *The Trial of Carlyle W. Harris*, 278.

7. Wellman and Simms, *The Trial of Carlyle W. Harris*, 280, 281.

8. Wellman and Simms, *The Trial of Carlyle W. Harris*, 283.

9. Wellman and Simms, *The Trial of Carlyle W. Harris*, 284, 285.

10. Wellman and Simms, *The Trial of Carlyle W. Harris*, 286.

11. Wellman and Simms, *The Trial of Carlyle W. Harris*, 287, 288.

12. Wellman and Simms, *The Trial of Carlyle W. Harris*, 289.

13. Wellman and Simms, *The Trial of Carlyle W. Harris*, 290.

14. Wellman and Simms, *The Trial of Carlyle W. Harris*, 290, 291.

15. Wellman and Simms, *The Trial of Carlyle W. Harris*, 292, 293.

16. Wellman and Simms, *The Trial of Carlyle W. Harris*, 293; *Hamlet*, act 2, scene 2.

17. Wellman and Simms, *The Trial of Carlyle W. Harris*, 294.

18. People v. Greenwall, 70 Sickels 520, 115 N.Y. 520, 526, 22 N.E. 180, 182 (1889).

19. Wellman and Simms, *The Trial of Carlyle W. Harris*, 295.

20. Mosley v. State, 46 So.3d 510 (Fla. 2016); People v. Brown, 26 A.D.3d 392, 812 N.Y.S.2d 561 (Sup.Ct., App.Div., 2nd Dept., New York County, 2006).

21. Wellman and Simms, *The Trial of Carlyle W. Harris*, 295.

22. Wellman and Simms, *The Trial of Carlyle W. Harris*, 297.

23. Wellman and Simms, *The Trial of Carlyle W. Harris*, 297, 298.

24. Wellman and Simms, *The Trial of Carlyle W. Harris*, 299.

25. Wellman and Simms, *The Trial of Carlyle W. Harris*, 300.

26. Wellman and Simms, *The Trial of Carlyle W. Harris*, 302.

27. "A Murderer's Double Life," *Harrisburg (PA) Patriot*, Feb. 4, 1892, http://genealogybank.com.

28. "Harris Feels Sure of a New Trial," *Herald*, Feb. 4, 1892.

29. "The Harris Conviction," *Tribune*, Feb. 4, 1892.

30. Transcript 470a.

31. "Harris Feels Sure of a New Trial."

32. "Carlyle Harris' Villany," *Boston (MA) Herald*, Feb. 4, 1892, http://www.genealogy.com; "New York's Young Murderer," *New Orleans (LA) Times-Picayune*, Feb. 4, 1892, http://www.genealogybank.com.

33. "A Murderer's Double Life."

34. "Harris Feels Sure of a New Trial," *Herald*, February 4, 1892.

35. Wellman and Simms, *The Trial of Carlyle W. Harris*, 303.

36. Wellman and Simms, *The Trial of Carlyle W. Harris*, 303.

37. Wellman and Simms, *The Trial of Carlyle W. Harris*, 304.

38. Wellman and Simms, *The Trial of Carlyle W. Harris*, 305–6.

39. Wellman and Simms, *The Trial of Carlyle W. Harris*, 306.

40. Wellman and Simms, *The Trial of Carlyle W. Harris*, 307.

41. Wellman and Simms, *The Trial of Carlyle W. Harris*, 307.

42. Wellman and Simms, *The Trial of Carlyle W. Harris*, 310.

43. Boswell and Thompson, *The Carlyle Harris Case*, 102.

44. Rovere, *The Weeper and the Blackmailer*, 68.

45. Rovere, *The Weeper and the Blackmailer*, 68.

46. Wellman, *Luck and Opportunity*, 27, 28.

47. "Harris Must Die," *Evening World*, Feb. 3, 1892.

48. Boswell and Thompson, *The Carlyle Harris Case*, 103.

49. "Summing Up."

50. "Murder in the First Degree," *Springfield (MA) Republican*, Feb. 3, 1892, http://genealogybank.com.

51. "Harris Is Found Guilty," *Times*, Feb. 3, 1892.

52. Wellman and Simms, *The Trial of Carlyle W. Harris*, 326, 327.

53. Boswell and Thompson, *The Carlyle Harris Case*, 105.

54. "The Harris Conviction,"

55. "Harris Is Found Guilty."

56. Boswell and Thompson, *The Carlyle Harris Case*, 108.

57. "Harris Is Found Guilty."

58. "When the Verdict Came," *Herald*, Feb. 3, 1892.

59. "Harris Must Die."

12. NEW EVIDENCE?

1. "Ready with Bail," *Evening World*, Mar. 21, 1891.

2. "The Harris Murder Trial," *Tribune*, Feb. 1, 1892.

3. "The Tide Turns and then Falls," *Philadelphia (PA) Inquirer*, Jan. 27, 1892, http://www.genealogybank.com.

4. "The Harris Case," *Times*, Feb. 3, 1892.

5. "'Give Him a Pill—I Can Fix That,'" *Herald*, Jan. 23, 1892.

6. "Harris Denies the Van Zandt Marriage," *Herald*, Feb. 5, 1892.

7. "Carlyle W. Harris's First Wife," *Tribune*, Feb. 5, 1892.

8. "His Record of the Worst," *Kansas City (MO) Times*, Feb. 4, 1892, http://genealogybank.com.

9. "A Most Foul Man," *Knoxville (TN) Journal*, Feb. 4, 1892, http://www.genealogybank.com; "Led a Double Life," *San Francisco Chronicle*, Feb. 4, 1892, http://www.genealogybank.com; "Gotham Gossip," *New Orleans Times-Picayune*, Feb. 10, 1892.

10. "Lawyer Jerome Talks," *Times*, Feb. 5, 1892.

11. Ledyard, *Articles, Speeches and Poems of Carlyle W. Harris*, 71.

12. Ledyard, *Articles, Speeches and Poems of Carlyle W. Harris*, 78.

13. "Heard His Doom Without Flinching," *Herald*, Feb. 9, 1892.

14. "Harris a Puzzle to the Warden," *Herald*, Feb. 6, 1892.

15. "Murderer Harris Is Sentenced," *New Haven (CT) Register*, Feb. 8, 1892, http://genealogybank.com.

16. "Heard His Doom Without Flinching."

17. "Helen Potts' Father Wants to Touch the Button that Ends Harris' Life," *Herald*, Feb. 8, 1892.

18. Ledyard, *Articles, Speeches and Poems of Carlyle W. Harris*, 95.

19. Ledyard, *Articles, Speeches and Poems of Carlyle W. Harris*, 107.

20. Ledyard, *Articles, Speeches and Poems of Carlyle W. Harris*, 103.

21. "Carlyle Harris on Life in the Tombs," *Evening World*, Mar. 5, 1892.

22. "Tomorrow's Sunday World," *Evening World*, July 9, 1892.

23. "Carlyle's Coolness," *Morning Olympian (WA)*, Feb. 17, 1892, http://genealogybank.com.

24. "Carlyle W. Harris' Life in the Tombs," *Herald*, Jan. 28, 1892.

25. "Used Morphine," *Trenton (NJ) Evening Times,* Feb. 12, 1892, http://genealogy
bank.com.

26. "It Is a Mystery," *Trenton Evening Times,* Feb. 13, 1892.

27. "It Is a Mystery."

28. "The Story Denounced as a Lie," *Trenton Evening Times,* Feb. 13, 1892.

29. "Miss Meeker Never Knew Harris' Friend," *Herald,* Feb. 13, 1892.

30. "May Be a Chance for Carlyle W. Harris," *Herald,* Feb. 14, 1892.

31. "Is Mrs. Kunn a Crank?" *Daily Eagle,* Feb. 15, 1892.

32. "Now They Say Haaman Is Harris' 'Pal' Prescott," *Herald,* Feb. 16, 1892.

33. "Now They Say Haaman Is Harris' 'Pal' Prescott."

34. "A Book About the Carlyle W. Harris Trial," *Times,* Mar. 12, 1892.

35. Wellman, *Gentlemen of the Jury,* 132.

36. "New Lawyers for Carlyle Harris," *Evening World,* May 21, 1892.

37. Wellman, *Luck and Opportunity,* 23, 24.

38. Rovere, *The Weeper and the Blackmailer,* 24.

39. Murphy, *Scoundrels in Law,* 105–9.

40. Boswell and Thompson, *The Carlyle Harris Case,* 119.

41. Boswell and Thompson, *The Carlyle Harris Case,* 96, 97, 107.

42. "The Appeal of Carlyle W. Harris," *Springfield Republican,* Dec. 7, 1892.

43. People v. Harris, 136 N.Y. 423, 33 N.E. 65, 66, (1893).

44. People v. Harris, 33 N.E. at 67.

45. The original text of this sentence reads "has often," which makes less
sense than "often has."

46. People v. Harris, 136 N.Y. 423, 33 N.E. 65, 73 (1893).

47. "Not a Judge for Harris," *Times,* Jan. 18, 1893.

48. "Carlyle W. Harris Agitated at Last," *Herald,* Jan. 18, 1893.

49. "Not a Judge for Harris."

50. "Not a Judge for Harris."

51. "Carlyle W. Harris to Die," *Tribune,* Jan. 18, 1893.

52. Ledyard, *Articles, Speeches and Poems of Carlyle W. Harris,* 35.

53. "A Response to the Appeal of Mrs. Harris," *Tribune,* Jan. 25, 1893.

54. "Mrs. Harris' Vain Search," *Herald,* Jan. 24, 1893.

55. "Experts in Murder Trials," *Times,* Apr. 23, 1893.

56. "In Behalf of Carlyle Harris," *Star,* Apr. 1, 1893.

57. Ledyard, *Articles, Speeches and Poems of Carlyle W. Harris,* 37.

58. "Senators Discuss the Harris Case," *Tribune,* Mar. 30, 1893.

59. "A Harris Mass Meeting," *Times,* Mar. 18, 1893.

60. "Mrs. Harris Visits Asbury Park," *Tribune,* Jan. 24, 1893; "Mrs. Harris' Vain
Search."

61. "A Response to the Appeal of Mrs. Harris."

62. "Phrenological Tests of Carlyle W. Harris," *Herald,* Jan. 29, 1893.

63. "Evidence for Harris," *Herald,* Feb. 3, 1893.

64. "Dr. Dixon Doubts Harris' Guilt," *Herald,* Feb. 6, 1893.

65. "Prayer in Harris' Cell," *Herald*, Mar. 27, 1893.

66. Dixon, *The Clansman*, dedication page.

67. "Dr. Dixon Doubts Harris' Guilt."

68. "Prayer in Harris' Cell."

69. See Hanson, *The Life and Works of the World's Greatest Evangelist, Dwight L. Moody.*

70. "Mrs. Harris Joins Her Daughter," *Buffalo (NY) Evening News*, Apr. 17, 1893, http://www.newspapers.com; "Carlyle W. Harris," *Watertown Daily Times*, Apr. 18, 1893.

71. See Czitrom, *New York Exposed*, and Parkhurst, *Our Fight with Tammany*.

72. "In a Death Grip," *San Francisco Morning Call*, Dec. 7, 1892, http://newspapers .com.

73. "Now Summing Up," *Evening World*, Feb. 7, 1893.

74. People v. Gardner, 144 N.Y. 119, 38 N.E. 1003 (1894).

75. "Giving Hope to Harris," *Evening World*, Jan. 18, 1893.

76. "Only Pity for Mrs. Harris," *Evening World*, Jan. 23, 1893.

77. "Asks Clemency for Harris," *Evening World*, Jan. 26, 1893.

78. "The Carlyle Harris Case," *Daily Eagle*, Jan. 31, 1893; "Carlyle W. Harris' Case Adjourned," *Herald*, Jan. 31, 1893; "The Carlyle Harris Case," *Watertown (NY) Daily Times*, Jan. 31, 1893.

79. "Carlyle Harris's Find," *Evening World*, Feb. 1, 1893.

80. "Carlyle Harris's Find."

81. "Efforts to Save Harris," *Times*, Feb. 3, 1893.

82. "Affidavits Against Harris," *Evening World*, Feb. 6, 1893.

83. "Carlyle W. Harris Is Angry," *Herald*, Feb. 6, 1893.

84. "Asks Clemency for Harris."

85. "Carlyle Harris's Hopes," *Evening World*, Jan. 28, 1893.

86. "New Witnesses Against Harris," *Herald*, Feb. 21, 1893.

87. This description comes from "Harris's Forlorn Hope," *Times*, Feb. 28, 1893, and "Carlyle Harris' Case," *Daily Eagle*, Feb. 27, 1893.

88. "Affidavits in Carlyle W. Harris's Case," *Tribune*, Mar. 4, 1893; "Harris Further Cheered," *Herald*, Mar. 8, 1893.

89. "Smyth Denies Carlyle Harris a New Trial," *Herald*, Mar. 17, 1893.

90. "A Harris Mass Meeting."

91. "Harris's Appeal Denied," *Times*, Mar. 17, 1893.

92. "Harris's Appeal Denied."

13. THE RAINES COMMISSION

1. "A Harris Mass Meeting," *Times*, Mar. 18, 1893.

2. "Carlyle Harris Is Defiant Now," *Herald*, Mar. 18, 1893.

3. "Appeal from Mrs. Harris," *Times*, Mar. 19, 1893.

4. *Dictionary of American Biography*, 4:83–86; Strong, *Joseph H. Choate*, 127–236.

5. "To Sentence Carlyle W. Harris," *Tribune*, Mar. 18, 1893.

6. "The Harris Mass Meeting," *Times*, Mar. 18, 1893.

7. "Mob Rule in the Case of Harris," *Daily Eagle*, Mar. 18, 1893.

8. "Carlyle Harris Is Defiant Now."

9. Foust, *Life and Dramatic Works of Robert Montgomery Bird*, 410–40.

10. Sherman, Telegram to Lt. Gen. Ulysses S. Grant, Oct. 9, 1864, Civil War Era NC, https://cwnc.omeka.chass.ncsu.edu/items/show/143.

11. "Carlyle Harris Is Defiant Now."

12. "Carlyle Harris Is Defiant Now."

13. "Harris Says He Is Ready to Die," *Herald*, Mar. 1, 1893.

14. "Carlyle Harris Must Die," *Times*, Mar. 21, 1893.

15. "Carlyle Harris Must Die."

16. "The Resentence of Harris," *Tribune*, Mar. 21, 1893.

17. "Carlyle Harris Must Die."

18. "The Resentence of Harris."

19. "Carlyle Harris Must Die."

20. "Carlyle Harris Must Die."

21. "The Resentence of Harris."

22. "Carlyle Harris Must Die."

23. "Harris Says He Is Vindicated," *Herald*, Mar. 22, 1893.

24. "Harris Says He Is Vindicated"; "Harris Goes to Sing Sing To-day," *Herald*, Mar. 23, 1893.

25. "Harris' Father Talks of His Case," *Herald*, Mar. 26, 1893.

26. "Harris Goes to Sing Sing To-day."

27. "How the Men Escaped," *Herald*, Apr. 22, 1893.

28. "Harris Waits by Death's Chair," *Herald*, Mar. 24, 1893.

29. "Harris Waits by Death's Chair."

30. For example, "Harris' Father Talks of His Case."

31. "Harris Awaits His Fate Coolly," *Herald*, Apr. 10, 1893.

32. "Some State Capital Echoes," *Watertown Daily Times*, Mar. 29, 1893.

33. "Carlyle Harris' Right to Appeal," *Herald*, Apr. 2, 1893.

34. "The Codes as Amended," *Tribune*, June 26, 1893.

35. "Harris Awaits His Fate Coolly."

36. "In Behalf of Carlyle W. Harris," *Tribune*, Apr. 4, 1893.

37. "Carlyle Harris's Hopes," *Times*, Apr. 4, 1893.

38. "Mr. Croker Has Done Nothing for Harris," *Tribune*, Apr. 5, 1893.

39. "To Plead for Harris on Monday," *Tribune*, Apr. 6, 1893.

40. *Dictionary of American Biography*, 6:479, 480.

41. "Local News from Albany," *Watertown Daily Times*, Apr. 8, 1893.

42. "Carlyle W. Harris," *Watertown Daily Times*, Apr. 10, 1893.

43. "Will Not Hear the Harris Case," *Herald*, Apr. 11, 1893.

44. "Two Murder Trials Postponed," *Herald*, Apr. 11, 1893.

45. "Harris's Petitions Presented," *Times*, Apr. 11, 1893.

46. "Carlyle W. Harris," *Watertown Daily Times*, Apr. 11, 1893; "Asking Life for Harris," *Tribune*, Apr. 12, 1893.

47. "Harris's Petitions Presented."

48. "Asking Life for Harris."

49. "One of Harris' Early Victims," *Herald*, Apr. 13, 1893.

50. "Carlyle W. Harris," *Watertown Daily Times*, Apr. 14, 1893.

51. "Carlyle W. Harris," *Watertown Daily Times*, Apr. 21, 1893.

52. "Escaped from Sing Sing," *Daily Eagle*, Apr. 21, 1893; "How the Men Escaped"; "The Escape from Sing Sing," *Watertown Daily Times*, Apr. 22, 1893.

53. "The Murderers Still Free," *Tribune*, Apr. 25, 1893.

54. "More Testimony in the Harris Case," *Herald*, Apr. 22, 1893.

55. "Harris Says He Is Ready to Die," *Herald*, Mar. 19, 1893.

56. "Flower-Harris Commission," *Daily Eagle*, Apr. 22, 1893.

57. "George Raines," *Times*, Nov. 28, 1908.

58. "Murderer Osmond Resentenced," *Times*, Apr. 25, 1893.

59. "Escaped from Sing Sing."

60. Conyes, *Fifty Years in Sing Sing*, 96.

61. "Raines' Report in Harris' Case," *Herald*, May 7, 1893.

62. This description of the hearing is compiled from "The Retrial of Harris," *Tribune*, Apr. 26, 1893; "Going Over the Old Ground," *Tribune*, Apr. 27, 1893; "Carlyle Harris' Case," *Watertown Daily Times*, Apr. 27, 1893; "The Harris Hearing," *Rochester (NY) Democrat and Chronicle*, Apr. 27, 1893, http://www.newspapers.com; "Sympathy for Mrs. Potts," *Tribune*, Apr. 29, 1894; "Two Women All in Black," *Times*, Apr. 29, 1893; and "The Harris Case Finished," *Watertown Daily Times*, Apr. 29, 1893.

63. "Close of the Harris Hearing," *Herald*, Apr. 30, 1893.

64. Wellman, *The Art of Cross-Examination*, 396; Wellman, *Luck and Opportunity*, 51–65.

65. "Accused of Poisoning His Wife," *Tribune*, Mar. 21, 1893.

66. "The Retrial of Harris."

67. "The Retrial of Harris."

68. "The Retrial of Harris."

69. "Going Over the Old Ground."

70. Clark, Dekle, and Bailey, *Cross-Examination Handbook*, 215.

71. "The Harris Hearing."

72. "Going Over the Old Ground."

73. "Referee Rains' Report," *Daily Eagle*, May 7, 1893.

74. "The Harris Hearing."

75. "Two Women All in Black."

76. "Two Women All in Black."

77. "Two Women All in Black."

14. THE CURTAIN FALLS

1. "What Purpose Can It Serve," *Times*, Apr. 30, 1893.

2. "What Purpose Can It Serve."

3. "Mr. Raines' Report Is Ready," *Daily Eagle*, May 2, 1893.

4. The following discussion of Raines's findings comes from the full text of his report, which was printed in "Raines' Report in Harris' Case," *Herald*, May 7, 1893; and "Referee Rains' Report," *Daily Eagle*, May 7, 1893.

5. Transcript, 429.

6. "Raines' Report in Harris' Case"; Wellman, *Luck and Opportunity*, 46.

7. "Death for Carlyle Harris," *Tribune*, May 5, 1893.

8. "Trying to Save Harris," *Daily Eagle*, May 5, 1893.

9. "To Be Electrocuted Monday," *Watertown Daily Times*, May 5, 1893.

10. "To Be Electrocuted Monday."

11. "All Are Resigned to Harris' Fate," *Herald*, May 6, 1893.

12. Conyes, *Fifty Years at Sing Sing*, 96.

13. "Harris Likely to Die Monday," *Times*, May 7, 1893.

14. "Raines' Report in Harris' Case."

15. "Francis McCready Harris," https://www.findagrave.com/memorial/113250950/frances-harris.

16. The following description of Harris's execution comes from "Last Act in the Harris Drama," *Watertown Daily Times*, May 8, 1893; "Carlyle W. Harris Is Dead," *Times*, May 8, 1893; "Carlyle Harris Killed," *Tribune*, May 9, 1893; "Harris Dies Pleading His Innocence," *Herald*, May 9, 1893; and "Executing the Murderer," *Herald*, May 9, 1893.

17. "Carlyle W. Harris' Funeral," *Watertown Daily Times*, May 9, 1893.

18. "Carlyle W. Harris' Funeral."

19. Ledyard, *Articles, Speeches and Poems of Carlyle W. Harris*, 98.

20. "Carlyle W. Harris' Funeral."

21. Albany Rural Cemetery, "Map of Famous Residents," http://albanyruralcemetery.org/historical-research/map-of-famous-residents-of-arc/. Although Harris's body is located in Section 4, Lot 11 of the famous cemetery, visitors to the cemetery's Web site will not find him on the Map of Famous Residents. "Carlyle Harris," https://www.findagrave.com/memorial/5788553/carlyle-harris.

22. "Harris' Body in the Grave," *Herald*, May 10, 1893.

23. "Visiting Carlyle Harris' Grave," *Daily Eagle*, May 10, 1893.

24. The information stated in this paragraph is taken from "She Loved Carlyle Harris," *New Haven Register*, May 11, 1893; "Gotham by 'Phone: Loved the Man Condemned to Die," *Philadelphia Inquirer*, May 12, 1893; "Harris Was Engaged," *Trenton Evening Times*, May 11, 1893.

25. "Denies She Was Harris' Betrothed," *Herald*, May 12, 1893.

26. "Harris Died Pleading His Innocence," *Herald*, May 9, 1893.

27. "Harris' Body in the Grave."

28. "Harris's Last Statement—His Innocence Stoutly Maintained," *Tribune,* May 10, 1893.

29. "The Case of Carlyle Harris," *The Illustrated American,* 584.

30. Howe, "Some Notable Murder Cases," 381, 382.

EPILOGUE

1. For example, the Heliocentric Universe, Newton's physics, and the indivisible atom, to name a few.

2. Instruction 3.7, *Florida Standard Jury Instructions in Criminal Cases,* http:// www.floridasupremecourt.org/jury_instructions/instructions-ch3.shtml.

3. WPIC 4.01, *Washington Pattern Jury Instructions—Criminal* (October 2016 Update), https://govt.westlaw.com/wcrji/Document/Ief9ba3b5e10d11daade1ae 871d9b2cbe?viewType=FullText&originationContext=documenttoc&transition Type=CategoryPageItem&contextData=(sc.Default).

4. Instruction E:3, *Colorado Jury Instructions Criminal 2016,* https://www. courts.state.co.us/userfiles/file/Court_Probation/Supreme_Court/Committees/ Criminal_Jury_Instructions/2016/COLJI-Crim%202016%20-%20Final.pdf.

5. Jacobellis v. Ohio, 378 U.S. 184, 197 (1964) (concurring opinion).

6. Hawley and McGregor, *The Criminal Law,* 16, 17.

7. Hilliard, *The American Law of Real Property,* 1:84–92.

8. Bedford, *The Law of Principal and Agent,* 1:44.

Bibliography

ABA Model Rules of Professional Conduct. American Bar Association, 2016. https:
//www.americanbar.org/groups/professional_responsibility/publications/model
_rules_of_professional_conduct/model_rules_of_professional_conduct_table
_of_contents/.

ABA Standards for Criminal Justice Prosecution Function. 3rd ed. ABA House of
Delegates, 1992. http://www.americanbar.org/content/dam/aba/publications/
criminal_justice_standards/prosecution_defense_function.authcheckdam.pdf.

Bedford, J. Claude. *The Law of Principal and Agent in Contract and Tort.* Vol. 1.
Philadelphia: The Blackstone Publishing Company, 1888. https://archive.org
/details/cu31924019245772.

"Bellevue Hospital Medical College, New York: Announcement for 1861–62." *The
Chicago Medical Journal* 4 (1861): 442. https://archive.org/details/chicagomedical
jo4186unse.

Boswell, Charles, and Lewis Thompson. *The Carlyle Harris Case.* New York: Collier
Books, 1961.

"Carlyle Harris Case, The." *Boston Medical and Surgical Journal* 128, no. 15 (1893):
378. https://books.google.com/books?id=RMAEAAAAYAAJ&pg=PA378&dq
=%E2%80%9CCarlyle+Harris+Case,+The.%E2%80%9D+Boston+Medical+
and+Surgical+Journal&hl=en&sa=X&ved=0ahUKEwjBkrGo9JrWAhXizFQ
KHZBPA1QQ6AEIJzAA#v=onepage&q=%E2%80%9CCarlyle%20Harris%20
Case%2C%20The.%E2%80%9D%20Boston%20Medical%20and%20Surgical
%20Journal&f=false.

"Carlyle Harris Case, The." *The Illustrated American* 13, no. 164 (Apr. 8, 1893):
429–30. https://books.google.com/books?id=VSMgAQAAMAAJ&printsec=
frontcover&dq=The+Illustrated+American&hl=en&sa=X&ved=0ahUKEw
jhn6749JrWAhXJsVQKHQZ2CUkQuwUIKTAA#v=onepage&q=carlyle%20
haris&f=false.

"Case of Carlyle Harris, The." *The Illustrated American* 13, no. 170 (May 20, 1893):
584. https://books.google.com/books?id=VSMgAQAAMAAJ&printsec=front
cover&dq=The+Illustrated+American&hl=en&sa=X&ved=0ahUKEwjhn6749

JrWAhXJsVQKHQZ2CUkQuwUIKTAA#v=onepage&q=carlyle%2oharis&f
=false.

Chapin, H. Gerald. "A Sequence in Crime." *The Green Bag* 14, no. 1 (1902): 36–44.
http://heinonline.org.lp.hscl.ufl.edu/HOL/Page?handle=hein.journals/tgb14
&div=18&start_page=36&collection=journals&set_as_cursor=0&men_tab=
srchresults.

Cicero. *Rhetorica ad Herennium*. Translated by Harry Caplan. Cambridge, MA:
Harvard Univ. Press, 1999.

Clark, Ronald H., George R. Dekle Sr., and William S. Bailey. *Cross-Examination
Handbook: Persuasion, Strategies, and Techniques*. 2nd ed. New York: Wolters-
Kluwer, 2015.

Colton, Charles Caleb. *Lacon; or Many Things in Few Words: Addressed to Those
Who Think*. Rev. ed. New York: E. Kearny, 1836. https://archive.org/details
/laconormanythin02coltgoog.

Conway, J. North. *The Big Policeman: The Rise and Fall of America's First, Most
Ruthless, and Greatest Detective*. Guilford, CT: Lyons Press, 2010.

Conyes, Alfred. *Fifty Years in Sing Sing: A Personal Account, 1879–1929*. Edited by
Penelope Kay Jarrett. Albany: State Univ. Press of New York, 2015.

Crothers, Thomas Davison. *Morphinism and Narcomanias from Other Drugs: Their
Etiology, Treatment, and Medicolegal Relations*. Philadelphia: W. B. Saunders
and Company, 1902. https://archive.org/details/1902CrothersMorphinism
AndNarcomaniaFromOtherDrugs.

Czitrom, Daniel. *New York Exposed: The Gilded Age Police Scandal that Launched
the Progressive Era*. New York: Oxford Univ. Press, 2016.

Daniels, Morris S. *The Story of Ocean Grove Related in the Year of Its Golden Jubilee*.
New York: The Methodist Book Concern, 1919. https://archive.org/details/story
ofoceangrooodani.

Dixon, Thomas J., Jr. *The Clansman: An Historical Romance of the Ku Klux Klan*.
New York: Grosset and Dunlap, 1905. https://archive.org/details/clansman
historicooindixo.

———. *The Fall of a Nation: A Sequel to The Birth of a Nation*. Chicago: M. A.
Donohue and Company, 1916. https://archive.org/details/fallanationaseqoo
dixogoog.

———. *The Leopard's Spots: A Romance of the White Man's Burden—1865–1900*.
New York: Doubleday, Page and Company, 1902. https://archive.org/details
/leopardsspotsaro1dixogoog.

Essig, Mark. "Poison Murder and Expert Testimony: Doubting the Physician in
Late Nineteenth-Century America." *Yale Journal of Law & Humanities* 14, no. 1
(2002): 177–210. http://heinonline.org.lp.hscl.ufl.edu/HOL/Page?handle=hein
.journals/yallh14&div=9&start_page=177&collection=journals&set_as_cursor
=0&men_tab=srchresults.

Evans, Colin. "Robert Buchanan Trial: 1893." In *Great American Trials*. 2002.
Encyclopedia.com. http://www.encyclopedia.com/doc/1G2–3498200109.html.

"Extensive Brain Lesion with Slight Symptoms." *Boston Medical and Surgical Journal* 113, no. 8 (Aug. 20, 1885): 187. https://books.google.com/books?vid =HARVARD:32044089568323&printsec=titlepage#v=onepage&q&f=false.

Florida Standard Jury Instructions in Criminal Cases. http://www.florida supremecourt.org/jury_instructions/instructions.shtml.

Foust, Clement E. *The Life and Dramatic Works of Robert Montgomery Bird.* New York: The Knickerbocker Press, 1919. https://archive.org/details/lifedramatic oofousrich.

Hamilton, Allan McLane. *The Intimate Life of Alexander Hamilton: Based Chiefly upon Original Family Letters and Other Documents, Many of Which Have Never Been Published.* London: Duckworth and Company, 1910. https://archive.org /details/intimatelifealeoomclagoog.

———. *A Manual of Medical Jurisprudence.* New York: Bermingham and Company, 1883. https://archive.org/details/cu31924031236338.

———. *Recollections of an Alienist: Personal and Professional.* New York: George H. Doran, 1916. https://archive.org/details/recollectionsano2hamigoog.

Hanson, J. W. *The Life and Works of the World's Greatest Evangelist, Dwight L. Moody: A Complete and Authentic Review of the Marvelous Career of the Most Remarkable Religious General in History.* Chicago: W. B. Conkey Company, 1900. https://archive.org/details/lifeworksofworldoohans.

Harsha, William M. "The Diagnostic Value of the Medical Laboratory." *Medicine: A Monthly Journal of Medicine and Surgery* 1, no. 2 (May 1895): 86–91. https: //books.google.com.

Hawley, John G., and Malcolm McGregor. *The Criminal Law.* 4th ed. Detroit: The Sprague Publishing Company, 1903.

Heidler, David S., and Jeanne T. Heidler, eds. *Encyclopedia of the American Civil War: A Political, Social, and Military History.* Vol. 3. Santa Barbara, CA: ABC-CLIO, 2000.

Hilliard, Francis. *The American Law of Real Property.* Vol. 1. 3rd ed. New York: Banks, Gould & Company, 1855. https://archive.org/details/americanlawof reaoihill.

Howe, William F. "Some Notable Murder Cases." *The Cosmopolitan Magazine,* Aug. 1900, 379–84. https://books.google.com/books?id=62hAAQAAMAAJ& printsec=frontcover&dq=editions:xWcuAzUrCUIC&hl=en&sa=X&ved=oah UKEwjLwImv-prWAhWCqVQKHTDLAUk4PBC7BQhQMAg#v=onepage&q =howe&f=false.

Johnson, Allen, ed. *Dictionary of American Biography.* Vol. 2, *Barsotti—Brazer.* New York: Charles Scribner's Sons, 1929. https://archive.org/details/dictionaryof amero2ilamer.

———. *Dictionary of American Biography.* Vol. 3, *Brearly—Chandler.* New York: Charles Scribner's Sons, 1929. https://archive.org/details/dictionaryofamer o3ilamer.

Johnson, Allen, and Dumas Malone, eds. *Dictionary of American Biography*. Vol. 4, *Chanfrau—Cushing*. New York: Charles Scribner's Sons, 1930. https://archive .org/details/dictionaryofamer04ilamer.

———. *Dictionary of American Biography*. Vol. 6, *Echols—Fraser*. New York: Charles Scribner's Sons, 1931. https://archive.org/details/dictionaryofamer06 ilamer.

Joyce, Howard C. *Treatise on the Law Governing Indictments with Forms*. Albany, NY: Matthew Bender and Company, 1908. https://archive.org/details/cu31924 020180273.

King, Moses. *Notable New Yorkers: 1896–1899*. New York: Bartlett and Company, 1899.

Ledyard, Hope, ed. *Articles, Speeches and Poems of Carlyle W. Harris*. New York: J. S. Ogilvie, Publisher, 1893. https://archive.org/details/cu31924064804168.

———. *Bible Stories and Scenes for Young People*. New York: Cassell and Company, 1883. https://archive.org/details/biblestoriessceno0harr.

Malone, Dumas, ed. *Dictionary of American Biography*. Vol. 13, *Mills—Oglesby*. New York: Charles Scribner's Sons, 1934. https://archive.org/details/dictionaryof amer12amer.

———. *Dictionary of American Biography*. Vol. 20, *Werden—Zunser*. New York: Charles Scribner's Sons, 1936. https://archive.org/details/dictionaryofamer 20amer.

McCaughey, Robert A. *Stand, Columbia: A History of Columbia University*. New York: Columbia Univ. Press, 2003.

Medical Times and Gazette: A Journal of Medical Science, Literature, Criticism, and News. Vol. 1 for 1863. London: John Churchill and Sons, 1863. https://archive .org/details/bub_gb_cRkCAAAAYAAJ.

Moyer, Harold N. *Medicine: A Monthly Journal of Medicine and Surgery*. Vol. 1. Detroit: George S. Davis, Publisher, 1895. https://books.google.com.

Murphy, Cait. *Scoundrels in Law: The Trials of Howe and Hummel*. New York: HarperCollins Books, 2010.

National District Attorneys Association. *National District Attorneys Association National Prosecution Standards*. 3rd ed. National District Attorneys Association, 2009. http://www.ndaa.org/pdf/NDAA%20NPS%203rd%20Ed.%20w%20 Revised%20Commentary.pdf.

Parkhurst, Charles W. *Our Fight with Tammany*. New York: Charles Scribner's Sons, 1895. https://archive.org/details/ourfightwithtammo0parkuoft.

People of the State of New York, Respondents, against Carlyle W. Harris, Appellant. Case on Appeal from Court of General Sessions of the Peace in and for the City and County of New York. New York: Martin B. Brown, Law Printer and Stationer, 1892. http://heinonline.org.lp.hscl.ufl.edu/HOL/Page?handle=hein.trials/abou 0001&div=2&start_page=[i]&collection=trials&set_as_cursor=0&men_tab= srchresults.

Philbrick, Frederick Arthur. *Language and the Law: The Semantics of Forensic English*. New York: Macmillan Company, 1949. http://heinonline.org.lp.hscl.ufl .edu/HOL/Page?handle=hein.beal/langlawo0001&div=7&start_page=56&collec tion=lbr&set_as_cursor=0&men_tab=srchresults.

Quintilian. *Institutes of Oratory: or Education of an Orator*. Vol. 1. Translated by John Selby Watson. London: George Bell and Sons, 1891. https://archive.org /details/quintiliansinsto5quingoog.

Robinson, Judith A., and H. W. Ling. "Blowpipe Dart Poison from Borneo." *British Journal of Pharmacology* 8, no. 1 (1953): 79–82. http://onlinelibrary.wiley .com/doi/10.1111/j.1476–5381.1953.tb00755.x/epdf.

Rovere, Richard H. *The Weeper and the Blackmailer: The True and Scandalous History of Howe and Hummel*. New York: Signet Books, 1950.

Smith, Edward Henry. *Famous American Poison Mysteries*. London: Hurst & Blackett, 1926. http://heinonline.org.lp.hscl.ufl.edu/HOL/Page?handle=hein.trials /famepomo0001&div=18&start_page=203&collection=trials&set_as_cursor= 0&men_tab=srchresults.

Snevily, H. M. "The Six Capsules." *Pearson's Magazine*, Jan. 1916, 230–35. https: //books.google.com/books?id=-GY3AQAAMAAJ&printsec=frontcover&dq= pearson's+magazine&hl=en&sa=X&ved=0ahUKEwj_v7aZgJvWAhXG31QKH VZ2DEcQuwUIKTAA#v=onepage&q=snevily&f=false.

Strong, Theron G. *Joseph H. Choate: New Englander, New Yorker, Lawyer, Ambassador*. New York: Dodd, Mead and Company, 1917. https://archive.org/details /josephhchoatenewoostro.

Stryker, L. P. *For the Defense: Thomas Erskine*. Garden City, NY: Doubleday, 1947.

"Symptoms Like Those of Poisoning by Opium—Pupils Contracted—Autopsy: Apoplexy of the Pons Varolii—Bright's Disease." In *Medical Times and Gazette: A Journal of Medical Science, Literature, Criticism, and News*, vol. 1. London: John Churchill and Sons, 1863. https://archive.org/details/bub_gb_cRkCAA AAYAAJ.

Taylor, Alfred Swaine. *A Manual of Medical Jurisprudence*. Edited by John James Reese. 7th American ed. Philadelphia: Henry C. Lea, 1873. https://archive.org /details/amanualmedicaljo2taylgoog.

———. *The Principles and Practice of Medical Jurisprudence*. Edited by Thomas Stevenson. Vol. 1. 3rd ed. Philadelphia: Henry C. Lea's Son & Company, 1883. https://archive.org/details/b21779077_0001.

Train, Arthur. *Courts and Criminals*. New York: Charles Scribner's Sons, 1926.

Transactions of the State Medical Society of Indiana at Its Twelfth Annual Session. Indianapolis: Elder & Harkness, Printers, 1861. https://books.google.com/books ?id=m7MRAAAAYAAJ&pg=PA1&dq=Transactions+of+the+State+Medical+ Society+of+Indiana+at+its+Twelfth+Annual+Session&hl=en&sa=X&ved= 0ahUKEwit3dnOhpvWAhVjxlQKHcReBkwQ6AEIJzAA#v=onepage&q=Trans actions%20of%20the%20State%20Medical%20Society%20of%20Indiana%20 at%20its%20Twelfth%20Annual%20Session&f=false.

Vibart, John. "A Famous New York Murder Case." *Police Journal* 6, no. 1 (1933): 84–102. hhttp://heinonline.org.lp.hscl.ufl.edu/HOL/Page?handle=hein.journals /policejl6&div=12&start_page=84&collection=journals&set_as_cursor=0&men _tab=srchresults.

Voorhees, David William. *The Holland Society: A Centennial History, 1885–1985.* New York: The Holland Society, 1985.

Wellman, Francis L. *The Art of Cross-Examination,* 4th ed. New York: Collier Books, 1970.

———. *Day in Court, Or, The Subtle Arts of Great Advocates.* New York: The Mac-Millan Company, 1921. https://archive.org/details/in.ernet.dli.2015.238271.

———. *Gentlemen of the Jury: Reminiscences of Thirty Years at the Bar.* New York: The Macmillan Company, 1944.

———. *Luck and Opportunity: The Recollections of Francis L. Wellman.* New York: The MacMillan Company, 1938.

Wellman, Francis L., and Charles E. Simms, eds. *The Trial of Carlyle W. Harris: For Poisoning His Wife, Helen Potts, at New York.* 1892. Reprint, Gale, Making of Modern Law Reprint, 2012.

Wellman, Francis L., et al. *Success in Court.* New York: The MacMillan Company, 1941.

West, Calvin. "Report on the Microscope." In *Transactions of the State Medical Society of Indiana at Its Twelfth Annual Session,* 34–38. Indianapolis: Elder & Harkness, Printers, 1861. https://books.google.com/books?id=m7MRAAAAYAA J&pg=PA1&dq=Transactions+of+the+State+Medical+Society+of+Indiana+at+ its+Twelfth+Annual+Session&hl=en&sa=X&ved=0ahUKEwit3dnOhpvWAhV jxlQKHcReBkwQ6AEIJzAA#v=onepage&q=Transactions%20of%20the%20 State%20Medical%20Society%20of%20Indiana%20at%20its%20Twelfth%20 Annual%20Session&f=false.

Whitman, James Q. *The Origins of Reasonable Doubt: Theological Roots of the Criminal Trial.* New Haven, CT: Yale Univ. Press, 2008.

Wood, Horatio C. *Reminiscences of an American Pioneer in Experimental Medicine.* Philadelphia: Reprinted from the Transactions of the Philadelphia College of Physicians and Surgeons, 1920. https://archive.org/details/reminiscencesofa oowood.

———. *Therapeutics: Its Principles and Practice.* 8th ed. Philadelphia: J. B. Lippincott Company, 1892. https://books.google.com/books?id=tz8zAQAAMAAJ& printsec=frontcover&dq=editions:bHp476TMVC4C&hl=en&sa=X&ved=0ah UKEwisgK-yh5vWAhVHrFQKHSQjDUoQ6AEIPTAE#v=onepage&q&f=false.

World 1908 Almanac and Encyclopedia. New York: Press Publishing Company, 1907. https://archive.org/details/worldalmanacency1908newy.

Wormley, Theodore G. *Micro-chemistry of Poisons: Including Their Physiological, Pathological, and Legal Relations.* 2nd ed. Philadelphia: J. B. Lippincott Company, 1885. https://archive.org/details/microchemistrypo3wormgoog.

Index

Page numbers in italics refer to illustrations.